ANIMAL RIGHTS

OPPOSING VIEWPOINTS®

Other Books of Related Interest in the Opposing Viewpoints Series:

Biomedical Ethics
The Environmental Crisis
The Health Crisis

Additional Books in the Opposing Viewpoints Series:

Abortion
AIDS
American Foreign Policy
American Government
American Values
America's Elections
America's Prisons
Censorship
Central America
Chemical Dependency
China
Civil Liberties
Constructing a Life Philosophy
Crime & Criminals
Criminal Justice
Death and Dying
The Death Penalty
Drug Abuse
Economics in America
Euthanasia
Israel
Japan
Latin America and U.S. Foreign Policy
Male/Female Roles
The Mass Media
The Middle East
Nuclear War
The Political Spectrum
Poverty
Problems of Africa
Religion in America
Sexual Values
Social Justice
The Soviet Union
The Superpowers
Teenage Sexuality
Terrorism
The Third World
The Vietnam War
War and Human Nature

ANIMAL RIGHTS

OPPOSING VIEWPOINTS®

David L. Bender and Bruno Leone, *Series Editors*
Janelle Rohr, *Book Editor*

OPPOSING VIEWPOINTS SERIES ®

Greenhaven Press, Inc.   PO Box 289009   San Diego, CA 92198-0009

Library of Congress Cataloging-in-Publication Data

Animal rights : opposing viewpoints / Janelle Rohr, book editor.
    p.   cm. — (Opposing viewpoints series)
    Bibliography: p.
    Include index.
    Summary: Presents thirty-two articles debating the question of whether animals have rights.
    ISBN 0-89908-415-X (pbk.)   ISBN 0-89908-440-0 (lib. bdg.)
    1. Animals, Treatment of. [1. Animals—Treatment.] I. Rohr, Janelle, 1963   . II. Series.
HV4711.A58 1989
174'.3—dc20   89-2227
                                            CIP
                                            AC

"Congress shall make no law . . . abridging the freedom of speech, or of the press."

First Amendment to the US Constitution

The basic foundation of our democracy is the first amendment guarantee of freedom of expression. The *Opposing Viewpoints Series* is dedicated to the concept of this basic freedom and the idea that it is more important to practice it than to enshrine it.

Contents

Why Consider Opposing Viewpoints?

"It is better to debate a question without settling it than to settle a question without debating it."

Joseph Joubert (1754-1824)

The Importance of Examining Opposing Viewpoints

The purpose of the Opposing Viewpoints books, and this book in particular, is to present balanced, and often difficult to find, opposing points of view on complex and sensitive issues.

Probably the best way to become informed is to analyze the positions of those who are regarded as experts and well studied on issues. It is important to consider every variety of opinion in an attempt to determine the truth. Opinions from the mainstream of society should be examined. But also important are opinions that are considered radical, reactionary, or minority as well as those stigmatized by some other uncomplimentary label. An important lesson of history is the eventual acceptance of many unpopular and even despised opinions. The ideas of Socrates, Jesus, and Galileo are good examples of this.

Readers will approach this book with their own opinions on the issues debated within it. However, to have a good grasp of one's own viewpoint, it is necessary to understand the arguments of those with whom one disagrees. It can be said that those who do not completely understand their adversary's point of view do not fully understand their own.

A persuasive case for considering opposing viewpoints has been presented by John Stuart Mill in his work *On Liberty*. When examining controversial issues it may be helpful to reflect on this suggestion:

> The only way in which a human being can make some approach to knowing the whole of a subject, is by hearing what can be said about it by persons of every variety of opinion, and studying all modes in which it can be looked at by every character of mind. No wise man ever acquired his wisdom in any mode but this.

Analyzing Sources of Information

The Opposing Viewpoints books include diverse materials taken from magazines, journals, books, and newspapers, as well as statements and position papers from a wide range of individuals, organizations and governments. This broad spectrum of sources helps to develop patterns of thinking which are open to the consideration of a variety of opinions.

Pitfalls To Avoid

A pitfall to avoid in considering opposing points of view is that of regarding one's own opinion as being common sense and the most rational stance and the point of view of others as being only opinion and naturally wrong. It may be that another's opinion is correct and one's own is in error.

Another pitfall to avoid is that of closing one's mind to the opinions of those with whom one disagrees. The best way to approach a dialogue is to make one's primary purpose that of understanding the mind and arguments of the other person and not that of enlightening him or her with one's own solutions. More can be learned by listening than speaking.

It is my hope that after reading this book the reader will have a deeper understanding of the issues debated and will appreciate the complexity of even seemingly simple issues on which good and honest people disagree. This awareness is particularly important in a democratic society such as ours where people enter into public debate to determine the common good. Those with whom one disagrees should not necessarily be regarded as enemies, but perhaps simply as people who suggest different paths to a common goal.

Developing Basic Reading and Thinking Skills

In this book carefully edited opposing viewpoints are purposely placed back to back to create a running debate; each viewpoint is preceded by a short quotation that best expresses the author's main argument. This format instantly plunges the reader into the midst of a controversial issue and greatly aids that reader in mastering the basic skill of recognizing an author's point of view.

A number of basic skills for critical thinking are practiced in the activities that appear throughout the books in the series. Some of the skills are:

Evaluating Sources of Information The ability to choose from among alternative sources the most reliable and accurate source in relation to a given subject.

Separating Fact from Opinion The ability to make the basic distinction between factual statements (those that can be demonstrated or verified empirically) and statements of opinion (those that are beliefs or attitudes that cannot be proved).

Identifying Stereotypes The ability to identify oversimplified, exaggerated descriptions (favorable or unfavorable) about people and insulting statements about racial, religious or national groups, based upon misinformation or lack of information.

Recognizing Ethnocentrism The ability to recognize attitudes or opinions that express the view that one's own race, culture, or group is inherently superior, or those attitudes that judge another culture or group in terms of one's own.

It is important to consider opposing viewpoints and equally important to be able to critically analyze those viewpoints. The activities in this book are designed to help the reader master these thinking skills. Statements are taken from the book's viewpoints and the reader is asked to analyze them. This technique aids the reader in developing skills that not only can be applied to the viewpoints in this book, but also to situations where opinionated spokespersons comment on controversial issues. Although the activities are helpful to the solitary reader, they are most useful when the reader can benefit from the interaction of group discussion.

Using this book and others in the series should help readers develop basic reading and thinking skills. These skills should improve the readers' ability to understand what they read. Readers should be better able to separate fact from opinion, substance from rhetoric and become better consumers of information in our media-centered culture.

This volume of the Opposing Viewpoints books does not advocate a particular point of view. Quite the contrary! The very nature of the book leaves it to the reader to formulate the opinions he or she finds most suitable. My purpose as publisher is to see that this is made possible by offering a wide range of viewpoints which are fairly presented.

David L. Bender
Publisher

Introduction

"What is man without the beasts? If the beasts were gone, man would die from a great loneliness of spirit. For whatever happens to the beasts soon happens to man."

Chief Seattle, after signing a peace treaty with the US government

Today's efforts to protect animals would seem completely alien to many people living in the United States one hundred years ago. Historian Thomas Dunlap asks, "What would they think of the battle over the snail darter [a tiny fish]? . . . Coming from a society that was seeking to kill every wolf on the continent, what would they make of our plans to reintroduce the timber wolf into parts of its old range?" Dunlap's comparison shows just how much Americans' views of animals have changed. These changes have led to a debate few people in the previous century would have considered seriously: Do animals have rights?

In nineteenth-century North America, this question could be answered with a resounding no. Many animal populations were decimated as white settlers spread westward. The bison population in North America was estimated at sixty million before European settlement; by 1825 all the bison east of the Mississippi River had been killed. Between 1872 and 1874, over a million buffalo were shot annually in the West. Predators, such as wolves, cougars, coyotes, hawks, and owls, were similarly threatened. Wolves were especially hated. William Hornaday, a conservationist and head of the New York Zoo, wrote at the turn of the century, "There is no depth of meanness, treachery, or cruelty to which [wolves] . . . do not cheerfully descend. They are the only animals on earth which make a regular practice of killing and devouring their wounded companions and eating their own dead." Settlers were paid bounties by the government for every wolf that they killed.

Few North Americans would advocate such harsh measures now. Why did our attitudes change? One reason was that at the same time such carnage was occurring, important new views about animals were gaining influence. Charles Darwin, in his theory of evolution, argued that humans were descendants of animals. Darwin wrote in his 1871 book *The Descent of Man,*

"There is no fundamental difference between man and the higher animals in their mental faculties." Lower animals "manifestly feel pleasure and pain, happiness and misery." While Darwin's views did not gain immediate public acceptance, they established a precedent for other scientists and for the study of human origins and human-animal relationships in general.

In addition, new knowledge about the role predators play in the population control of other animals overturned many people's prejudices against predators. A startling example occurred when conservationists established a preserve for deer at Kaibab National Forest on the rim of the Grand Canyon. To safeguard the deer, all the large predators in this area, including wolves, mountain lions, and coyotes were exterminated. When the deer population exploded and deer began starving to death, hunters and conservationists recognized why predators were essential. While some states still offer bounties for predators, the bounties are intended to keep animal populations in balance, not to exterminate completely a particular type of animal.

In the twentieth century, knowledge about animals continues to expand. Scientists have studied animal behavior and found that animals have social rules that guide the way they interact and communicate. Thus animals do not act simply by instinct, but have and use more intelligence than scientists previously believed. This new scientific information, like Darwin's views a century before, continues to inspire debate over how animals should be treated.

Does increasing knowledge about animals inevitably lead to a conviction that animals deserve more consideration than society gives them now? Not necessarily. As the viewpoints in this book show, the issues related to animal rights are hotly debated. *Animal Rights: Opposing Viewpoints,* focuses on five key topics: Do Animals Have Rights? Is Animal Experimentation Justified? Should Animals Be Used for Food? Does Wildlife Need To Be Protected? and How Can the Animal Rights Movement Improve Animal Welfare? As people learn more about animals and reassess the human-animal relationship, controversy over animal rights will continue.

Do Animals Have Rights?

Chapter Preface

Recent studies have vastly improved people's understanding of animals. Many of these studies show that animals are far more intelligent than previously thought. Studies of animal communication, in particular, have led to new insights about animal intelligence. In 1971, a chimp called Washoe became the first to memorize and respond to human sign language. Since Washoe, several other chimps have learned sign language and have used it to respond to complex commands. University of Hawaii professor Lou Herman has taught dolphins to understand, interpret, and respond to hand gestures. According to Harvard psychologist Richard Herrnstein, even pigeons, with their tiny brains, can memorize the precise contents of hundreds of photographs.

Outside the laboratory setting, scientists have found that wild animals are also intelligent and capable of communication. Wolves, for example, use posture to indicate dominance or submission to other members of their packs. They howl and leave scent markings to establish their territory, and packs generally respect each others' borders.

These recent findings have inspired greater respect for animals' intelligence and abilities. This recognition has led to serious consideration of a question few would have raised decades ago: Do animals have rights? The following chapter features viewpoints that discuss this question.

> *"The tyranny of human over nonhuman animals . . .has caused and today is still causing an amount of pain and suffering that can only be compared with . . . tyranny by white humans over black humans."*

The Case for Animal Rights

Peter Singer

The book *Animal Liberation* has been called the bible of the animal rights movement. The author, Peter Singer, is a philosophy professor and director of the Centre for Human Bioethics at Monash University in Australia. In the following viewpoint, excerpted from *Animal Liberation,* Singer argues that because animals have nervous systems and can suffer just as humans can, it is wrong for humans to use animals for research, food, or clothing. He maintains that ending discrimination and abuse against animals will require a massive shift in public attitudes.

As you read, consider the following questions:

1. How does Singer define "speciesism"?
2. What relationship does Singer see between the women's rights movement, the civil rights movement, and the animal rights movement?

Peter Singer, *Animal Liberation: A New Ethics for Our Treatment of Animals.* New York: Avon Books, 1975. Reprinted with permission.

This [viewpoint] is about the tyranny of human over nonhuman animals. This tyranny has caused and today is still causing an amount of pain and suffering that can only be compared with that which resulted from the centuries of tyranny by white humans over black humans. The struggle against this tyranny is a struggle as important as any of the moral and social issues that have been fought over in recent years.

Most readers will take what they have just read to be a wild exaggeration. Five years ago I myself would have laughed at the statements I have now written in complete seriousness. Five years ago I did not know what I know today. . . .

Changing Prejudicial Attitudes

A liberation movement demands an expansion of our moral horizons. Practices that were previously regarded as natural and inevitable come to be seen as the result of an unjustifiable prejudice. Who can say with any confidence that none of his or her attitudes and practices can legitimately be questioned? If we wish to avoid being numbered among the oppressors, we must be prepared to rethink all our attitudes to other groups, including the most fundamental. . . .

I believe that our present attitudes are based on a long history of prejudice and arbitrary discrimination. I argue that there can be no reason—except the selfish desire to preserve the privileges of the exploiting group—for refusing to extend the basic principle of equality of consideration to members of other species. I ask you to recognize that your attitudes to members of other species are a form of prejudice no less objectionable than prejudice about a person's race or sex. . . .

"Animal Liberation" may sound more like a parody of other liberation movements than a serious objective. The idea of "The Rights of Animals" actually was once used to parody the case for women's rights. When Mary Wollstonecraft, a forerunner of today's feminists, published her *Vindication of the Rights of Women* in 1792, her views were widely regarded as absurd, and before long an anonymous publication appeared entitled *A Vindication of the Rights of Brutes.* The author of this satirical work (now known to have been Thomas Taylor, a distinguished Cambridge philosopher) tried to refute Mary Wollstonecraft's arguments by showing that they could be carried one stage further. If the argument for equality was sound when applied to women, why should it not be applied to dogs, cats, and horses? The reasoning seemed to hold for these "brutes" too; yet to hold that brutes had rights was manifestly absurd; therefore the reasoning by which this conclusion had been reached must be unsound, and if unsound when applied to brutes, it must also be unsound when applied to women, since the very same arguments had been used in each case. . . .

One way in which we might reply is by saying that the case for equality between men and women cannot validly be extended to nonhuman animals. Women have a right to vote, for instance, because they are just as capable of making rational decisions about the future as men are; dogs, on the other hand, are incapable of understanding the significance of voting, so they cannot have the right to vote. There are many other obvious ways in which men and women resemble each other closely, while humans and animals differ greatly. So, it might be said, men and women are similar beings and should have similar rights, while humans and nonhumans are different and should not have equal rights.

Equal Consideration of Rights

The reasoning behind this reply to Taylor's analogy is correct up to a point, but it does not go far enough. There *are* important differences between humans and other animals, and these differences must give rise to *some* differences in the rights that each has. Recognizing this obvious fact, however, is no barrier to the

MAN
DEMONSTRATING HIS
SUPERIORITY OVER
ANIMALS.

R. Cobb. Reprinted with permission from SACA NEWS, published by the Student Action Corps for Animals, PO Box 15588, Washington, DC 20003.

case for extending the basic principle of equality to nonhuman animals. The differences that exist between men and women are equally undeniable, and the supporters of Women's Liberation are aware that these differences may give rise to different rights. Many feminists hold that women have the right to an abortion on request. It does not follow that since these same feminists are campaigning for equality between men and women they must support the right of men to have abortions too. Since a man cannot have an abortion, it is meaningless to talk of his right to have one. Since a dog can't vote, it is meaningless to talk of its right to vote. There is no reason why either Women's Liberation or Animal Liberation should get involved in such nonsense. The extension of the basic principle of equality from one group to another does not imply that we must treat both groups in exactly the same way, or grant exactly the same rights to both groups. Whether we should do so will depend on the nature of the members of the two groups. The basic principle of equality does not require equal or identical *treatment;* it requires equal *consideration.* Equal consideration for different beings may lead to different treatment and different rights. . . .

The Basis of Equality

Although, it may be said, humans differ as individuals there are no differences between the races and sexes *as such.* From the mere fact that a person is black or a woman we cannot infer anything about that person's intellectual or moral capacities. This, it may be said, is why racism and sexism are wrong. The white racist claims that whites are superior to blacks, but this is false—although there are differences among individuals, some blacks are superior to some whites in all of the capacities and abilities that could conceivably be relevant. The opponent of sexism would say the same: a person's sex is no guide to his or her abilities, and this is why it is unjustifiable to discriminate on the basis of sex. . . .

It is an implication of this principle of equality that our concern for others and our readiness to consider their interests ought not to depend on what they are like or on what abilities they may possess. Precisely what this concern or consideration requires us to do may vary according to the characteristics of those affected by what we do: concern for the well-being of a child growing up in America would require that we teach him to read; concern for the well-being of a pig may require no more than that we leave him alone with other pigs in a place where there is adequate food and room to run freely. But the basic element—the taking into account of the interests of the being, whatever those interests may be—must, according to the principle of equality, be extended to all beings, black or white, masculine or feminine, human or nonhuman. . . .

When in the 1850s the call for women's rights was raised in the United States, a remarkable black feminist named Sojourner Truth [spoke] . . . at a feminist convention:

> They talk about this thing in the head; what do they call it? ["Intellect," whispered someone near by.] That's it. What's that got to do with women's rights or Negroes' rights? If my cup won't hold but a pint and yours holds a quart, wouldn't you be mean not to let me have my little half-measure full?

It is in accordance with this principle that the attitude that we may call "speciesism," by analogy with racism, must also be condemned. Speciesism—the word is not an attractive one, but I can think of no better term—is a prejudice or attitude of bias toward the interest of members of one's own species and against those members of other species. . . .

Moral Zombies

The plain fact is, it is not just society that needs changing. The struggle for animal rights is also a struggle with the self. What we are trying to do is transform the moral zombie that society would like us to be into the morally advanced beings we are capable of becoming. All liberation movements have this common theme.

Tom Regan, quoted in *Minneapolis Star & Tribune,* March 29, 1987.

Many philosophers and other writers have proposed the principle of equal consideration of interests, in some form or other, as a basic moral principle; but not many of them have recognized that this principle applies to members of other species as well as to our own. Jeremy Bentham was one of the few who did realize this. In a forward-looking passage written at a time when black slaves had been freed by the French but in the British dominions were still being treated in the way we now treat animals, Bentham wrote:

> The day *may* come when the rest of the animal creation may acquire those rights which never could have been withholden from them but by the hand of tyranny. The French have already discovered that the blackness of the skin is no reason why a human being should be abandoned without redress to the caprice of a tormentor. It may one day come to be recognized that the number of the legs, the villosity of the skin, or the termination of the *os sacrum* are reasons equally insufficient for abandoning a sensitive being to the same fate. What else is it that should trace the insuperable line? Is it the faculty of reason, or perhaps the faculty of discourse? But a full-grown horse or dog is beyond comparison a more rational, as well as a more conversable animal, than an infant of a day or week or even a month, old.

> But suppose they were otherwise, what would it avail. The question is not, Can they *reason?* nor Can they *talk?* but, *Can they suffer?*

In this passage Bentham points to the capacity for suffering as the vital characteristic that gives a being the right to equal consideration. The capacity for suffering—or more strictly, for suffering and/or enjoyment or happiness—is not just another characteristic like the capacity for language or higher mathematics. Bentham is not saying that those who try to mark "the insuperable line" that determines whether the interests of a being should be considered happen to have chosen the wrong characteristic. By saying that we must consider the interests of all beings with the capacity for suffering or enjoyment Bentham does not arbitrarily exclude from consideration any interests at all—as those who draw the line with reference to the possession of reason or language do. The capacity for suffering and enjoyment is *a prerequisite for having interests at all,* a condition that must be satisfied before we can speak of interests in a meaningful way. It would be nonsense to say that it was not in the interests of a stone to be kicked along the road by a schoolboy. A stone does not have interests because it cannot suffer. Nothing that we can do to it could possibly make any difference to its welfare. A mouse, on the other hand, does have an interest in not being kicked along the road, because it will suffer if it is.

No Excuse for Ignoring Suffering

If a being suffers there can be no moral justification for refusing to take that suffering into consideration. No matter what the nature of the being, the principle of equality requires that its suffering be counted equally with the like suffering—in so far as rough comparisons can be made—of any other being. If a being is not capable of suffering, or of experiencing enjoyment or happiness, there is nothing to be taken into account. So the limit of sentience (using the term as a convenient if not strictly accurate shorthand for the capacity to suffer and/or experience enjoyment) is the only defensible boundary of concern for the interests of others. To mark this boundary by some other characteristic like intelligence or rationality would be to mark it in an arbitrary manner. Why not choose some other characteristic, like skin color?

The racist violates the principle of equality by giving greater weight to the interests of members of his own race when there is a clash between their interests and the interests of those of another race. The sexist violates the principle of equality by favoring the interests of his own sex. Similarly the speciesist allows the interests of his own species to override the greater interests of members of other species. The pattern is identical in each case.

"Animals . . . have no rights, and they can have none."

The Case Against Animal Rights

Carl Cohen

The question of whether animals should be treated humanely is far less controversial than the question of whether animals have rights. In the following viewpoint, Carl Cohen argues that while humans have an obligation to treat animals humanely, animals cannot have rights. Granting a being a right depends on that being also accepting the rules of society, Cohen argues. Animals have no sense of morality and they do not recognize the rights of others. Cohen concludes that this necessitates treating animals differently from how one treats other human beings. Cohen is a professor at the University of Michigan Medical School in Ann Arbor.

As you read, consider the following questions:

1. The author argues that animals have no capacity for making moral judgments. How does this argument support his belief that animals do not have rights?
2. What obligations do humans have to animals, in Cohen's opinion?
3. Why does Cohen defend speciesism?

Carl Cohen, "The Case for the Use of Animals in Biomedical Research," *The New England Journal of Medicine*, Vol. 315, pp. 865-870, 1986. Reprinted with permission.

Using animals as research subjects in medical investigations is widely condemned on two grounds: first, because it wrongly violates the *rights* of animals, and second, because it wrongly imposes on sentient creatures much avoidable *suffering*. Neither of these arguments is sound. The first relies on a mistaken understanding of rights; the second relies on a mistaken calculation of consequences. Both deserve definitive dismissal.

Why Animals Have No Rights

A right, properly understood, is a claim, or potential claim, that one party may exercise against another. The target against whom such a claim may be registered can be a single person, a group, a community, or (perhaps) all humankind. The content of rights claims also varies greatly: repayment of loans, nondiscrimination by employers, noninterference by the state, and so on. To comprehend any genuine right fully, therefore, we must know *who* holds the right, *against whom* it is held, and *to what* it is a right.

Alternative sources of rights add complexity. Some rights are grounded in constitution and law (e.g., the right of an accused to trial by jury); some rights are moral but give no legal claims (e.g., my right to your keeping, the promise you gave me); and some rights (e.g., against theft or assault) are rooted both in morals and in law.

The differing targets, contents, and sources of rights, and their inevitable conflict, together weave a tangled web. Notwithstanding all such complications, this much is clear about rights in general: they are in every case claims, or potential claims, within a community of moral agents. Rights arise, and can be intelligibly defended, only among beings who actually do, or can, make moral claims against one another. Whatever else rights may be, therefore, they are necessarily human; their possessors are persons, human beings.

The attributes of human beings from which this moral capability arises have been described variously by philosophers, both ancient and modern: the inner consciousness of a free will (Saint Augustine); the grasp, by human reason, of the binding character of moral law (Saint Thomas Aquinas); the self-conscious participation of human beings in an objective ethical order (G.W.F. Hegel); human membership in an organic moral community (F.H. Bradley); the development of the human self through the consciousness of other moral selves (G.H. Mead); and the underivative, intuitive cognition of the rightness of an action (H.A. Prichard). Most influential has been Immanuel Kant's emphasis on the universal human possession of a uniquely moral will and the autonomy its use entails. Humans confront choices that are purely moral; humans—but certainly not dogs or mice—lay down

24

moral laws, for others and for themselves. Human beings are self-legislative, morally *auto-nomous.*

Animals (that is, nonhuman animals, the ordinary sense of that word) lack this capacity for free moral judgment. They are not beings of a kind capable of exercising or responding to moral claims. Animals therefore have no rights, and they can have none. This is the core of the argument about the alleged rights of animals. The holders of rights must have the capacity to comprehend rules of duty, governing all including themselves. In applying such rules, the holders of rights must recognize possible conflicts between what is in their own interest and what is just. Only in a community of beings capable of self-restricting moral judgments can the concept of a right be correctly invoked.

Humans have such moral capacities. They are in this sense self-legislative, are members of communities governed by moral rules, and do possess rights. Animals do not have such moral capacities. They are not morally self-legislative, cannot possibly be members of a truly moral community, and therefore cannot possess rights. In conducting research on animal subjects, therefore, we do not violate their rights, because they have none to violate. . . .

Respect for Human Life

People involved in the animal rights movement consider the life of a cat, dog, chicken or pig to be equal to the life of a human. It just shows how far some of us have fallen in respect for human life.

Lawrence Wade, *The Washington Times,* August 2, 1987.

Genuinely moral acts have an internal as well as an external dimension. Thus, in law, an act can be criminal only when the guilty deed, the actus reus, is done with a guilty mind, mens rea. No animal can ever commit a crime; bringing animals to criminal trial is the mark of primitive ignorance. The claims of moral rights are similarly inapplicable to them. Does a lion have a right to eat a baby zebra? Does a baby zebra have a right not to be eaten? Such questions, mistakenly invoking the concept of right where it does not belong, do not make good sense. Those who condemn biomedical research because it violates "animal rights" commit the same blunder.

In Defense of Speciesism

Abandoning reliance on animal rights, some critics resort instead to animal sentience—their feelings of pain and distress. We ought to desist from the imposition of pain insofar as we can. Since all or nearly all experimentation on animals does impose pain and could be readily forgone, say these critics, it should be stopped.

25

The ends sought may be worthy, but those ends do not justify imposing agonies on humans, and by animals the agonies are felt no less. The laboratory use of animals (these critics conclude) must therefore be ended—or at least very sharply curtailed.

Argument of this variety is essentially utilitarian, often expressly so; it is based on the calculation of the net product, in pains and pleasures, resulting from experiments on animals. Jeremy Bentham, comparing horses and dogs with other sentient creatures, is thus commonly quoted: "The question is not, Can they reason? nor Can they talk? but, Can they suffer?"

Biomedical Research Must Still Proceed

Animals certainly can suffer and surely ought not to be made to suffer needlessly. But in inferring, from these uncontroversial premises, that biomedical research causing animal distress is largely (or wholly) wrong, the critic commits two serious errors.

The first error is the assumption, often explicitly defended, that all sentient animals have equal moral standing. Between a dog and a human being, according to this view, there is no moral difference; hence the pains suffered by dogs must be weighed no differently from the pains suffered by humans. To deny such equality, according to this critic, is to give unjust preference to one species over another; it is "speciesism." The most influential statement of this moral equality of species was made by Peter Singer:

> The racist violates the principle of equality by giving greater weight to the interests of members of his own race when there is a clash between their interests and the interests of those of another race. The sexist violates the principle of equality by favoring the interests of his own sex. Similarly the speciesist allows the interests of his own species to override the greater interests of members of other species. The pattern is identical in each case.

This argument is worse than unsound; it is atrocious. It draws an offensive moral conclusion from a deliberately devised verbal parallelism that is utterly specious. Racism has no rational ground whatever. Differing degrees of respect or concern for humans for no other reason than that they are members of different races is an injustice totally without foundation in the nature of the races themselves. Racists, even if acting on the basis of mistaken factual beliefs, do grave moral wrong precisely because there is no morally relevant distinction among the races. The supposition of such differences had led to outright horror. The same is true of the sexes, neither sex being entitled by right to greater respect or concern than the other. No dispute here.

Between species of animate life, however—between (for example) humans on the one hand and cats or rats on the other—

26

the morally relevant differences are enormous, and almost universally appreciated. Humans engage in moral reflection; humans are morally autonomous; humans are members of moral communities, recognizing just claims against their own interest. Human beings do have rights; theirs is a moral status very different from that of cats or rats.

Speciesism Is Necessary

I am a speciesist. Speciesism is not merely plausible; it is essential for right conduct, because those who will not make the morally relevant distinctions among species are almost certain, in consequence, to misapprehend their true obligations. The analogy between speciesism and racism is insidious. Every sensitive moral judgment requires that the differing natures of the beings to whom obligations are owed be considered. If all forms of animate life—or vertebrate animal life—must be treated equally, and if therefore in evaluating a research program the pains of a rodent count equally with the pains of a human, we are forced to conclude (1) that neither humans nor rodents possess rights, or (2) that rodents possess all the rights that humans possess. Both alternatives are absurd. Yet one or the other must be swallowed if the moral equality of all species is to be defended. . . .

Rampant Anthropomorphism

So far as I can see, unless one is initially prepared to adopt a rather rampant anthropomorphism in respect to animals, they can have no rights.

R.G. Frey, *Interests and Rights: The Case Against Animals,* 1980.

Those who claim to base their objection to the use of animals in biomedical research on their reckoning of the net pleasures and pains produced make a second error, equally grave. Even if it were true—as it is surely not—that the pains of all animate beings must be counted equally, a cogent utilitarian calculation requires that we weigh all the consequences of the use, and of the nonuse, of animals in laboratory research. Critics relying (however mistakenly) on animal rights may claim to ignore the beneficial results of such research, rights being trump cards to which interest and advantage must give way. But an argument that is explicitly framed in terms of interest and benefit for all over the long run must attend also to the disadvantageous consequences of not using animals in research, and to all the achievements attained and attainable only through their use. The sum of the benefits of their use is utterly beyond quantification. The elimination of horrible disease, the increase of longevity, the avoidance of great pain, the

27

saving of lives, and the improvement of the quality of lives (for humans and for animals) achieved through research using animals is so incalculably great that the argument of these critics, systematically pursued, establishes not their conclusion but its reverse: to refrain from using animals in biomedical research is, on utilitarian ground, morally wrong.

When balancing the pleasures and pains resulting from the use of animals in research, we must not fail to place on the scales the terrible pains that would have resulted, would be suffered now, and would long continue had animals not been used. Every disease eliminated, every vaccine developed, every method of pain relief devised, every surgical procedure invented, every prosthetic device implanted—indeed, virtually every modern medical therapy is due, in part or in whole, to experimentation using animals. Nor may we ignore, in the balancing process, the predictable gains in human (and animal) well-being that are probably achievable in the future but that will not be achieved if the decision is made now to desist from such research or to curtail it. . . .

The Absurd Consequences of Animal Rights

Finally, inconsistency between the profession and the practice of many who oppose research using animals deserves comment. This frankly ad hominem observation aims chiefly to show that a coherent position rejecting the use of animals in medical research imposes costs so high as to be intolerable even to the critics themselves.

One cannot coherently object to the killing of animals in biomedical investigations while continuing to eat them. Anesthetics and thoughtful animal husbandry render the level of actual animal distress in the laboratory generally lower than that in the abattoir. So long as death and discomfort do not substantially differ in the two contexts, the consistent objector must not only refrain from all eating of animals but also protest as vehemently against others eating them as against others experimenting on them. No less vigorously must the critic object to the wearing of animal hides in coats and shoes, to employment in any industrial enterprise that uses animal parts, and to any commercial development that will cause death or distress to animals. . . .

Scrupulous vegetarianism, in matters of food, clothing, shelter, commerce, and recreation, and in all other spheres, is the only fully coherent position the critic may adopt. At great human cost, the lives of fish and crustaceans must also be protected, with equal vigor, if speciesism has been forsworn. A very few consistent critics adopt this position. It is the reductio ad absurdum of the rejection of moral distinctions between animals and human beings.

"To go (sometimes literally) out of our way to help animals, . . . to feel with them their suffering and to be moved by it—these are surely signs of spiritual greatness."

Christianity Supports Animal Rights

Andrew Linzey

Andrew Linzey is the chaplain and director of studies at the Center for the Study of Theology at the University of Essex in Great Britain. In the following viewpoint, Linzey questions traditional interpretations of the Old and New Testaments as they relate to animals. He argues that passages in these writings and in later Christian writings challenge humans to treat all creatures compassionately and do not endorse human exploitation of animals.

As you read, consider the following questions:

1. What teachings of Jesus does Linzey cite to support his argument that Jesus opposed animal sacrifices?
2. What does Linzey believe is the religious lesson in the stories of saints who cared for animals?
3. What facts lead the author to conclude that the treatment of animals is a major moral problem?

From CHRISTIANITY AND THE RIGHTS OF ANIMALS edited by Andrew Linzey. Copyright © 1987 by Andrew Linzey. Reprinted by permission of The Crossroad Publishing Company.

Understanding animal sacrifice (*zebach*) in the Old Testament is notoriously difficult. Why is it that Noah's first response to God after the Flood consists in taking 'clean' (that is, non-carnivorous) animals and offering them as 'burnt offerings'? What is meant by God 'smelling' (that is, literally breathing in) these 'pleasing odours'? And why is it that this response leads God to the reversing of his curse and the promise that he will never again 'destroy *every living creature* [animals as well as humans] as I have done'? At first sight, the practice is surely paradoxical: God is seen to delight in the gratuitous destruction of the creatures he has made. Doubtless for many centuries this has been the dominant, popular view. Animals are there seen as simply expendable as signs of human penitence. According to this view, sacrifice consists almost entirely in the death of the subject, indeed it is the slaying nature of sacrifice that most characterizes it. And yet this view is obviously open to all kinds of difficulties. For if the *destruction* of life is the core of sacrifice, how can God *receive* what is offered? If death is the end of animal life, what is there to offer? Moreover, why (in this particular instance at least) does the offering of sacrifice lead to the establishment of blessing for all living creatures both human and animal? The only way forward in grappling with the rationale of the practice of sacrifice has to be to move away from the simple equation of sacrifice with the infliction of death.

The Real Meaning of Sacrifice

'In modern discussions of the significance of Old Testament sacrifices', writes Frances Young, 'it is frequently claimed that the animal victim died as a substitute for the offerer.' And yet as Young shows this idea is 'unfounded'. The central issue is whether the essential feature of the act of sacrifice 'was the death of the victim or the offering of lifeblood'. But what did it mean to offer lifeblood (*nephesh*) to the Creator? First of all, it meant that all life was a gift from God and therefore belonged to him. Secondly, the act of return to the Creator was probably understood (by those who practised it) as the offering of life. Thirdly, and perhaps most importantly, the practice of sacrifice thereby assumed that the life of the individual animal continued beyond mortal death. In these ways it is possible to understand the historic practice of sacrifice as affirming the value of the individuals slain and not simply as their gratuitous destruction. The tradition of sacrifice did not *necessarily* involve a low view of animal life.

And yet it would not be fair to the Jewish tradition to suppose that the practice did not pass without objection and protest. 'What to me is the multitude of your sacrifices?' says the Lord in Isaiah. 'I have had enough of burnt offerings of rams and the fat of fed beasts; I do not delight in the blood of bulls, or of lambs, or of he-goats.' What the Lord requires is not substitutionary sacrifice but the exercise of justice. . . . Before we reach the time of Christ, there are strong signs that, under the weight of widespread criticism, the sacrificial system was beginning to wane. 'So it was that Judaism was able to develop from a religion in which sacrifice played a most important part to a religion in which sacrifice had no place', [according to Young].

The Challenge of Jesus

It is only in the light of this that we can see both the continuity and the challenge of Jesus. Whatever the justification for animal sacrifices, the Christian Church effectively abolished them. In this it is difficult not to see the hand of Jesus. Few scholars have reflected, for example, on the radical significance for the animals themselves of the well-known incident concerning the cleansing of the temple of 'those who sold pigeons' and by implication all those who traded animals in the temple precincts. When it is combined with the later passage in Mark concerning the ineffectiveness of sacrifice, we are able to see Jesus as expressing the continuity of moral protest illustrated so well by the prophets themselves. Moreover, there is no hint in the Gospels of Jesus' support for the practice of sacrifice itself; neither he nor his disciples practised it. In this, and the subsequent theology of sacrifice, Jesus clearly posed a radical challenge to the tradition. Although sacrifice was arguably on the wane, the advent of the followers of Jesus was to hasten the decline of an already questionable practice. . . .

Rigidly Set Apart

The glaring folly, we might almost say superstition, of speciesism, [is] the belief that the stratum of creation we label as human should be considered as rigidly set apart from the rest of the animal kingdom. The notion stemmed in large part from a misinterpretation of some phrases in *Genesis*, where the word "dominion" is taken to mean "domination," and all that word implies by way of absolute superiority and authority. It is a word which has put enmity between man and his fellow-animals for untold centuries.

Liam Brophy, *The AV Magazine,* October 1988.

While dogmatic theology has been slow to extend the spirit of Christian sacrifice to animals, there are signs that this insight has not been lost within the saintly tradition. Frequently hagiographers are bemused by the 'antics' of even celebrated saints who go out of their way to express concern for the non-human, 'preaching the Gospel to them', celebrating their gift of life and being scrupulous even in the smallest matters where either life or well-being are concerned. This 'wildness' and 'folly' gave St Francis of Assisi 'a profound rapport with all living things'. As in their own day, these 'fools for Christ' are apt to be despised and ridiculed, and many today who care for animals are similarly despised. But who can deny that these 'fools' preserve for us an essential element of the gospel of sacrificial love? The moral point is aptly put by Austin Farrer. 'If Jesus is willing to be in us, and to let us show him to the world, it's a small thing that we should endure being fools for Christ's sake'. Happily this 'folly' is still enjoined today in the Principles of the Society of St Francis. They are to follow Christ 'in the way of renunciation and sacrifice' and by so doing exemplify loving service to the world. Moreover, they 'must remember that they follow the Son of Man' who 'loved the birds and the flowers', and particularly 'They will rejoice in God's world and all its beauty and its living creatures, calling nothing common or unclean'. In this the Christian tradition has much to learn from the modern-day followers of St Francis. The recent signs of concern among them for the lost tradition of cosmic awareness and the welfare of animals in particular should be heeded.

And yet St Francis was not the first, and certainly not the last, Christian saint to recognize the spiritual unity of all God's creatures and to befriend them. Several of the Georgian saints, for example, many hundreds of years before Francis, were distinguished by their love of animals. 'St John Zedazneli made friends with bears near his hermitage' and 'St Shio employed an obliging but rather inefficient wolf to guide the donkeys which brought supplies to his lonely grotto'. In particular, the stories of St David of Garesja and his protection of deer and birds from the hunters of his day abound with moral protest. 'He whom I believe in and worship looks after and feeds all his creatures, to whom He has given birth,' is his reply to those who wish to kill them. The early Celtic saints too, who lived in Ireland, Wales, Cornwall and Brittany in the fifth and sixth centuries after Christ, showed extraordinary consideration to animals, not only befriending them, but also praying for them and healing them of injury.

True Spirituality

The point to be grasped from the saintly tradition is that to love animals is not sentimentality (as we now know it) but true spirituality. Of course there can be vain, self-seeking loving, but to go (sometimes literally) out of our way to help animals, to expend effort to secure their protection and to feel with them their suffering and to be moved by it—these are surely signs of spiritual greatness. Such, at least, is the verdict of countless numbers of story-tellers and sages within Christendom. We do well to listen to them if our present vision of God's Kingdom is not to be severely diminished.

In our urbanized communities it might now be possible for some people to grow up without actually seeing a live animal, let alone witnessing an act of cruelty or neglect. If a good number of Christians react rather unbelievingly to the suggestion that our ill-treatment of animals is a major moral problem, then it could be in part a simple result of 'not seeing is not believing'. The irony is that although a whole range of public spectacles involving wantonness towards animals have disappeared from view, we actually utilize more animals today than ever before. In the two major areas of farming and experimentation alone, approximately a hundred billion animals are killed in the world every year. Use of experimental animals in the United States is conventionally estimated in the region of seventy to a hundred and twenty million. World-wide the total is probably somewhere around five hundred million. When it comes to farming, in the United Kingdom alone there are approximately forty-five million laying hens in intensive conditions, and in the United States this figure probably exceeds a billion at least. These figures, even if exaggerated, indicate a scale of animal usage hitherto unknown in the history of humankind. We eat, ride, shoot, fish, wear, trap, hunt, farm and experiment upon billions of animals world-wide every year. Even if we only grant animals some minimal moral status, it could be seriously claimed that in terms of pain, suffering and deprivation alone, the treatment of the non-human ranks among the most important moral issues confronting the human species. To include animals among the class of right-holders in a world where they are almost universally disregarded is surely a bold act of faith.

"Our major religious and historical traditions contain strong elements . . . urging us toward the experimental use of animals for the benefit of man."

Christianity Does Not Support Animal Welfare

Harold J. Morowitz

In the following viewpoint, Harold J. Morowitz cites passages from the Bible to argue that humans are considered more important than other animals. Old Testament prophets and Jesus used animals for human benefit, he writes, so humans today are justified in using animals for experiments that improve health. Morowitz is Robinson professor of biology and natural philosophy at George Mason University in Fairfax, Virginia.

As you read, consider the following questions:

1. What passages does Morowitz cite to argue that the Bible supports using animals for human benefit?
2. On what basis has Christianity denied rights to animals, according to the author?
3. What cultural traditions does the author argue justify using animals for experiments?

Harold J. Morowitz, "Jesus, Moses, Aristotle, and Laboratory Animals," *Hospital Practice,* January 15, 1988. Reprinted with permission.

In granting permission to use this article, the author wishes to note that Animal Rights *is an improper title, using the rhetoric of propaganda generated by the animal movement. The dictionary states that a "right" is that which belongs to a person by law, nature, or tradition. Rights stem from the social compact between humans. To shift the word "right" from people to animals is to deny those unique aspects of humanness which are central to our culture. In accepting the misuse of rights, the editors have from the outset biased the argument. I object and hope the readers will see how this manipulation of language is an improper approach to fair and rational debate.*

Issues such as the use of animals in research do not arise as isolated abstractions, as many "animal rights" advocates would have us believe, but are embedded in a cultural framework that goes back over 25 centuries. For contemporary American and European society, the moral structure of that framework has two principal foundations: the Judeo-Christian religious development and the rationalist-humanist school, which has its roots in Greek culture, particularly in the thinking of Aristotle and the Athenian Academy. While animal experimentation per se was not an issue in the classical world, contemporary attitudes on related issues established the basic approaches.

Central to Judaism is the Pentateuch, the first five books of the Bible, which are closely identified with Moses. The book of Leviticus contains elaborate descriptions of animal sacrifices: the burnt offering, the peace offering, the sin offering, and congregational sacrifices. The notion of animal sacrifices, while clearly not the same as research on animals, nonetheless carries the message that animals are killed for human benefit. Indeed, the language of that practice has held to the present day: When experimental animals are killed, scientific journals use the phrase, "The animals were sacrificed."

The New Testament

By the time of the New Testament, animal sacrifice was no longer predominant. Nevertheless, the concept of animals serving as surrogates for ailing humans was still present. There occurs a most dramatic story in the Gospel According to St. Mark:

> And they came over unto the other side of the sea, into the country of the Gadarenes. And when [Jesus] was come out of the ship, immediately there met him out of the tombs a man with an unclean spirit, . . .
>
> And always, night and day, he was in the mountains, and in the tombs, crying, and cutting himself with stones.
>
> But when he saw Jesus afar off, he ran and worshipped him.
>
> And cried with a loud voice, and said, What have I to do with thee, Jesus, thou Son of the most high God? I adjure thee by God, that thou torment me not.

35

For he said unto him, Come out of the man, thou unclean spirit.
And he asked him, What is thy name? And he answered, saying, My name is Legion: for we are many. . . .
Now there was there nigh unto the mountains a great herd
of swine feeding.
And all the devils besought him, saying, Send us into the swine,
that we may enter into them.
And forthwith Jesus gave them leave. And the unclean spirits
went out, and entered into the swine: and the herd ran violently
down a steep place into the sea, (they were about two thousand;)
and were choked in the sea.

Mark 5:1-2, 5-9, 11-13

What is noteworthy is the willingness of Jesus to sacrifice 2,000
higher mammals to save one human being from his afflictions.
That attitude, which pervades both Judaism and Christianity,
comes originally from Genesis and the concept of man's dominion
over the animals:

And God said, Let us make man in our image, after our
likeness: and let them have dominion over the fish of the sea,
and over the fowl of the air, and over the cattle, and over all
the earth. . . .
And God blessed them, and God said unto them, Be fruitful,
and multiply, and replenish the earth, and subdue it: and have
dominion over the fish of the sea, and over the fowl of the air,
and over every living thing that moveth upon the earth.

Gen. 1:26, 28

A central theme of biblical morality is the sacredness of each
human life. Since man is the purpose of all creation, the notion
of dominion follows in a natural way.

The tradition that has developed within the Roman Catholic
branch of Christianity was explicitly expressed in *Moral Philosophy
of Ethics and Natural Law* (1889) by Joseph Rickaby, S.J. The book
was part of a series called Manuals of Catholic Philosophy.

Brute beasts, not having understanding and therefore not being
persons, cannot have any rights. . . . The conclusion is clear. We
have no duties to them,—not of justice, as is shown; not of
religion, unless we are to worship them, like the Egyptians of
old; not of fidelity, for they are incapable of accepting a promise.
The only question can be of charity. Have we duties of charity
to the lower animals? Charity is an extension of the love of
ourselves to beings like ourselves, in view of our common nature
and our common destiny to happiness in God. It is not for the
present treatise to prove, but to assume, that our nature is not
common to brute beasts, but immeasurably above theirs, higher
indeed above them than we are below the angels. . . . We have
then no duties of charity, nor duties of any kind, to the lower
animals, as neither to sticks and stones. . . . Much more in all
that conduces to the sustenance of man may we give pain to
brutes, as also in the pursuit of science.

Father Rickaby's point of view closely follows the writings of St. Thomas Aquinas. However, disagreement with this perspective on grounds of Christian charity and mercy was expressed by C.W. Hume in the *Dictionary of Christian Ethics* (1967).

A Protestant affirmation of Rickaby's view is found in Elmer Smick's entry in *Baker's Dictionary of Christian Ethics* (1973):

> Not all forms of life, however, are equally sacred: there are levels of creation with man at the top. There should be no question of man's right to life above the animal world because he bears the Creator's image and has a spiritual nature.

Aristotle and Animals

The classical rationalist secular view lacks a single categorical statement, but its beginnings may be seen in the works of Aristotle, who as an experimental biologist had probably done hundreds of animal vivisections and dissections. He fully understood the importance of animal models in the study of human anatomy, physiology, and disease. . . .

The extension of the Aristotelian perspective into the age of science is seen most forcefully in the writings of Claude Bernard. In his book *Experimental Medicine* (1865), he addressed the issue of animal use and gave what I believe is still the scientist's justification for work on higher mammals:

> Have we the right to make experiments on animals and vivisect them? As for me, I think we have this right, wholly and absolutely. No hesitation is possible; the science of life can be established only through experiment, and we can save living beings from death only after sacrificing others. Experiments must be made either on man or on animals. Now I think that physicians have already made too many dangerous experiments on man, before carefully studying them on animals. I do not admit that it is moral to try more or less dangerous or active remedies on patients in hospitals, without first experimenting with them on dogs; for I shall prove, further on, that results obtained on animals may all be conclusive for man when we know how to experiment properly. If it is immoral, then, to make an experiment on man when it is dangerous to him, even though the result may be useful to others, it is essentially moral to make experiments on an animal even though painful and dangerous to him, if they may be useful to man.

Thus, our major religious and historical traditions contain strong elements not only permitting us, but in a certain sense urging us toward, the experimental use of animals for the benefit of man. Those traditions also direct us to be compassionate to the animals being used.

"Medical science won't advance far without putting the needs of man above those of animals."

Human Needs Are More Important than Animal Rights

Jay Stuller

When faced with the choice of sparing an animal's life or saving a human being, most people would reasonably choose to save the human, according to the author of the following viewpoint, Jay Stuller. Stuller argues that food shortages and the need for cures to life-threatening illnesses justify human use of animals to meet those needs. Stuller is a free-lance writer whose articles have appeared in *Audubon, Oceans,* and *Reader's Digest.*

As you read, consider the following questions:

1. What does Stuller find baffling about the arguments of animal rights groups?
2. Why does the author believe it is harmful to anthropomorphize animals?
3. What might be the consequences of granting animals rights equal to those humans have, according to Stuller?

Jay Stuller, "Do Animals Have Rights?" *Kiwanis* magazine, September 1988. Reprinted with permission.

Since mankind first developed the intelligence to ponder such things, the natural order that placed humans above animals seemed clear. Though the strength and beauty of various species always have warranted admiration and respect, Western cultures generally have ranked the interests of wildlife and domesticated stock below that of men, women, and children.

Faced with a choice of starvation or eating the beautiful deer grazing in the glen, "Bambi," sorry to say, invariably wound up on the spit.

Man, of course, had the brains and ability to enforce this system—most of the time, sharks notwithstanding. Viewed as a renewable resource for clothing, transportation, nutrition, and labor, animals have "served" man in countless ways. In fact, most of the major medical advances of the past century have sprung from experiments and tests conducted upon rats, rabbits, dogs, cats, and primates.

Animals in a Different Light

There is a large and fast-growing movement, however, that perceives animals in a different light. Drawing support from the public, the news media, and politicians in North America, Europe and, to some degree, other parts of the globe, this crusade has many factions with several hundred animal-interest organizations representing an estimated 10 million members.

And though these groups include conventional conservationists who mainly are concerned with preserving wildlife populations, there is a radical element to this movement that is gaining increasingly broader support.

Led by humans who have made a moral determination that all *creatures* are created equal, the campaign for animal rights (which differs from concerns for their welfare) vests nearly all beasts with a moral and legal status comparable to that usually granted humans. Such activists seek to prohibit the use of animals for food, clothing, shoes, sport, and, in particular, scientific and medical research. . . .

Baffling Protests

Some of the more recent animal-rights protests have been, well, unusual, if not baffling, to folks raised in rural regions. Largely of North American and European origin, the campaigns must seem incomprehensible to people in parts of the world with food shortages.

For example: "Behind virtually every slice of bacon and every innocuous looking egg," warns a Humane Society of the United States newsletter, "lurks a long, hidden history of unbearable suffering." Featuring photos of suffering sows and distressed chickens confined in small pens and crowded cages, the society asked that recipients donate money to stop what's known as "factory farming."

Conditions in the pork and poultry industries, it states, make a plate of bacon and eggs nothing less than "the breakfast of cruelty."

Then there's an organization of attorneys called the Animal Legal Defense Fund that files lawsuits to stop fur trappers from using leg-hold traps, to prevent farmers from raising "milk-fed" veal calves, and to save geese from *pâtés de foie gras* (a fat goose liver and truffles dish).

Only in the Industrialized West

The central assertion of animal liberation—that animals and humans share equal moral status—glosses over the complexity of human relationships to animals worldwide. Peter Singer, the Australian philosopher and animal rights advocate, posits a dichotomy only comprehensible to urban inhabitants of the industrialized West and few other societies when he writes, "We treat [animals] as if they were things to be used as we please, rather than as beings with lives of their own to live" (1985). The recognition of animals as sentient beings in the world of nature and yet different from humans in moral status is implicit in the attitudes and behavior of people in many other cultures. For instance, among the Kung San, gatherer-hunters of southern Africa, the hunter is pragmatic about his desire for meat but asks forgiveness of the animal's spirit after the kill. In this example, the animal is neither a thing nor the equal of a human being. . . . Animal liberation posits too ethnocentric and narrow a view of the human-animal relationship, a view that has little application outside the privileged enclaves of the industrial West.

Susan Sperling, *Animal Liberators*, 1988.

And the American Society for the Prevention of Cruelty to Animals wants to halt carriage rides like those around New York City's Central Park, which, it alleges, "are responsible for the death or injury to many horses every year."

So much for breakfast, fine dining, and romance.

A Moral Dilemma

The most emotional arena for the animal-rights crusade, however, concerns medical and scientific experimentation. The thought of a dog, cat, or monkey suffering in a research lab is wrenching for all but the most heartless. But it also creates one of the greatest of moral dilemmas.

"Animal research," explains Frederick A. King, director of the Yerkes Regional Primate Center of Emory University in Atlanta, Georgia, "has produced virtually all modern vaccines against infectious diseases, the invention of surgical approaches to eye disorders and bone and joint injuries, the discovery of insulin and other hormones, and the testing of new drugs and antibiotics. Polio could not have been stopped without the use of primates."

Biofeedback, which had its origin in studies of rats, can be used to control blood pressure and hypertension to prevent heart attacks. Neural and behavioral studies of the early development of vision in cats and primates have led to advances in pediatric ophthalmology that can prevent irreversible brain damage and loss of vision.

Current animal studies are beginning to provide clues to Alzheimer's disease. And research on primates, according to King, will be a key to developing a vaccine for the most dreaded disease of modern times—AIDS. . . .

A Reign of Fear

"There's really a reign of fear in the scientific community," says Don White of the American Psychological Association. "Labs are forced to put more money into expensive security equipment, and universities are cutting back on commitments to basic animal research. And at the same time, the federal funds available are dwindling, because animal research is not popular." . . .

James McGaugh of the University of California at Irvine frames the issue simply and elegantly: "The fundamental question here is: 'Are humans more important than other animals?' If you grant animals equal rights, you must also accept the consequences." . . .

The questions raised by the animal-rights movement are about human life versus animal life. For the foreseeable future, medical science won't advance far without putting the needs of man above those of animals—if that is the wish of the majority of the people.

"It's been said that during war, there are no atheists in the trenches," says McGaugh. "I wonder how an animal-rights person dying of a catastrophic illness might feel if one more animal test could find a cure."

"Animals are the victims of a vast human-regulated system of slavery."

Human Needs Are Not More Important than Animal Rights

Spence Carlsen

A common argument of philosophers who support animal rights is that it is impossible to justify rights for humans, who are a type of animal, and deny rights to non-human animals. In the following viewpoint, Spence Carlsen argues that animals have a right to life just as humans have a right to life. He believes that human morality must expand to acknowledge and respect the rights of non-human animals. Carlsen serves on the advisory boards of two national animal rights groups, Fund for Animals and Mercy Crusade.

As you read, consider the following questions:

1. How do humans turn animals into objects, according to the author?
2. What are the excuses humans use to justify their treatment of animals, according to Carlsen?
3. What is the basis of Carlsen's contention that animals are slaves for humans?

Spence Carlsen, "Animals Are Victims of Vast Human-Regulated System of Slavery," *Los Angeles Times,* April 22, 1987. Reprinted with permission.

People are nervous and uncomfortable around things that they don't easily understand. Sometimes, amid all the discussion that surrounds it, a new idea is either misunderstood completely or not understood at all. Such confusion surrounds the idea that non-human animals have rights. Many people think that this is either too ridiculous to be taken seriously or too complicated for anyone except philosophers. As usual, this kind of polarization disguises the much simpler truth of the matter: If human animals have rights, such as the right to life, so do non-human animals.

A common mistake, and a probable cause of much of the confusion, is the belief that human animals are radically different creatures from non-human animals. We are raised from childhood to see other animals as creatures that are in some way less than human and distinctly separate from us by nature. Most of us never even see animals, other than dogs and cats, except in pictures or zoos. Our separation is physical as well as mental.

Animals as Objects

We think about animals as objects whose purpose in the order of things is to serve human ends. We learn a whole set of unquestioned beliefs and a very specialized vocabulary that keep us from realizing the abuses that non-human animals undergo to satisfy these ends. A cow who has been killed, skinned, dismembered and ground up or sliced is "beef," "leather," "hindquarter," "hamburger." A laboratory rat is a "research tool" or "model." A deer or a fox on a wildlife "refuge" becomes a "resource" deserving of "conservation." Using these words, it is hard, if not impossible, to understand non-human animals as creatures that, like ourselves, experience pain and suffering and have complicated emotional lives.

Most of us know that what we do to animals we would never do to people. We understand that people have certain rights that keep them from being eaten, worn or experimented on by other people. What we don't realize, until we really examine our beliefs about animals, is that these rights cannot belong exclusively to human beings. There is no non-arbitrary way to exclude such things as the right to life from non-human animals.

A Relationship Based on Power

In order to continue to do what we have always done, we dream up excuses to hide the bolder truth. The excuses range from the unscientific "God gave them to us to use" to the pseudo-scientific "Animals are machines, not substantially different from clocks in their working." These mind-boggling distortions prevent most of us from realizing that the human relationship with other animals is based on power. We are stronger than they are. We do whatever we want, whenever we want, because non-human animals are unable to stop us. In the same way in which people holding power deny the rights of people with less power, human animals deny the rights of non-human animals.

Animals are in laboratories because we are powerful enough to keep them there, not because it is where they belong. Once they are restrained and caged, we can burn, irradiate, infect, electrocute, poison and "sacrifice" them. The extent of experimentation is limited by imagination, not law.

Question the System

The realization that the animals we enslave, the animals we turn into *things*, the animals who slave for us that we might eat some luxury from their bodies, are *alive*, are as possessive of their lives as you or I, this realization would throw a wrench into the system. If this realization were reached, people would have to change an aspect of their lifestyle. And this is why many people resist thinking about it, resist questioning the system, and fail to know the obvious. Which greatly pleases the slave-*owners*, those who directly profit from the lives of animals and from our passive and active acceptance of slavery and oppression. For if individuals did question it, and refused to participate any longer, the system would collapse.

Marjorie Spiegel, *The Dreaded Comparison: Human and Animal Slavery,* 1988.

Animals are on our dinner tables because we are powerful enough to control their lives from birth. We confine them in the smallest possible spaces, breed or artificially inseminate them, take their babies away from them, give them hormones, overfeed them and, finally, kill them. Animal skins, with and without their fur, are on our bodies because we are powerful enough to hunt, trap, club, shoot and harpoon other animals. We maintain wilderness habitats for fur-bearing animals in order to harvest them. We control the natural predator population to "conserve" the stock.

Enslaved Animals

Animals are the victims of a vast human-regulated system of slavery. They serve our desires and whims, whether for the taste of their flesh, the feel of their skin or the profit that can be made. To see this enslavement for what it is, and to comprehend the suffering that it causes, is the first step toward understanding the meaning of animals' rights—that is, the rights that are possessed by human and non-human animals alike. The next step is to respond to the call that this places on our conscience and do something to restore the rights that naturally belong to what Henry Beston called "other nations," in a disturbing and beautiful passage in his book *The Outermost House.*

a critical thinking activity

Distinguishing Between Fact and Opinion

This activity is designed to help develop the basic reading and thinking skill of distinguishing between fact and opinion. Consider the following statement: "More than 10 million people belong to animal rights groups." This is a factual statement because it could be proved by checking how many members each animal rights group has. But the statement, "The people involved in animal rights groups have mixed-up morals," is an opinion. Someone who agrees with animal rights groups would have a different idea of what is moral than someone who does not agree.

When investigating controversial issues it is important that one be able to distinguish between statements of fact and statements of opinion. It is also important to recognize that not all statements of fact are true. They may appear to be true, but some are based on inaccurate or false information. For this activity, however, we are concerned with understanding the difference between those statements which appear to be factual and those which appear to be based primarily on opinion.

Most of the following statements are taken from the viewpoints in this chapter. Consider each statement carefully. *Mark O for any statement you believe is an opinion or interpretation of facts. Mark F for any statement you believe is a fact. Mark I for any statement you believe is impossible to judge.*

If you are doing this activity as a member of a class or group, compare your answers with those of other class or group members. Be able to defend your answers. You may discover that others come to different conclusions than you do. Listening to the reasons others present for their answers may give you valuable insights in distinguishing between fact and opinion.

O = opinion
F = fact
I = impossible to judge

1. Rights cannot belong exclusively to human beings.

2. In the 1850s a black feminist named Sojourner Truth spoke at a feminist convention.

3. It is essentially moral to experiment on an animal.

4. When Mary Wollstonecraft published her *A Vindication of the Rights of Women* in 1792, her views were widely regarded as absurd.

5. God created animals for man to use.

6. Christianity did not employ animal sacrifice, except in isolated instances.

7. Most of today's modern medical miracles would not exist if experimental animals had not been available.

8. Christians engage in a sacramental meal in which the body and blood of the Saviour are symbolically devoured.

9. There is an organization of attorneys called the Animal Legal Defense Fund that files lawsuits to stop fur trappers from using leg-hold traps.

10. The book of Leviticus contains elaborate descriptions of animal sacrifices.

11. If a being suffers there can be no moral justification for refusing to take that suffering into consideration.

12. Western cultures generally have ranked the interests of wildlife and farm animals below that of men, women, and children.

13. Our major religious and historical traditions contain strong elements that not only permit us, but urge us toward the experimental use of animals for the benefit of people.

14. Because animals can suffer, they deserve equal consideration.

15. More than a hundred million animals are used in US labs every year.

16. Brute beasts, not having understanding and therefore not being persons, cannot have any rights.

17. Animal liberation posits too narrow a view of the human-animal relationship.

Periodical Bibliography

The following articles have been selected to supplement the diverse views presented in this chapter.

Ronald Bailey — "Non-Human Rights," *Commentary*, October 1985.

Kim Bartlett — "The 'Divine Right' of Humans," *The Animals' Agenda*, December 1987.

Patrick Buchanan — "Animal Rights and Ideology," *The Washington Times*, December 5, 1988.

Arthur L. Caplan — "Beastly Conduct: Ethical Issues in Animal Experimentation," *Annals of the New York Academy of Sciences*, 1981.

Karen Davis — "Farm Animals and the Feminine Connection," *The Animals' Agenda*, January/February 1988.

Harper's Magazine — "Just Like Us? Toward a Notion of Animal Rights," August 1988.

Harper's Magazine — "Letters: Facing Our Own Savagery," November 1988.

Gabriel Moran — "Dominion over the Earth," *Commonweal*, December 4, 1987.

Timothy Noah — "Have You Hugged Your Lab Animal Today? Monkey Business," *The New Republic*, June 2, 1982.

Christine Pierce — "Can Animals Be Liberated?" *Philosophical Studies*, July 1979.

Steve F. Sapontzis — "Moral Community and Animal Rights," *American Philosophical Quarterly*, July 1985.

Carolyn See — "Lured to the Whales When It's So Hard To Rescue People in Need," *Los Angeles Times*, October 28, 1988.

Trans-Species Unlimited — "Animal Rights: What's It All About?" Available from Trans-Species Unlimited, PO Box 1553, Williamsport, PA 17703.

Alice Walker — "Am I Blue?" *Ms.*, July 1986.

Debra Blake Weisenthal — "The Other Michael Fox: An Interview with the Humane Society's Visionary," *Vegetarian Times*, January 1989.

Is Animal Experimentation Justified?

ANIMAL RIGHTS

Chapter Preface

The debate over the ethics of animal experimentation has a long and contentious history. French philosopher René Descartes was an early advocate of experimentation. In 1637 in his *Discourse on the Method,* he recommends to those not versed in anatomy that they have "cut up before their eyes the heart of some large animal which has lungs." By doing this, they would become familiar with how the heart and other organs work. This example illustrates Descartes's view that humans are superior to animals and can freely use animals to increase scientific knowledge. He believes human superiority lies in the ability to make rational, intelligent decisions and to communicate. Animals, in contrast, act purely on instinct.

In the 1700s, British philosopher Jeremy Bentham argued against Descartes's view. He believed that pain, not intelligence or ability to communicate, was the standard that should be used to assess the ethics of animal experimentation. Bentham argued that since animals can feel pain, humans must not inflict pain on them. In a footnote in his 1789 text, *The Principles of Morals and Legislation,* he links the struggle to end animal suffering with the struggle to end human suffering. Just as some "have already discovered that the blackness of skin is no reason why a human being should be abandoned without redress to the caprice of a tormentor" so one day people might recognize that suffering should not be inflicted on animals.

The views of Descartes and Bentham are often quoted today when people debate whether it is ethical for humans to use animals in scientific experiments. The authors in the following chapter discuss many of the same issues that these philosophers first raised.

49

"Many, if not most, of today's modern medical miracles would not exist if experimental animals had not been available to medical scientists."

Animal Experimentation Is Ethical

Richard C. Simmonds

Richard C. Simmonds is a veterinarian who specializes in the care of laboratory animals. He is the president of the American Association for Laboratory Animal Science and the treasurer of Scientists Center for Animal Welfare. In the following viewpoint, Simmonds argues that as long as laboratory animals are well-cared for, using them in biomedical research is ethical. He concludes that the life-saving medical advances produced by animal testing are adequate justification for continuing to use animals for humane research.

As you read, consider the following questions:

1. What does Simmonds mean by the term "basic research"?
2. Why is it ethical for humans to use animals for human benefit, according to Simmonds?
3. What does the author predict might happen if teachers could no longer use animals in their medical classes?

Richard C. Simmonds, "Should Animals Be Used in Research and Education?" *The New Physician*, March 1986. Reprinted with permission.

A recent public opinion poll indicated that 81 percent of the people across the nation believe it is necessary to use animals for some medical research, and 72 percent thought researchers should be allowed to use pound animals. Given the current public furor over the use of animals in biomedical research, this high percentage of public support is surprising and heartening. Yet in the same poll, 76 percent indicated they believed animals "have rights," and 46 percent of those people thought the "use of animals in medical experiments violates the animals' rights."

My interpretation of these responses is that the public still overwhelmingly supports medical research using animals but believes that doing so involves some ethical "costs." However, I do not believe the public accepts that animals have "rights" as postulated by a number of modern philosophers. Rather, I believe our society's ethic is more utilitarian in nature, asserting that such use of animals is justified so long as the potential gain in preventing human suffering or amassing new knowledge is significant enough to outweigh the ethical "cost" of the animals' deaths.

The Need for Basic Research

This position leads to certain questions: How does one judge the utilitarian (or "ethical") value versus cost of any particular experiment? Who should be the judge? What ratio of value to cost is acceptable? No answers will satisfy everyone, but research would probably be acceptable to most members of our society if the experiment is directly related to improving human health dramatically, i.e., "applied" rather than "basic" research.

Basic research that frequently seems frivolous and esoteric to many people is more difficult to judge. The fact that major medical discoveries of today are based on bits and pieces of information generated by basic research decades ago is poorly understood by many people. Open heart surgery today is based on discoveries from the 17th century that involved disciplines quite remote from medicine, such as engineering and materials sciences, yet scientists have not effectively conveyed such information to the public or their legislators.

Animals and Medical Miracles

It is a simple fact that many, if not most, of today's modern medical miracles would not exist if experimental animals had not been available to medical scientists. It is equally a fact that, should we as a society decide the use of animal subjects is ethically unacceptable and therefore must be stopped, medical progress will slow to a snail's pace. Such retardation will in itself have a huge ethical "price tag" in terms of continued human and animal suffering from problems such as diabetes, cancer, degenerative cardiovascular diseases, and so forth. The exquisite complexity of living organisms has not yet been duplicated by any non-animal or in vitro system. Thus, if medical science is to continue to advance, intact live animal subjects are necessary.

An Ethical Responsibility

The ability of biomedical scientists to enhance the well-being of humans and animals depends directly on advancements made possible by research, much of which requires the use of experimental animals. The scientific community has long recognized both a scientific and an ethical responsibility for the humane care of animals, and all who care for or use animals in research, testing, and education must assume responsibility for their general welfare.

National Institutes of Health, *Guide for the Care and Use of Laboratory Animals,* 1985.

True, we can decide that the human species should accept the cost of slowed medical progress in order to spare nonconsenting sentient animals, but we do not have to make that decision. According to the natural order of life on earth, all living organisms exist at the expense of other organisms. Plants require certain microorganisms to get nutrients from the soil and depend on decaying organic matter (including animal carcasses) for many of their nutritional needs. Herbivorous animals eat the plants and carnivorous animals eat the plant-eaters. Nature imposes no limitations on how one species may exploit another for survival, and I submit that humans have a natural "right" to exploit other species for our survival and benefit. I include the development of medical cures and treatments as part and parcel of our survival. However, I also believe that as the only species endowed with the intellect to develop abstract concepts such as "ethics" and "morals," we have an obligation to treat animals used for our benefit as humanely as possible; that obligation is to our own humanity, not to the animals.

Science Education

The use of animals in programs of biomedical education poses related ethical questions. I have been quoted as saying there are no data to support the benefit of using live animal laboratories to enhance the competence of medical practitioners, either physicians or veterinarians. This is a true statement. What is usually omitted, however, is that I also say there are no data to support the position that such labs are not of value; nor is it likely that any such data will ever be obtained. But studies do indicate there are short-term educational gains from such experiences for most students, and a large majority of educators believe subjectively that such laboratory exercises are very valuable. I personally believe I learned a great deal from my laboratory experiences as a veterinary student. Furthermore, without such labs, health care professionals will learn certain skills on the job, which probably will increase the number of errors they initially make. Our society may decide the risk to humans of such on-the-job training is a "cost" we should pay, in lieu of what some see as the unethical use of animals. However, people should be fully informed that such risks are definitely part of such a position.

The obligation to treat animal subjects humanely requires, in my opinion, a full commitment by all involved persons, from the scientist who designs the experimental or teaching protocols to the technicians and veterinarians responsible for the animal care program, to the administrators who are responsible for institutional resources and priorities. Today, with analytical equipment that can detect subtle physiological changes caused by minor environmental variations, quality science really does require quality animal care, and such care is expensive. Institutions that want to continue doing research involving live, intact animals *must* fully commit themselves to having quality animal care and use programs. Such programs should implement the three "Rs" of Russell and Burch (*The Principles of Humane Experimental Techniques*): *R*eplacement (of animals with non-animal alternatives), *R*efinement (of techniques to minimize the need for animals or the distress imposed upon them), and *R*eduction (of the number of animals required by better experimental design), as well as the fourth "R" of Paton (*Man & Mouse: Animals in Research*)—*R*esponsibility (for accomplishing quality science in a quality manner).

Limited Ethical Cost

In conclusion, the use of animals in biomedical research is the only form of animal exploitation by mankind that has the potential for unlimited benefit at limited ethical cost; that is, any new information derived can be used from the time of discovery through all future generations, *ad infinitum*. The polio vaccine discovered in the early 1950s will prevent multitudes of cases of that dreaded disease and will continue to do so until the virus can be eliminated. It truly would be unwise, and I believe ethically immoral, not to continue using animal subjects in biomedical research. At the same time, we must do so with a full commitment to providing the best care possible and to using animals only when there is no other way to achieve the research objectives.

*"The infliction of suffering and death on
animals in the laboratory is morally wrong."*

Animal Experimentation Is Unethical

The American Anti-Vivisection Society

Founded in 1883, The American Anti-Vivisection Society has remained a vocal opponent of conducting research tests on animals. In the following viewpoint, the Society objects to animal research because they believe it inflicts great suffering upon animals. Such research, the Society contends, does not help humans because many of the tests are redundant and other tests are useless.

As you read, consider the following questions:

1. What point does the American Anti-Vivisection Society make when comparing scientists to priests?
2. Why is it harmful to use animals as testing models in science classes, according to the Society?
3. Why does the author believe that cancer research that uses animals is a waste of taxpayers' money?

The American Anti-Vivisection Society, *The Case Book of Experiments with Living Animals*, August 1988. Reprinted with permission.

We oppose vivisection because it is morally wrong, cruel and fruitless! The American Anti-Vivisection Society is a national organization dedicated to the abolition of vivisection. We are motivated by the conviction that the infliction of suffering and death on animals in the laboratory is morally wrong, and that animals have a right to be free from such exploitation. In addition to that ethical concern, our programs, campaigns and literature reflect our belief that animal experiments are characterized by fundamental scientific limitations, chief among them the difficulty of transferring results to human beings with any degree of reliability.

By What Right?

When a murder is committed—when a man or woman takes the life of another—it is regarded as a crime against the state, which also means a crime against society. It is The State versus John Doe, and he is tried by a jury drawn from the people. Life is not to be taken lightly. To deprive one of it is a capital offense.

Curiously enough, little thought is given to the murder of animals, or to the excruciating tortures to which they may be subjected in the process. The tendency on the part of many people has been to regard them as insensate, or even as little more than inanimate objects. If, like Walt Whitman, you looked upon them as fellow beings, you might be regarded as a sentimentalist but hardly as the realist which you actually are.

Or again, if you are a person who has not been conditioned to witnessing pain or torture, if you do not wear the cold exterior armor that reveals neither concern nor compassion, or the chilling interior indifference that has become a part of your nature because of innumerable slayings at your hands, then you could know only horror at the atrocities performed upon animals in experimental laboratories. These creatures are defenseless, innocent of wrongdoing, unable to understand what is being done to them and why, but their nerves shriek and their bodies tremble or they sicken and retch with injected or ingested poisons, and sometimes they expire in agony. To them a speedy bullet and oblivion would be welcomed. But that is not the purpose of their murderers who wear the holy mantle of science, though they perform their rites much as an Aztec priest at a human sacrifice. The priest was placating the gods; the scientist courts the demons of disease. Like the Aztec, the scientist defends his acts on holy grounds. His god is his own invention; it is called Science, and everyone is supposed to bow down to it and to him as its prophet. See how alike they are. He executes his experiments, his torture and his murder of animals in the name of this god, and he cunningly justifies his acts not with a promise of abundant harvests but with a promise to cure disease—a promise, incidentally, less often fulfilled than that of abundant crops, though there is a striking similarity—both are more often the achievements of nature than of the efforts of priests or vivisectionists. Nevertheless there was, and is, much prestige and often wealth attached to both vocations. . . .

For years, the vivisectors and related groups have promoted themselves as the high priests of medicine whose judgment is beyond question. However, over the past decade, there has been growing interest in the philosophy of animal rights and the morality of animal research. The litany of concerned voices comes from members of the academic community as well as from the lay public.

No Privileged Status for Humans

One of the principal areas of controversy is whether different species should have equal consideration and treatment in research. Richard Ryder in the introduction to his book *Victims of Science* states:

> The most important qualities that men share with the other animals are life and sentience. There is as much evidence to believe that another animal can suffer as there is to believe that another individual of one's own species can suffer. There is good evidence that pain is a function of the nervous system and that many animals have nervous systems very much like our own— so, is it not reasonable to assume that when a wounded animal screams and struggles it is suffering in a way similar to that in which a wounded man can suffer? The capacity to suffer is the crucial similarity between men and animals that binds us all together and places us all in a similar moral category.

Mr. Ryder is not alone in this judgment. A recent editorial in the *New England Journal of Medicine* titled, "Immoral and Moral Use of Animals" makes a similar point:

> It is fair to say that no one has yet given good reasons to accept a moral perspective that grants a privileged moral status to all and only human beings . . . The exclusion of animals from the moral domain . . . is, in any case, arbitrary and unfounded in good moral argument.

Furthermore, the author of this article states:

> Scientists who perform experiments on animals rarely see the need to justify them, but when they do they almost always stress the seriousness of the research. Although it may be regrettable that animals are harmed, their suffering is seen as an unavoidable casualty of scientific progress. The moral philosopher must still ask: is the price in animal misery worth it? . . .

The question to be asked is how many scientists really do make a conscientious effort to avoid using and harming animals. Few of the cases outlined in this [viewpoint] are encouraging in this regard. . . .

A 1970 study concluded that at least 3 million animals per year are used in the United States for secondary school and university educational purposes. Many of these animal studies are not experiments at all, but simply demonstrations, and there is little objective evidence that manipulative exercises on live animals are necessary in educational courses. (In Great Britain, under the Cruelty to Animals Act, a license is required to experiment on living vertebrates. No student below the University level has ever been licensed; however, students do dissect living insects and other invertebrate animals.). . . .

Stop Vivisection

Vivisection should be stopped so that animals no longer suffer and die in laboratory experiments. Then scientists would have to introduce better and safer methods of research so we would all be better off.

Robert Sharpe, *Greenscene*, no. 2.

One of the greatest cruelties in medical research is the deliberate infliction of burns on animals. With so many tragic cases of burn victims in the wards of hospitals around the world, it seems totally unnecessary to inflict such suffering on sentient animals.

Vivisectors in the Department of Physiology, Louisiana State University Medical Center, New Orleans, appear to have made a career out of publishing burn studies which they undertook utilizing guinea pigs.

In these studies, guinea pigs were immersed for three seconds in 100°C water. This produced "full skin-thickness burns" over 50% or 70% of the body surface of each animal. In addition, the animals were conscious during these procedures; the only anesthesia being halothane during the scalding. In all three reports, the authors note similar investigations by others; however, they have changed a few variables to justify their work. . . .

Psychology Research

Animal experimentation plays a predominant role in psychology research. "Countless animals have been surgically dismembered, drugged, starved, fatigued, frozen, electrically shocked, infected, cross-bred, maddened, and killed in the belief that their behaviour closely observed, would cast light on the nature of humankind."

Hundreds of articles appear in numerous journals each year chronicling the pernicious nature of psychology research with animals. . . .

Fear, punishment and aggression are other popular subjects of research for psychologists who torment rats. In laboratories throughout the United States, supported by federal, state and

Ed Gamble. Reprinted with permission.

university funds, this research goes on under the mantle of "scientific inquiry." Outside the laboratory, these activities would be illegal. . . .

Infrequently, a vivisector will realize the horror of this type of research. Dr. Roger Ulrich, who for many years was inducing aggression in animals by causing them pain, is one of the few psychologists who has repudiated his work. In a poignant letter to the American Psychological Association Monitor, March 1978, he states:

> When I finished my dissertation on pain-produced aggression, my Mennonite mother asked me what it was about. When I told her she replied, 'Well, we knew that. Dad always warned us to stay away from animals in pain because they are more likely to attack.' Today I look back with love and respect on all my animal friends from rats to monkeys who submitted to years of torture so that like my mother I can say, 'Well, we knew that.'

"Research involving animals is absolutely essential to maintaining and improving the health of the American people."

Animal Experimentation Benefits Human Health

American Medical Association

Animals have been used in medical research for centuries. Animals were used in early studies to discover how blood circulates through the body, the effect of anesthesia, and the relationship between bacteria and disease. In the following viewpoint, the American Medical Association argues that animal experimentation is essential to learning about the human body. The AMA was founded in 1847 and is a leading national professional organization for physicians. Its publications, including the *Journal of the American Medical Association,* are highly influential in the medical field.

As you read, consider the following questions:

1. What qualities do animals have that make them particularly useful for experimentation, according to the American Medical Association?
2. What benefits do the authors see in psychological research that uses animals?
3. How do the authors respond to arguments that there are alternatives to using animals for research?

Use of Animals in Biomedical Research: The Challenge and Response, published in March 1988 as an AMA White Paper. Copyright © 1988, American Medical Association.

Today, animals are used in experiments for three general purposes: (1) biomedical and behavioral research, (2) education, (3) drug and product testing.

Biomedical research increases understanding of how biological systems function and advances medical knowledge. Biomedical experiments are conducted in accordance with the principles of the scientific method developed by the French physiologist, Claude Bernard, in 1865. This method established two requirements for the conduct of a valid experiment: (1) control of all variables so that only one factor or set of factors is changed at a time, and (2) the replication of results by other laboratories. Unless these requirements are met, an experiment is not considered scientifically valid. Behavioral research is a type of biomedical research that is directed toward determining the factors that affect behavior and how various organisms and organs respond to different stimuli. Much behavioral research is environmental in nature but some involves the study of responses to physical stimuli or manipulation of biological systems or organs, such as the brain.

Educational experiments are conducted to educate and train students in medicine, veterinary medicine, physiology, and general science. In many instances, these experiments are conducted with dead animals.

Animals also are employed to determine the safety and efficacy of new drugs or the toxicity of chemicals to which humans or animals may be exposed. Most of these experiments are conducted by commercial firms to fulfill government requirements. . . .

Using Animals Rather than Humans

A basic assumption of all types of research is that man should relieve human and animal suffering. One objection to the use of animals in biomedical research is that the animals are used as surrogates for human beings. This objection presumes the equality of all forms of life; animal rights advocates argue that if the tests are for the benefit of man, then man should serve as the subject of the experiments. There are limitations, however, to the use of human subjects both ethically, such as in the testing of a potentially toxic drug or chemical, and in terms of what can be learned. The process of aging, for instance, can best be observed through experiments with rats, which live an average of two to three years, or with some types of monkeys, which live 15 to 20 years. Some experiments require numerous subjects of the same weight or genetic makeup or require special diets or physical environments; these conditions make the use of human subjects difficult or impossible. By using animals in such tests, researchers can observe subjects of uniform age and background in sufficient numbers to determine if findings are consistent and applicable to a large population.

Animals are important in research precisely because they have complex body systems that react and interact with stimuli much as humans do. The more true this is with a particular animal, the more valuable that animal is for a particular type of research. One important property to a researcher is discrimination—the extent to which an animal exhibits the particular quality to be investigated. The greater the degree of discrimination, the greater the reliability and predictability of the information gathered from the experiment.

For example, dogs have been invaluable in biomedical research because of the relative size of their organs compared to humans. The first successful kidney transplant was performed in a dog and the techniques used to save the lives of "blue babies," and babies with structural defects in their hearts, were developed with dogs. Open heart surgical techniques, coronary bypass surgery and heart transplantation all were developed using dogs.

Another important factor is the amount of information available about a particular animal. Mice and rats play an extensive role in research and testing, in part because repeated experiments and controlled breeding have created a pool of data to which the findings from a new experiment can be related and given meaning. Their rapid rate of reproduction also has made them important in studies of genetics and other experiments that require obser-

Animals used for research in 1986 and some of the benefits—		
	Primates 49,000	AIDS research, vaccine development, studies of Alzheimer's and Parkinson's diseases
	Cats 54,000	Vision research
	Dogs 180,000	Heart-surgery research
	Rats, mice 12-15 mil.	Cancer research, safety testing of new drugs

USN&WR—Basic data: U.S. Dept. of Agriculture, Office of Technology Assessment

vation over a number of generations. Moreover, humans cannot be bred to produce "inbred strains" as can be done with animals; therefore, humans cannot be substituted for animals in studies where an inbred strain is essential. . . .

Nobel Prize Winners

One demonstration of the critical role that animals play in medical and scientific advances is that 54 of 76 Nobel Prizes awarded in physiology or medicine since 1901 have been for discoveries and advances made through the use of experimental animals. Among these have been the Prize awarded in 1985 for the studies (using dogs) that documented the relationship between cholesterol and heart disease; the 1966 Prize for the studies (using chickens) that linked viruses and cancer; and the 1960 Prize for studies (using cattle, mice, and chicken embryos) that established that a body can be taught to accept tissue from different donors if it is inoculated with different types of tissue prior to birth or during the first year of life, a finding expected to help simplify and advance organ transplants in the future. Studies using animals also resulted in successful culture of the poliomyelitis virus; a Nobel Prize was awarded for this work in 1954. The discovery of insulin and treatment of diabetes, achieved through experiments using dogs, also earned the Prize in 1923.

In fact, virtually every advance in medical science in the 20th century, from antibiotics and vaccines to antidepressant drugs and organ transplants, has been achieved either directly or indirectly through the use of animals in laboratory experiments. The result of these experiments has been the elimination or control of many infectious diseases—smallpox, poliomyelitis, measles—and the development of numerous life-saving techniques—blood transfusions, burn therapy, open-heart and brain surgery. This has meant a longer, healthier, better life with much less pain and suffering. For many, it has meant life itself. . . .

Behavioral Research

Behavioral research has been of immense benefit to humans. For example, fundamental information on how people learn was discovered by experiments on animals in laboratories; the learning principles and behavior modification therapies discovered or developed through such experiments are today being used to treat conditions such as anuresis (bed-wetting), addictive behaviors (tobacco, drugs, alcohol), and compulsive behaviors such as anorexia nervosa. . . .

Experiments on cats have enhanced the understanding of the corpus callosum, a band of fibers that connects the left and right sides of the brain needed for transfer of information from one side to another. This finding, for which a Nobel Prize was awarded in 1981, led directly to the development of new treatments for patients with strokes, language disorders, brain damage, intractable epilepsy, and other neurologic conditions.

One objection of animal rights advocates to behavioral research is their belief that many tests are conducted merely to confirm or prove long-accepted or obvious concepts, such as that a child will suffer when deprived of love or a parenting figure. However, what appears to be an obvious truth often proves to be false when subjected to close scrutiny in experiments. This includes the idea that all animals suffer when separated from a parent. In tests conducted over a number of years with rhesus monkeys, scientists discovered that, whereas some infants became withdrawn and anxious, others grew stronger and showed fewer stress-related symptoms when exposed to new or threatening situations. This has prompted new research into possible genetic and physiologic reasons why people react differently to stress and which types of persons are more likely to develop conditions such as depression.

Integral to Biomedicine

Research with laboratory animals has been so integral to the progress of biomedicine that it is difficult to exaggerate the contribution. Virtually every medical innovation of the last century—and especially the last four decades—has been based to a significant extent upon the results of animal experimentation. Had laboratory scientists studied only relatively simple living systems such as invertebrates, microorganisms, and cell cultures or had clinical scientists lacked avenues of inquiry apart from human experimentation with all its necessary ethical constraints, mystery would reign in many areas where invaluable knowledge now exists.

William Raub, *Health Benefits of Animal Research.*

Other behavioral research utilizing animals is leading to a deeper understanding of links between the mind and the body that may have important ramifications for the prevention and treatment of disease. Studies conducted with mice and monkeys have helped to establish and explore the relationship between stress and conditions such as heart disease, hypertension, and breakdowns in the immune system that leave individuals vulnerable to disease. Such studies may lead to an understanding of the nature of psychosomatic illnesses in humans. . . .

Unnecessary Duplication?

Criticism by animal rights adherents is directed at three types of experiments: those that are conducted for educational purposes; those that are conducted merely to "prove the obvious"; and those that repeat experiments already conducted.

Fewer animals are used for education than for any other purpose. They are used either to instruct students in courses such as physiology or to teach techniques, such as surgery. The use of animals in education varies from school to school and from program to program, even within medical schools. Educators generally agree, however, that students are better trained and patients better served when the students are given "hands-on" experience with living tissue, especially for training in surgery. Even the British, who otherwise ban the use of animals for educational purposes, accept the necessity of using animals under anesthesia to teach the techniques of microsurgery.

The Need To Duplicate Experiments

Animal rights activists also object to the duplication of experiments including those conducted for educational purposes and those that have failed elsewhere. The performance of experiments when the result is known in advance is a sound educational technique and is employed in many fields that do not involve animals, such as mathematics, physics, and chemistry. By utilizing an experiment in which the result is known in advance, it can be determined whether the experiment is performed correctly or incorrectly.

The criticism relating to the repetition of failed experiments has some merit, scientists agree, and emphasizes the need to improve communication among scientists in both the research and testing communities. Commercial firms that perform many of the testing experiments, such as drug and chemical companies, have taken steps both directly and through their trade associations to respond to this need by establishing mechanisms for sharing of data and results among firms. The creation of a comprehensive data bank for all research and testing is a far more complex undertaking, however, and an attempt by a private firm to establish a limited system failed earlier this decade.

A third reason for duplication of experiments is the requirement of the scientific method for a new finding to be verified by scientists in other laboratories before the finding can be considered valid. Such replication is necessary and quite often uncovers a mistake in technique or design or some other flaw in the original experiments that will render it invalid.

Both economic pressure and the peer review process used to evaluate research proposals make the conduct of unnecessary experiments unlikely. Research today involves intense competition for funding; for example, only about 25% of studies proposed to, and approved by, federal agencies each year are actually funded. Therefore, scientists on research evaluation committees are not likely to approve redundant or unnecessary experiments. Also, given the competition for funds, scientists are unlikely to waste valuable time and resources conducting unnecessary or duplicative experiments. . . .

Primates are used in experiments in relatively few numbers—approximately one-half of 1% of all animals used. However, their contributions to both biological and behavioral sciences have been numerous, significant, and in some cases crucial. . . .

No Real Alternatives

Individuals and groups opposed to animal research . . . say that so-called alternative methods could have solved the problem without the use of animals. While it is indeed now possible to produce certain vaccines through the use of microbiological and cell cultures, these methods were not applicable at the time of the development of the polio vaccine. In the case of polio, should we have waited for an undeveloped technology whose potential uses for vaccine development were not even recognized? If we had, some of you, or your children, would likely not be living today. And who among us would subject their families and children to a vaccine untested for safety on animals?

Frederick A. King, speech to the American Association for Laboratory Animal Science, September 10, 1986.

Primates played three different roles in the development of the poliomyelitis vaccines, all of them essential. Although many studies on poliomyelitis in humans were conducted in the late 19th century, the cause of the disease remained unknown until scientists were able to transmit the virus to monkeys in 1908. There followed many years of research with primates until scientists were able, in the early 1950s, to grow the virus in human cell cultures and development of a vaccine became possible. At that point, to ensure the safety and effectiveness of the vaccines, tests were conducted with monkeys. To produce the vaccines in pure form in great quantities, it was necessary to use kidney tissue taken from monkeys. Today, the use of the monkey kidney tissue is no longer necessary because vaccines now are produced through self-propagating cells—an alternative to the use of animals developed through appropriate research. . . .

AIDS

The chimpanzees may play a critical role in developing a therapy for AIDS. Medical researchers note that, in contemporary medicine, AIDS is the first infectious disease that is virtually 100% fatal. The chimpanzee has been the only animal that scientists have been able to infect with the AIDS virus. To date, none have developed the disease, leading some animal rights activists and even some scientists to question its value in the research. However, the fact that the chimpanzee does not become ill may in itself provide a clue to combating the disease if the reason can be discovered through research. Primates will be vitally important in the development and testing of vaccines for AIDS. . . .

Animal rights activists have insisted that certain experimental methods that investigators have developed can be used in lieu of animal experiments. Thus, as used in the debate, the word "alternatives" has become virtually synonymous with the word "substitutes" and animal rights activists have tended to focus on two: *in vitro* research (cell, tissue, and organ cultures) and computer simulation of biological systems in the form of mathematical models.

Both of these methods play important roles in biomedical research and have allowed the performance of experiments not possible with animals. In addition, both have avoided the need to use animals in some stages of research. However, they cannot serve, either individually or in combination with any other research method, as total replacement for use of live animals in experiments, for they cannot reproduce exactly the intact biological system provided by live animals. Each method suffers from at least some inherent deficiency.

Cell Cultures

The technology and use of cell cultures has grown dramatically during the past 20 years, making possible the performance of experiments that were previously impossible. Cells in isolation, however, do not act or react the same as cells in an intact system. As the Congressional Office of Technology Assessment noted in a report it prepared for Congress, *Alternatives to Animal Use in Research, Testing, and Education:* " . . . isolated systems give isolated results that may bear little relation to results obtained from the integrated systems of whole animals."

The same is true of tissues and organs placed in cultures. In addition, scientists point out, tissue and organs are difficult to nourish and maintain and tend to disintegrate automatically or lose their ability to function when maintained in cultures for long periods.

Computer Simulations

Computer simulations, often promoted as the great hope of the future by animal rights activists, have been invaluable in developing or suggesting new lines of scientific inquiry and in developing new mechanisms or techniques. However, both computers and computer simulations have inherent limitations that make it unlikely that they will ever totally replace animals in experiments. One of these limitations is the nature of simulation. The validity of any model depends on how closely it resembles the original in every respect. Much about the body and the various biological systems of humans and animals is not known. For example, how the body breaks down each chemical or drug or the manner in which brain cells transmit the sensory signals that create vision are not known; therefore, they cannot be programmed into any model. Until full knowledge of a particular biological system is developed, no model can be constructed that will in every case predict or accurately represent the reaction of the system to a given stimulus. . . .

No other method of study can exactly reproduce the characteristics and qualities of a living intact biological system or organism. Therefore, in order to understand how such a system or organism functions in a particular set of circumstances or how it will react to a given stimulus, it becomes necessary at some point to conduct an experiment or test to find out. There simply is no alternative to this approach and therefore no alternative to using animals for most types of health related research. . . .

One testing procedure for which a concerted effort to develop an alternative has been made is the Draize test in which chemicals and other substances are sprayed into the eyes of rabbits to determine potential toxic effects. This test, which can cause pain and blinding, has been the special target of one particular animal rights group and through its efforts several million dollars have been contributed by cosmetics companies, foundations, and animal welfare organizations to seek substitute tests. Although attempts are being made by scientists to limit the use of this test and some alternatives seem promising, no adequate replacements have yet been devised that would provide accurate information to protect the public from toxic new drugs, household products, and other chemicals. Work is continuing in this area. . . .

Absolutely Essential

Biomedical research using animals is essential to continued progress in clinical medicine. Animal research holds the key for solutions to AIDS, cancer, heart disease, aging and congenital defects. In discussing legislation concerning animal experimentation, the prominent physician and physiologist, Dr. Walter B. Cannon, stated in 1896 that " . . . the antivivisectionists are the second of the two types Theodore Roosevelt described when he said, 'Common sense without conscience may lead to crime, but conscience without common sense may lead to folly, which is the handmaiden of crime.'"

The American Medical Association has been an outspoken proponent of biomedical research for over 100 years, and that tradition continues today. The Association believes that research involving animals is absolutely essential to maintaining and improving the health of the American people.

"Animal research has contributed little to human health."

Most Animal Experimentation Does Not Benefit Human Health

Stephen Kaufman

The author of the following viewpoint, Stephen Kaufman, argues that for decades the value of animal research has been grossly overstated. Many important medical advances have been made by clinical research and close observation of human patients, not animal research, according to Kaufman. Furthermore, he argues, because animal research is well-funded, there is an entrenched community that exaggerates the value of this research so that scientists are ensured continued funding. Kaufman is a senior resident in ophthalmology at New York University and the vice-chairman of the Medical Research Modernization Committee, a New York group of health professionals who work to improve biomedical research.

As you read, consider the following questions:

1. In Kaufman's opinion, how has some animal research actually harmed human health?
2. Why does the author argue that most psychiatric research on animals is useless?

Stephen Kaufman, "Most Animal Research Is Not Beneficial to Human Health," position paper written December 18, 1988. Reprinted with permission.

Increasing numbers of scientists and clinicians have criticized animal research on scientific grounds. Animal studies have always been unreliable and of tenuous value, but proponents have argued that there were no alternatives. Today, there are many alternatives that are less expensive and more valid. However, we continue to waste billions of tax dollars on irrelevant, often misleading animal research. This situation, which is tragic for both people and animals, occurs in large part because the thousands of scientists who make a living doing animal research defend the status quo vigorously and effectively. They claim that animal research has been valuable to human health and that it will continue to benefit human patients.

Scientists frequently make statements such as, "Animal experimentation is an essential component of biomedical and behavioral research, a critical part of efforts to prevent, cure, and treat a vast range of ailments."[1] However, Reines showed that most of the key discoveries in several areas, such as heart disease and cancer, were made by clinical research, observations of patients, and human autopsies.[2] Animal research served primarily to "prove" in animals what had already been demonstrated in people.

Historical Impact of Animal Research

The scientific tradition that medical hypotheses must be "proven" in the lab has had unfortunate consequences. Frequently, effective therapies have been delayed because of the difficulty of finding an animal model that "works." For example, research with the animal model of polio resulted in a misunderstanding of the mechanism of infection. This delayed the development of the tissue culture, which was critical to the discovery of a vaccine.[3]

Misleading animal tests can be devastating for human health. For example, prior to 1963, every prospective and retrospective study of human patients, dozens in all, demonstrated that cigarette smoking causes cancer. Unfortunately, health warnings were delayed for years, and thousands of people subsequently died of cancer, because laboratory results were conflicting. In fact, a leading scientist wrote in the 1950s, "The failure of many investigators . . . to induce experimental cancers, except in a handful of cases, during fifty years of trying, cast serious doubt on the validity of the cigarette-lung cancer theory."[4]

How could widespread beliefs about the value of animal models be inaccurate? Academic researchers, many of whom do animal research, teach medical students and graduate students, write the textbooks students study, and edit the journals that all professionals read. Thus, they have the ability to disseminate widely among professionals a self-serving interpretation of medical history. For example, it is widely believed that the surgical therapy that cured the "blue babies", who suffered from a congenital heart defect known as tetralogy of Fallot, was derived from laboratory research. In fact, Dr. Taussig suggested a helpful surgical procedure based on human autopsy studies. In order to "prove" that the surgery would help, scientists tried to create an animal "model". Since it was impossible to produce tetralogy of Fallot in dogs, researchers cut out lung tissue of lab dogs instead. Thus, the lab animal "model" and the babies with tetralogy of Fallot had fundamentally different disease processes. Indeed, the only similarity was that they were both blue. Then, a surgical procedure, which was different from the one that was later used in patients, was tried on the dogs. While most dogs did poorly, some seemed to do a little better. Despite the irrelevance and poor outcome of the laboratory research, scientists claimed that this was an animal research success story. For example, Glaser wrote, "The experiments were so successful and confirmed Dr. Taussig's theory so completely that Blalock felt he could venture to operate on one of the poor children. . . ."[5]

An Expensive Failure

In the past thirty years, 400,000 chemicals have been screened mainly on mice suffering from leukemia, and some with lung tumors, but though drugs were found that acted against these cancers in mice, chemical trials with human lung cancer victims have been disappointing. This principal thrust of the "war against cancer" has been, in the main, an expensive failure based on the excessive reliance which has been placed on animal experiments and tests.

The nation needs to fund original thinkers to bring additional alternative methods to light, to develop and implement them for the benefit of the public health.

Christine Stevens, Statement before the House Subcommittee on Labor, Health, and Human Services, April 30, 1987.

While scientists have attempted to re-write medical history, many clinicians have recognized the primary role of clinical research. For example, renowned physician Paul Beeson, reviewing the history of hepatitis, concluded:

> Progress in the understanding and management of human disease must begin, and end, with studies of man. . . . Hepatitis, although an almost 'pure' example of progress by the study of man, is by no means unusual; in fact, it is more nearly the rule. To cite other examples: appendicitis, rheumatic fever, typhoid fever, ulcerative colitis and hyperparathyroidism.[6]

It is surprising that animal research has contributed little to human health, given the billions of dollars invested in animal experimentation annually. An underlying problem with animal research is that it is difficult, if not impossible, to gain insight into a human disease by studying a superficially similar but fundamentally different nonhuman disease in a nonhuman animal. Even though dogs with surgically removed lungs and babies with tetralogy of Fallot were both blue, the dog "model" was not valid. Animal models of human disease have never been reliable, but researchers have argued that they were needed to study ongoing disease processes. While autopsies have always been a vital clinical research tool, they are rarely useful for the study of human disease before its lethal stage. However, many modern research techniques, such as CAT scans, PET scans, needle biopsies, and tissue cultures, permit safe, ethical investigation of human diseases with human patients and human tissues.

Contemporary Animal Models: Cancer

In 1971, the National Cancer Act initiated a "War on Cancer," which many sponsors predicted would cure cancer by 1976. However, despite spending over one billion dollars a year on cancer research, the program has been, according to Harvard's Dr. John Bailar III, a "qualified failure." Bailar reported in 1986 that, "Age-adjusted mortality rates (from cancer) have shown a slow and steady increase over several decades, and there is no evidence of a recent downward trend."[7] However, in order to encourage continued support for cancer research, scientists have misled the public. According to the U.S. General Accounting Office, the National Cancer Institute's statistics, " . . . artificially inflate in the amount of 'true' progress."[8] The GAO found that simple five year survival statistics used by the NCI did not consider important statistical biases. Furthermore, claims of cancer "cures" based on five year survival ignore the fact that certain cancers, such as breast cancer and melanoma, often kill the patient more than five years after detection.

Why has progress against cancer failed to be commensurate with the research effort? One possibility is that, in our enthusiasm to cure cancer, we have uncritically funded many less-promising projects. In addition, Dr. Irwin Bross noted that, since cancer reflects failure of the body's own defense system, substantial differences between man and animals have hindered efforts to cure cancer with animal models.[9] Dr. Bailar, commenting on the discouraging results of our research efforts on cancer treatment, stated that " . . . the more promising areas are in cancer prevention. . . ."[7]

Recently, researchers have advocated use of animal models of AIDS. However, no immunologically normal animal besides man

BLOOM COUNTY

BLOOM COUNTY by Berke Breathed. © 1989 Washington Post Writers Group. Reprinted with permission.

develops the AIDS syndrome. Only chimpanzees can be infected with the virus, but they develop a mild flu-like illness only. Furthermore, since AIDS is an infectious disease, the chimpanzees must be kept in isolation. This is very stressful for chimpanzees, who are social animals. Since stress affects the immune system and since AIDS attacks the immune system, this animal "model" of AIDS is of dubious value.

Because chimpanzees are a threatened species, many researchers are studying simian (monkey) AIDS. However, Power et al. wrote, " . . . a molecular clone of the prototype SAIDS virus . . . has no notable similarity in either genetic organization or sequence to the human AIDS retroviruses."[10] Not surprisingly, the critical insights into the understanding, prevention, and treatment of human AIDS has come from research using human subjects and tissues. Although future advances against this disease are most likely to come from clinical investigation, a large fraction of the research on AIDS is being devoted to animal research.

Psychiatry

Animal models of psychiatric diseases have come under particularly vigorous attack. For examples, there have been hundreds of "learned helplessness" studies, in which animals are repeatedly shocked or otherwise traumatized until they stop trying to escape. This "learned helplessness," researchers maintain, is similar to human depression, in which patients feel helpless and hopeless. However, these animals do not have other symptoms of human depression, such as sleeplessness, loss of appetite, guilt, or suicidal behavior and ideas. Psychiatrist Dallas Pratt wrote, "Surely these experimenters are contributing little or nothing to an understanding of the complexities of human anxiety or depressive states. If anything, these tortured and terrified dogs appear to be suffering from a traumatic reaction, similar to the soldier's 'shell-shock'. . . ."[11] Indeed, we do not know if animals exhibiting "learned helplessness" are experiencing depression, anxiety, shock, or a type of mental state unfamiliar to our species. As in all animal models of psychiatric diseases, it is not possible to determine the mental state of the animal, because it cannot communicate its feelings. The only way to understand human depression is to interview and study depressed people.

Similarly, Midgely criticized Harlow's monkey maternal deprivation experiments, in which infants were separated from their mothers and consequently exhibited "depression" and other psychopathology:

> The existences of the species barrier confronts experimenters like Harlow with only two clear alternatives: (1) Human beings and rhesus monkeys are indeed very closely comparable emotionally. In this case his results, though slight, may have some validity for human beings, and he is guilty of cruelty so enormous that hardly any theoretical advance could justify it. (2) Human beings and rhesus monkeys are not closely comparable emotionally. In this case he may be guilty of callousness . . . but is convicted of enormous and wasteful intellectual confusion, and his results are void.[12]

Harlow himself wrote, " . . . most experiments are not worth doing and the data obtained are not worth publishing."[13] Indeed, former behavioral psychologist Roger Ulrich recalled, "When I finished my dissertation on pain-producing aggression, my Mennonite mother asked me what it was about. When I told her she replied, 'Well, we knew that. Dad always warned us to stay away from animals in pain because they are more likely to attack.'"[13]

Important Differences

Animals and humans differ in medically important ways. Therefore, effects of drugs and other treatments studied are not necessarily seen in humans, and many effects that do occur in humans have no apparent counterparts or are not readily observable in animals (e.g. nausea, headache).

The Humane Society of the United States, "Fact Sheet: Alternatives," 1986.

Giannelli concluded:

> I believe the most valuable things we have learned through animal experimentation are insights into the human mentality. These insights have arisen from direct analysis of researchers at work, not from tenuous extrapolations to ourselves based on animal behavior in highly artificial laboratory environments. We have learned that otherwise compassionate people can become remarkably desensitized and detached from the suffering they inflict upon animals. We have learned that highly intelligent people can be engaged in the most trivial or eccentric research yet convince themselves that their work is important.[14]

Regarding the development of drugs for psychiatric diseases, Reines observed, " . . . the antidepressants and antipsychotics were discovered by clinical serendipity. This was common knowledge among psychopharmacologists until N.E. Miller and other animal research enthusiasts started rewriting medical history."[15]

Toxicity Tests

Several prevalent animal toxicity tests have been widely criticized by toxicologists and humanitarians. For example, the LD50 test, which determines how much of a drug, chemical, or cosmetic is needed to kill 50% of test animals, uses about 60-100 animals, most of whom suffer greatly. However, it has several scientific flaws.[16] First, extrapolation of results from rodents to man is highly unreliable. Second, since the results can depend on such variables as strains within species, age, sex, and weight, different laboratories often obtain widely disparate results for the same substances. Third, LD50 data cannot be applied to most human poisoning victims, because the quantity and even the type of substance(s) ingested are often unknown. Finally, in an emergency, one needs to know how much of a substance is dangerous and which organs are at risk, but the LD50 indicates only the meaningless statistic of how much is lethal to 50% of individuals. While the LD50 is nearly worthless, alternative protocols could yield more relevant information while using 80-90% fewer animals.[17]

Similarly, the Draize eye irritation test, in which unanesthetized rabbits have substances instilled in their eyes, is scientifically unsound. Fundamental anatomical differences between rabbits and people in the eyelids, tearing mechanisms, and corneas make the Draize results of dubious validity. In fact, when Draize data for 14 household and cosmetic products were compared to accident human eye exposures, they differed by a factor 18 to 250. On the other hand, modern *in vitro* assays have compared well with existing databases.[18] A battery of *in vitro* tests would be less expensive, and probably more accurate, than the Draize test.

Animal tests for cancer causing substances are notoriously unreliable. Of the 19 known human oral carcinogens, only seven caused cancer in the NCI protocol. This standard screening test is so insensitive that a substance that did not appear to be carcinogenic in experimental animals could still cause cancer in up to one million Americans.[19] On the other hand, an international study demonstrated that new *in vitro* tests were more sensitive and more accurate than the animal tests.[20]

Why Animal Research Persists

If animal experimentation is indeed of little value, why does it persist? There are several possible explanations. First, animal research is easy. It is simple to take a well-defined animal model, change a variable, and produce a paper for publication. This is a strong incentive to do animal research in the "publish or perish" world of academia. Second, animal research is fast. Human diseases tend to span over many years, but laboratory animals, with shorter lifespans, tend to have more rapidly progressive disease processes. This again facilitates quick publication of papers. Third, many scientists are trained in and comfortable with animal research techniques. They are reluctant to adopt alternative methodologies, such as tissue cultures, which would require extensive re-training. A final attraction is that scientists can control research variables much more tightly in animal experiments than is possible with human clinical research. It is possible to take genetically similar animals, give identical disease conditions, and then try two different research strategies to see which works better. The problem, however, is known as "garbage in, garbage out." If the animal model is irrelevant to human disease, it is most unlikely to provide information of clinical value. The ability to control variables, which permits consistent, reproducible results, has led to a widespread belief among scientists that animal research is more "scientific" than clinical research. While controlling variables is desirable, it does not justify the use of poorly conceived animal models.

Redirect Animal Research Funds

In conclusion, it appears that, for political reasons, the historical value of animal research has been grossly overstated. Not all animal research is irrelevant, but its value is severely limited by anatomical, physiological, and pathological differences between people and nonhuman animals. Most of the billions of dollars invested annually in animal research could be used much more effectively in clinical research or public health programs.

1. Committee on the Use of Laboratory Animals in Biomedical and Behavioral Research: *Use of Laboratory Animals in Biomedical and Behavioral Research.* Washington, D.C., National Academy Press, 1988.
2. Reines BR. *Masked Men of Medicine.* New York, Paragon House, 1989 (in press).
3. Paul JR. *A History of Poliomyelitis.* New Haven, Yale University Press, 1971.
4. Northrup E. Men, mice, and smoking. *Science looks at smoking.* New York, Coward-McCann, 1957, p.133.
5. Glaser H. *The Miracle of Heart Surgery.* London, Lutterworth Press, 1961, p.59.
6. Beeson PB. The growth of knowledge about a disease: hepatitis. *American Journal of Medicine.* Vol 67; 1979: pp. 366-370.
7. Bailar JC, Smith EM. Progress against Cancer? *New England Journal of Medicine.* Vol 314; 1986: pp. 1226-1232.
8. U.S. General Accounting Office. *Cancer Patient Survival: What Progress has been Made?* Washington, D.C., General Accounting Office, 1987.
9. Bross I. *Crimes of Official Science.* Buffalo, Biomedical Metatechnology Press, 1987.
10. Power JD, Marx PA, Bryant ML, Gardner MB, Barr PJ, Luciw PA: Nucleotide sequence or SRV-1, a type D simian acquired immune deficiency syndrome retrovirus. *Science* Vol 231; 1987: pp. 438-446.
11. Pratt D. *Alternatives to Pain in Experimentation on Animals.* New York, Argus Archives, 1980, p. 68.
12. Midgely M. Why knowledge matters. In Sperlinger D (ed). *Animals in Research.* New York, John Wiley & Sons, 1981.
13. Rollin BE. *Animal Rights and Human Morality.* Buffalo, Prometheus Books, 1981.
14. Giannelli MA: Three blind mice, see how they run: a critique of behavioral research with animals. In Fox MW, Mickley LD (eds). *Advances in Animal Welfare Science 1985/86.* Washington, D.C., Humane Society of the United States, 1985.
15. Reines BR. Animal rights and research. *American Journal of Psychiatry.* Vol 145; 1987: pp. 539-540.
16. Zbinden G, Flury-Roversi M: Significance of the LD50 test for the toxicological evaluation of chemical substances. *Archives of Toxicology.* Vol 47; 1981: pp. 77-99.
17. Schutz E, Fuchs H: A new approach to minimizing the number of animals used in acute toxicity testing and optimizing the information of test results. *Archives of Toxicology.* Vol 51; 1982: pp. 197-200.
18. Goldberg AM (ed). *In Vitro Toxicology: Approaches to Validation.* New York, Mary Ann Liebert, 1987.
19. Rowan AN. *Of Mice, Models, & Men: A Critical Evaluation of Animal Research.* Albany, SUNY Press, 1984.
20. De Serres FJ. Panel discussion. In *Trends in Bioassay Methodology: in vivo, in vitro and mathematical approaches.* Washington, D.C., U.S. Department of Health and Human Services, 1981.

"The animals in our reputable research laboratories are not being wantonly tortured by sadistic scientists."

Animal Experimentation Is Adequately Regulated

Robert J. White

Animal research laboratories that receive federal funding are regulated by the Animal Welfare Act and institutional animal care committees. An important part of the debate on the issue of animal research is how well those two mechanisms regulate such research to ensure that the tests being conducted are humane and necessary. Robert J. White argues in the following viewpoint that animal research is adequately regulated and any further restrictions would make such research prohibitively expensive. The result, White warns, will be stymied medical progress and poorer human health. White is director of neurological surgery at Cleveland Metropolitan General Hospital and teaches neurosurgery at the Case Western Reserve University Medical School in Cleveland.

As you read, consider the following questions:

1. What reasons does the author cite to reject the argument that scientists abuse lab animals?
2. How have animal rights groups hurt medical research, according to the author?
3. In White's opinion, why are there no real alternatives to many kinds of animal research?

Four years ago I was part of a surgical team trying to remove a malignant tumor from the brain of a nine-year-old girl. The operation failed because we could not stem the hemorrhaging in the brain tissue. We were unable to separate the little girl from the cancer that was slowly killing her. To buy time, we put her on a program of radiation.

Concurrently we were experimenting in our brain-research laboratory with a new high-precision laser scalpel. Working with monkeys and dogs that had been humanely treated and properly anesthetized, we perfected our operating technique. Then, in July 1985, my associate, pediatric neurosurgeon Matt Likavec, and I used the laser to remove all of that little girl's tumor. Now 13, she is healthy, happy, and looking forward to a full life. The animal experiments had enabled us to cure a child we could not help 15 months earlier.

Essential Research

There is virtually no major treatment or surgical procedure in modern medicine that could have been developed without animal research. Work with dogs and other animals led to the discovery of insulin and the control of diabetes, to open-heart surgery, the cardiac pacemaker and the whole area of organ transplantation. Polio, which once killed some 30,000 people annually and crippled thousands of children, has been almost totally eradicated in the United States by preventive vaccines perfected on monkeys. By working with animals, researchers have raised the cure rate for children afflicted with acute lymphocytic leukemia from four percent in 1965 to 70 percent in 1987.

Animal research has vanquished smallpox and enabled us to immunize our children against mumps, measles, rubella and diphtheria, and to defend them against infections by means of an arsenal of medical "magic bullets" called antibiotics.

Animals, too, have profited from this research. Many a family pet has had cataracts removed, has undergone open-heart surgery or wears a pacemaker, and many animals have benefited from vaccines for rabies, distemper, anthrax, tetanus and feline leukemia.

Regulatory Straitjacket

The dramatic medical strides of the past 50 years far exceed the progress in all of previous history. Unhappily, the next 50 years may not see comparable accomplishments. We owe this cloudy outlook to a radical element within the animal-rights movement, spearheaded by People for the Ethical Treatment of Animals (PETA) and other anti-vivisectionist groups, whose leaders insist that *all* research involving animals must cease. These extremists are applying pressure at every level of government, trying to fashion a regulatory straitjacket that is sure to slow medical progress.

Rep. Robert Mrazek (D., N.Y.) and Sen. Wendell Ford (D., Ky.) have introduced companion bills in Congress that would effectively prohibit the sale of pound animals for any medical research funded by the National Institutes of Health (NIH). Twelve states already have banned such sales, and five more have similar legislation under active consideration.

In addition, Rep. Charles Rose (D., N.C.) has introduced a bill that would, in effect, give animals "standing" in court. Should the bill pass, anyone who decides that an animal has been misused in an animal-research facility could file suit in the animal's behalf against the government. Thus, misguided radicals could choke our courts with nuisance suits.

Economic Realities

It is not hard to understand why opponents of research with animals have received such a sympathetic response. The idea conjures up images of experiments on beloved family pets. But the fact is that over 90 percent of the more than 20 million animals used annually in medical research are mice, rats and other rodents. A small percentage are farm animals and monkeys, and less than one percent are dogs and cats.

Good Research Subjects

Scientists cannot afford to mistreat research animals. To be a good research subject, the animal must be adequately fed and housed and kept free of any disease other than the one that may be under investigation. Poor care and treatment will reduce the reliability of the results of the study, something researchers must prevent.

California Biomedical Research Association, *Animal Research: Fact vs. Myth.*

About 200,000 dogs and cats are abandoned *each week* in the United States. These are animals that people have left to roam the streets, forage in garbage dumps and run wild. After a waiting period in the pound, during which time any pet picked up accidentally may be claimed by its owner or adopted, the animals are put to death. It is only after this waiting period has expired that medical researchers purchase a few already doomed animals—in 1986, for example, less than two percent of them. That same year, about one-tenth of our dog and cat populations—some ten million animals—were destroyed.

Researchers obtain animals from pounds because the cost for each is usually $15 or less, while animals bred by commercial suppliers for research purposes cost several hundred dollars. If medical centers are prohibited from purchasing pound animals, many researchers will not be able to afford to continue their work.

This is nowhere more evident than in Massachusetts, one of the world's most productive medical-research centers and the first state to ban totally the sale of pound animals for medical-research purposes. The high cost of commercially supplied dogs has forced noted Harvard Medical School physiologist Dr. A. Clifford Barger to cut back on work aimed at finding cures for hypertension and coronary-artery disease. "The dog is essential to the study of such diseases," says Dr. Barger. "In the end, it's the public that is going to suffer."

In the November 1986 issue of *The Washingtonian* magazine, Katie McCabe recounted another aspect of the Massachusetts pound law: at Massachusetts General Hospital "cost factors have forced Dr. Willard Daggett to limit his cardiovascular studies to the rat heart, which severely limits the research questions that can be explored and applied to human cardiac patients."

Additionally, regulations governing the way we care for research animals have already increased costs substantially, and animal-rights activists continue to make new proposals to drive costs higher. "It has even been proposed that dogs used in research have individual, isolated runs so they can defecate in privacy," says Dr. Mark Ravitch, surgeon-in-chief-emeritus at the University of Pittsburgh's Montefiore Hospital. "All of this has little to do with dog welfare, and everything to do with raising the price of medical research."

Shackled Experiments

The public should have confidence that the animals used in our medical-research laboratories are well treated. Every federally funded facility has an "institutional animal-care-and-use committee," one of whose functions is to ascertain that animals are being cared for properly. The committee must include a medical-research scientist, a non-scientist, someone not affiliated with the institution, and a veterinarian. Additional monitoring is provided by federal agents.

I certainly have no objection to these safeguards. Government-funded projects involve many thousands of scientists in some 800 institutions, and the probability that there won't be some carelessness is zero. But all good researchers insist that animals be treated humanely—not only out of compassion but also because valid work depends on clean, healthy research subjects that are not victims of physical or emotional stress.

Charles McCarthy, Director of NIH's Office for Protection from Research Risks, says: "We have had a half-dozen abuse cases since 1981. Either animals have not been properly cared for—usually over a long weekend—or an attendant has not conscientiously provided an animal with adequate anesthetics. But we have *never* run into a sadist who got his kicks inflicting pain on animals."

My main objection is to regulations requiring animal-care-and-use committees to pass on all research proposals involving animals. While experiments begin with specific goals, a scientist never knows at the outset where the research will lead. Yet he may not deviate from the original plan—in order to pursue an unexpected opportunity—without first filling out costly, time-consuming paper work to obtain committee approval. New regulations governing the use of animals have already increased the financial burden on the nation's 127 medical schools by many millions of dollars annually. "But the real cost is that there will be less research," says Carol Scheman of the Association of American Universities, "and when research is slowed, people die."

Damaging Setbacks

Public-opinion polls have shown that nearly 80 percent of us approve of the use of animals in medical experimentation. I am convinced that most Americans are unaware of the devastating effect animal-rights extremists are having on such research. Frankie L. Trull, president of the Foundation for Biomedical Research, says, "People don't realize that they are being steamrollered. They may not recognize what is happening until a lot of damage has been done."

The damage is already considerable. For example, Stanford University's proposal to build a state-of-the-art animal laboratory and a new biology building met with opposition from the Palo Alto Humane Society. First objecting to the lab, partly out of concern for the well-being of Stanford's animals, the Society later joined in an appeal to delay construction of the biology building on the basis of possible environmental damage. These delays will cost Stanford some $2 million.

Proper and Humane

The care and treatment of laboratory animals in U.S. research institutions is, in the overwhelming majority of cases, both proper and humane. Good science and human decency require no less.

Foundation for Biomedical Research, *Caring for Laboratory Animals,* January 1986.

What are the human stakes? Stanford University scientists have already developed a permanent cure for diabetes in mice. It isn't known yet whether this will lead to a permanent cure for human diabetes, but there is a strong basis for optimism. If this dream is to be realized, research must proceed with more mice, then with larger animals.

Animal-rights activists like to claim that work accomplished with animals can be done by other means, that we can unlock medical mysteries with computers and with cell cultures grown in test tubes. But, as yet, there is no computer that can even come close to matching the nervous system that tells a mouse how to move a leg or a monkey a finger.

How can researchers using cell cultures, which do not have bones, develop a treatment for arthritis or other bone diseases? How can cell cultures help us to perfect the surgical techniques used in organ transplantation? For the foreseeable future the answers to such questions can be found only by scientists working with living species.

Intimidation Tactics

Not content to impose their views through lawful means, fringe elements of the animal-rights movement have resorted to terrorist activity. [In] April [1987], intruders who left behind graffiti and vandalized university vehicles set afire an unfinished veterinary diagnostic laboratory at the University of California's Davis campus, causing damage estimated at $3.5 million. A few months later a group calling itself "The Band of Mercy" took 28 cats from a Department of Agriculture research center in Beltsville, Md. Eleven of these cats had been infected with a parasite, Toxoplasm gondii, which infects pregnant women and causes some 2000 birth defects annually in the United States. The incident severely hampered the work of researchers who were investigating the effects of the parasite in animals as a potential source for infection in not only pregnant women but also victims of AIDS and other diseases that weaken the immune system. . . .

Resisting False Propaganda

We are a people who love animals, but we must be realistic. Through the ages we have harvested animals for food, clothing, shelter, and in this century alone medical scientists working with animals have played a major role in increasing our average life-span from 50 to 75 years. What a tragic disservice to ourselves and future generations if we allow the animal-rights extremists to quell this marvelous momentum!

What to do? First, an important don't: Don't be misled by emotional and false propaganda. The animals in our reputable research laboratories are *not* being wantonly tortured by sadistic scientists. Such reports should not be taken seriously. . . .

Do we want to wipe out leukemia? Alzheimer's? AIDS? Diabetes? Do we want better vaccines, more effective treatments and cures for high blood pressure, coronary-artery disease, stroke and myriad other ills? All of these things and more are possible within the next 25 years, some of them sooner, because of the work medical scientists are now doing with animals. But they can't be accomplished if we surrender to the mindless emotionalism and intimidation of the animal-rights fanatics. The choice is ours.

"No law in this country prohibits painful or frivolous experiments."

Animal Experimentation Is Underregulated

New England Anti-Vivisection Society

The controversy over animal research has been heightened by animal rights groups that have broken into laboratories and taken pictures of research animals. Animal rights activists believe these pictures prove that much of the research conducted is inhumane and even sadistic. In the following viewpoint, the New England Anti-Vivisection Society refutes ten common statements made in support of animal research. The Society contends federal regulations on animal research are so poorly enforced that they are useless. The Society is a Boston-based national lobbying organization that conducts educational programs opposing animal research.

As you read, consider the following questions:

1. Name two reasons the authors give to support their argument that animal research does not improve human health.
2. Why does the author believe the Animal Welfare Act is inadequate?
3. Why does animal research continue, according to the Society?

New England Anti-Vivisection Society, "Reading the Truth About Animal Testing Will Take 5 Minutes and a Very Strong Stomach," *The New York Times,* July 16, 1988. Reprinted with permission.

[T hose] whose careers depend on experimenting on animals want to scare you into thinking that we must choose between people and animals. To hear them tell it, we'll all die tomorrow if animal experiments are regulated or ended. But blind trust in the people who profit most from animal research misleads and scares the public and keeps us in the dark ages of science.

The Animals' Side of the Story

We believe you should know what the approximately 60 million animals used and killed in experiments each year cannot tell you. Their side of the story is important to learn, because their lives and yours are threatened daily by animal experiments.

1. "Animal research is necessary to advance human health."

The use of nonhuman animals to develop drugs and treatments for human beings is a two-sided coin: Human and nonhuman animals respond similarly to treatments in some cases, but most often they do not. It is probable that drugs and treatments that might help people today were never developed because tests on other species were not successful. The physiological differences between different species and the fact that the stress and confinement suffered by animals in laboratories does in fact alter reactions to the experiments, makes animal experiments highly unreliable.

Many drugs developed in animals, including DES, thalidomide, and many arthritis medicines, actually harm human beings. Some drugs developed using animals cause such severe side effects in humans after being released on the market that consumers must initiate lawsuits to have their use banned.

History shows that the decline of many diseases, including tuberculosis, pneumonia, measles, whooping cough, and scarlet fever resulted more from increased standards of living, better diets, improved sanitation like clean water and uncontaminated foods, and natural immunities than from drugs and vaccines.

Alternatives To Using Animals

2. "Viable alternatives to animal research do not yet exist."

There are many alternatives to animal research, the most obvious being the study of illness in human beings under controlled conditions (clinical studies), and the study of naturally occurring disease patterns in human populations (epidemiology). People in need of immediate health care currently are denied the opportunity to help themselves and to advance medical knowledge at the same time.

Clinical and epidemiological studies, cadavers, tissue cultures, cell cultures from human organs, and sophisticated computer simulators (like "HUMTRN," which can process 10 million intricate pieces of information about the effects of substances on the human body) are just a few of the cheaper, much more reliable alternatives to animal research. We can now test irritancy on egg membranes, produce vaccines from human tissues, and perform pregnancy tests using blood samples instead of killing rabbits. With more funding and a genuine effort to develop and use them, non-animal tests can advance human health more quickly than archaic animal-based methods. The unfortunate truth is that many experimenters simply prefer using animals because they can be conveniently caged, used at will, and discarded, without the human-based complexities of scheduling conflicts, transportation, and the threat of malpractice lawsuits from human subjects.

3. "All of our major medical advances have resulted from animal research."

In the past, some major medical advances came from the use of animals because that was often the only method tried. The discovery of antibiotics, sulpha drugs, anesthetics, x-rays, aspirin, digitalis, radium and mercury therapy disinfectants, opium and morphine, and bacteriology did not come from animals, and the most promising major medical advances today, including CAT scans, magnetic resonance, and the Ames cancer test, have come from non-animal sources.

A Price We Should Pay

New regulations and laws will create some dilemmas—and make some kinds of research more costly. But it is a price that we should pay. We can no longer pretend that animals are simply "resources." They are individuals, and they deserve a measure of respect.

Neal Barnard, *The Scientist*, May 30, 1988.

Results from tests on one species cannot be accurately applied to another. Ultimately, everything tested on nonhuman animals must be tested on human beings before it becomes an accepted practice. The time, money, and resources wasted on animal studies can be better spent by studying diseases where and how they normally occur.

AIDS Research

The AIDS case is a classic example of the futility of animal-based experiments. The AIDS virus was isolated in human blood, the AZT treatment for AIDS came from cell cultures, and animal experimenters cannot find any animals other than human beings who get AIDS as we do. Yet the National Institutes of Health is now funding a multi-million dollar program to breed endangered chimpanzees for use in highly exploitive and cruel AIDS experiments. The fact remains that chimpanzees do not even get AIDS even after they have been injected with the AIDS virus.

4. "Animal research is acceptable because 90 percent of the animals used are rats and mice; only a small percentage are cats, dogs, or monkeys."

Anyone with even a basic knowledge of the biology of guinea pigs, rats, squirrels, and mice knows that they have nervous systems and social bonds virtually identical to those of dogs, cats, and primates, and yet the Animal Welfare Act does not cover rats and mice. This allows researchers to use them like paperclips, tossing millions of them into experiments—and then into the trash—each year. An animal's ability to suffer is unrelated to his or her popularity or the perceived "inferiority" of his or her species.

When you hear percentages of animal totals quoted instead of actual numbers, remember that when you're talking about 60 to 100 million animals, even a "small percentage" translates into millions of suffering individuals.

Inadequate Regulations

5. "The Animal Welfare Act protects animals from abuse."

The Animal Welfare Act regulates housing and sanitation in laboratories, not experimental procedures. What little it covers is poorly enforced by the U.S. Department of Agriculture. In fact, a 1985 General Accounting Office study found that USDA inspections often occurred only once a year, if at all; half of all the facilities in California and New York were not inspected during a one-year period. No law in this country prohibits painful or frivolous experiments. Once the laboratory door closes, no humane or independent authority monitors the care and use of animals in experiments.

Despite the provisions of the Animal Welfare Act, cases of animal abuse in laboratories abound. In 1981, Dr. Edward Taub became the first federally funded vivisector convicted of animal cruelty, based on experiments in which he surgically damaged the spinal cords and limbs of macaque monkeys, and then tormented them in efforts to make them use their deadened arms. His conviction was later overturned by a Maryland Court of Appeals on the grounds that the state anti-cruelty law did not apply to federal research. In 1985, the University of Pennsylvania's Head Injury Clinic was shut down by the Secretary of Health and Human Services after the lab's own videotapes showed brain damage experiments being performed on semi-conscious baboons while experimenters laughed at their struggles, smoked during surgery, and used contaminated instruments. Experiments at the City of Hope medical center in California were suspended after gross negligence was uncovered.

6. "Institutional Animal Care and Use Committees ensure that animals are not used unnecessarily or cruelly."

Institutional Animal Care and Use Committees (IACUCs), required by an amendment to the Animal Welfare Act, are usually composed of members handpicked by the institution performing the research—as Judge Edwin Allen recently described the IACUC of the University of Oregon, "It's the closest thing to letting the foxes guard the chickens." Because they are "rubber stamp" committees consisting primarily of animal researchers who simply approve each others' proposals. Their meetings are usually not open to the public. The humane community is now bringing lawsuits to gain public access.

Pound Animals

7. "Since dogs and cats in pounds are going to die anyway, they might as well be put to good use in experiments."

Pounds and shelters were created to provide safe and humane refuges for abandoned, lost, or stray animals. To turn them into laboratory supply houses cheats the taxpayer as well as the animals. Because experimenters prefer the same young, healthy, friendly animals that potential adopters want, giving such animals to laboratories defeats the goal of placing them with loving families. Animals used to non-threatening human companionship become terrified when they are caged and experimented upon. An unlimited supply of animals from pounds encourages frivolous

" THIS ONE WE GOT FROM THE COUNTY POUND IS HOUSEBROKEN AND EVERYTHING. AND LOOK ... HE EVEN KNOWS HOW TO BEG! "

Wayne Stayskal. Reprinted by permission: Tribune Media Services.

and unnecessary experiments, which waste enormous amounts of money.

8. "Experimenters respect the animals they use and care for them well."

Vivisectors are trained to regard animals as tools; only desensitized individuals can cut, burn, poison, mutilate, drown, strangle, shock, or torment them. Vivisection is a business, first and foremost. Billions of taxpayer dollars are poured into animal research every year, yet the cancer rate is rising, birth defects are increasing, and heart disease remains the leading cause of death. The U.S. is only 17th in the world in life expectancy, despite spending more on medical research than the first 16 countries combined.

Animal research continues because of outdated traditions, and because a multitude of individual experimenters, laboratories, pharmaceutical companies, food and equipment suppliers, and animal breeders and dealers comprise a giant, multi-billion dollar industry.

The Philosophy of Animal Rights

9. "The people who oppose animal experiments put animals before people."

Increasing numbers of concerned people are opposing animal research as they learn how cruel, unnecessary, wasteful and unproductive it is. Although most experiments are hidden from public view, many people have taken the time to learn the real facts about animal research, and they are appalled at what they see.

Recent cases, like the Silver Spring Monkeys case, the baboon head-bashing experiments at the University of Pennsylvania, the infant monkey blindings at the University of California at Riverside, the cosmetic and household products industry's blinding and poisoning of dogs and rabbits to market makeup, shampoos, and detergents (tests which columnist Dear Abby describes as "cruel and inhuman"), the view of the military's irradiation of primates in the movie "Project X," the "live storage" of chimpanzees at the SEMA laboratory in Maryland, and many other cases of large-scale animal abuse have demonstrated that the public does care about the way animals are used in experiments and will act to stop such abuse.

Groups of physicians, nurses, psychologists, students, veterinarians, disabled persons, and others who care about their fellow creatures are promoting productive, humane, and progressive science. They are teaching people how to prevent illness—including heart disease, cancer, diabetes, and stroke—with proper diet and exercise. They are working to reduce life-threatening pollution and environmental contamination. They are working, too, to promote home care and treatment centers for the disabled, and for the use of sophisticated and sensible research methodologies. And they believe that neither animals nor humans should be forced to suffer.

10. "Animal rights activists support terrorism."

Even the most "militant" underground animals rights groups, such as the Animal Liberation Front (ALF) and other groups who rescue animals from laboratories and destroy vivisection equipment, are opposed to violence. Their rescue of cats with electrodes implanted in their brains, monkeys with eyes sewn shut, or beagles forced to inhale pollutants is designed to prevent violence and expose the horror of such experiments to those who pay for them: the American taxpayers. Members of animal protection groups are schoolteachers, veterans, business professionals, parents, and others who have become frustrated with the lack of humane legislation and proper enforcement, and the misinformation given the public by animal researchers who claim that all is well in laboratories.

Exposing Animal Research

Although the actions of animal liberationists are not supported by everyone, their actions nevertheless have provided the public with an uncensored look at the animal experiments that experimenters deliberately keep hidden. They may destroy the instruments used to inflict pain, but they do not threaten human or animal life. They try to educate the public while freeing innocent beings from the painful doom of vivisection.

Scanty Protection

Legal protection for laboratory animals is scanty. The Animal Welfare Act does require that minimal standards be met for handling, housing, feeding, watering, sanitation, ventilation, shelter, and veterinary care. But while the care of animals before and after experiments is covered, the Animal Welfare Act specifically omits from coverage any animals involved in experiments. . . . Moreover, violations of the Animal Welfare Act are not subject to criminal prosecution.

Physicians Committee for Responsible Medicine, *PCRM Update*, September/October 1987.

As George Bernard Shaw once wrote, "Whoever doesn't hesitate to vivisect will hardly hesitate to lie about it." The more you learn about animal experiments, the more you realize that the pro-vivisection industry lies. If you're concerned about human health, what your taxes pay for, and how animals are abused in laboratories, take the time to learn what the animal research industry doesn't want you to know.

"At . . . primate research centers, humane treatment is practiced as a matter of routine and as a matter of both ethical and scientific concern."

Primate Research Is Humane

Frederick A. King

Frederick A. King is a leading expert on primate research and the director of the Yerkes Regional Primate Research Center at Emory University in Atlanta, Georgia. In the following viewpoint, King responds to criticism of primate researchers by describing the procedure followed at the Yerkes Center. According to King, numerous safeguards exist to ensure research is necessary and beneficial, and federal regulations regarding the proper care of primates are rigorously followed.

As you read, consider the following questions:

1. What is the purpose of the federally-funded regional primate centers, according to the author?
2. What safeguards does King cite as proof that the Yerkes Center and others like it conduct research that is necessary and humane?

Frederick A. King, "Significance and Problems of Primate Research in the Behavioral and Biomedical Sciences," a paper given at the Annual Meeting of the American Psychological Association at Anaheim, CA on August 27, 1983. Also includes portions from "Primates," *Science*, June 10, 1988 and "Studying a Kindred Species," *Emory Medicine*, Fall 1987. Reprinted with permission.

Behavioral and biomedical research with animals has been coming under increasing fire by individuals and organizations of a wide variety of persuasions. At one end of this spectrum are the extremist proponents of animal rights who believe that all captive animals should be freed and returned to their natural habitats; for this group, not only is research with animals wrong, but so are zoos and the eating of meat. Then there are the antivivisectionists who would stop most animal research, especially studies that involve experimental and invasive procedures. Toward the opposite end of the spectrum are moderates who simply and reasonably want to insure the welfare and humane treatment of animals in research, while recognizing the benefits that these studies have brought to humankind. It is this last group that we, as scientists, should work with and listen to, while making our best efforts possible to persuade the first two groups of the importance of animal research to our nation's welfare. . . .

Federally Funded Primate Centers

The question of the value of research with primates is a crucial issue. When the seven NIH-sponsored primate research centers were established in the early 1960s, they were charged with the mission of developing both basic and applied research programs which could benefit human and animal health by focusing on the unique behavioral and biological characteristics of primates and the striking similarities between non-human primates and humans. The Yerkes Center and the other primate centers are therefore committed to research that can best be accomplished with these species.

The Centers were established on a regional basis to provide resources and expertise across the nation. In their two decades of existence, the primate centers have demonstrated that primates are not only valuable, but in many respects, essential for progress in the fields of reproductive biology, hormones and behavior, mental development and retardation, neurobiology, heart disease, infectious diseases, environmental health, disorders of the central nervous system, immunology, nutrition, cancer and diseases of the newborn. . . .

Questions About Humane Care

Whenever the role of primates in experimentation is discussed, concerns for the humane care and treatment of the animals are immediately raised. To elaborate this, I will use the Yerkes Center as an example, but I am certain that with regard to research proposals, the care of the animals, and the rules for the conduct of research, procedures and standards at the other primate centers are similar, if not virtually identical.

Before any Yerkes animals can be used in research, the scientist proposing the study must present a written proposal to be evaluated by the Yerkes Animal Resources Committee and the Emory Institutional Animal Care and Use Committee. The Yerkes research review and monitoring procedures, which the center established in 1981, not only meet but exceed current U.S. Public Health Service regulations for the review of research proposals by each institution. The federal government requires that the research study comply with Public Health Service regulations regarding the care and treatment of laboratory animals, and Yerkes also requires that the study be well designed, scientifically or medically valuable, and conducted humanely.

1. Are primates necessary for the proposed study, or can the work be as well conducted with another species or an alternative, nonanimal method?

2. Is the particular primate species selected appropriate biologically or behaviorally for the proposed investigation?

Excellent Models

Nonhuman primates are excellent animal models for human diseases because of their close relationship to humans. Indeed, comparisons of the chromosomes and DNA homologies between primates and humans testify to the commonality of the genetic material between these phylogenetically related species.

W.H. Stone, R.C.S. Treichel, and J.L. VandeBerg, in *Animal Models,* 1987.

---

3. Is the study likely to contribute significantly to scientific knowledge or to human or animal health?

4. Is the investigator scientifically and technically qualified to conduct the study?

5. Will the study be conducted in a humane fashion, with proper consideration for the welfare of the animal, and in compliance with existing regulations?

6. If invasive procedures or others likely to produce pain or discomfort are proposed, are they essential to the study?

7. In proposals involving potentially painful procedures or surgery, has provision been made for elimination or minimization of pain or discomfort including proper anesthesia, analgesia, and round-the-clock post-operative care and surveillance?

8. If the research is replication of previous or other ongoing studies, is it justified and needed?

9. Is the number of animals to be used and the research design adequate to produce clearly interpretable results, but not excessive?

10. Will the study limit reproductive capacity in a way that will be injurious to breeding in the particular primate colony or to the species itself?

Once approval of the project has been achieved within the Center the proposals of the project are again reviewed with similar criteria by review panels and site visitors of the funding agency or foundation to which it has been submitted. Once a project has been initiated at the Yerkes Center, its progress is monitored by a Yerkes committee, as well as the Center's veterinarians. Annual progress reports of all work are submitted to NIH, and to any other agency supporting or involved in the project. These are available to the public through the Freedom of Information Act.

Yerkes scientists rigorously adhere to federal guidelines for the housing and care of animals as well as those of professional and scientific associations. The U.S. Department of Agriculture periodically inspects all scientific institutions which receive federal support to insure that animal feeding, housing, cleanliness and other aspects of treatment and care conform to the government rules, as does yet another monitoring group, the Animal Care Committee of our University.

At our Center and the other NIH-sponsored primate research centers, humane treatment is practiced as a matter of routine and as a matter of both ethical and scientific concern.

Expert Health Surveillance

One key to a first class animal care program is expert health surveillance. At the Yerkes Center the animal care team includes three full-time clinical veterinarians, two additional veterinarians in clinical pathology, and another veterinarian who specializes in reproductive biology, a registered nurse, three veterinary technicians and over 30 animal care attendants. As a team they continually monitor the health status of the primates. All apes and monkeys at the Center are visited and inspected daily so that any health problem can be detected and treated early. Clinical consultants in human medical specialties are also called upon for unusual cases.

The nurseries of the Center specialize in the care of young great apes and monkeys and provide temporary or long-term care and special diets and treatments for premature infants and those whose mothers are ill or lack mothering skills. Young primates in the nursery are returned to their mothers or to an appropriate social living group as soon as possible.

Complete Medical Exams

In addition to the daily checks, each ape and monkey at the Center periodically receives a complete medical examination. In research surgery and other invasive procedures which are carefully controlled and monitored by our veterinary staff, veterinarians and scientists alike use the same anesthetics and sterile procedures followed in human hospitals. Post-operative care includes around-the-clock veterinary surveillance, and regular administration of analgesics and other medications whenever required.

The NIH-sponsored primate centers also are important national and international resources to scientists from many universities around the country and overseas. They provide researchers and students with opportunities that would otherwise be impossible or impractical. The unique concentration of specialized facilities, personnel, and primate species that are available at the primate centers would be almost impossible to duplicate in most institutions.

An additional contribution of the primate centers is in the breeding and conservation of endangered primate species and the development of new knowledge, diagnostic procedures and treatment in animal medicine and improved methods of animal care that have been adopted in zoos as well as research institutions.

Informing the Public

The value of primate studies and primate centers, as well as research with other animals, for the improvement of scientific knowledge and the betterment of the human condition has been, I believe, clearly and amply demonstrated. It is now up to us to inform the public about what we are doing and why it is essential to continue our work, or suffer the consequences of unwarranted, but unanswered attacks on our purposes, practices and achievements.

"Room after room was lined with small, bare cages . . . in which monkeys circled round and round and chimpanzees sat huddled, far gone in depression and despair."

Primate Research Is Inhumane

Jane Goodall

Some people believe that primate research is more inhumane than research on other animals because primates closely resemble humans and are known to have psychological needs and high intellectual abilities. The author of the following viewpoint, Jane Goodall, has directed the field study of chimpanzees for almost thirty years at the Gombe Research Stream Center in Tanzania. An active and well-known conservationist, Goodall has written many books and articles and produced television specials for *National Geographic.* Goodall writes that most primate laboratories are inhumane because they neglect chimpanzees' psychological needs.

As you read, consider the following questions:

1. How does Goodall describe the habitat and customs of chimpanzees in the wild?
2. Why is the housing at primate labs cruel, in Goodall's opinion?
3. Why are scientists obligated to treat primates humanely, according to the author?

Jane Goodall, "A Plea for the Chimps," *The New York Times Magazine,* May 17, 1987. Copyright © 1987 by The New York Times Company. Reprinted by permission.

The chimpanzee is more like us, genetically, than any other animal. It is because of similarities in physiology, in biochemistry, in the immune system, that medical science makes use of the living bodies of chimpanzees in its search for cures and vaccines for a variety of human diseases.

There are also behavioral, psychological and emotional similarities between chimpanzees and humans, resemblances so striking that they raise a serious ethical question: are we justified in using an animal so close to us—an animal, moreover, that is highly endangered in its African forest home—as a human substitute in medical experimentation?

In the long run, we can hope that scientists will find ways of exploring human physiology and disease, and of testing cures and vaccines, that do not depend on the use of living animals of any sort. A number of steps in this direction already have been taken, prompted in large part by a growing public awareness of the suffering that is being inflicted on millions of animals. More and more people are beginning to realize that nonhuman animals—even rats and guinea pigs—are not just unfeeling machines but are capable of enjoying their lives, and of feeling fear, pain and despair.

But until alternatives have been found, medical science will continue to use animals in the battle against human disease and suffering. And some of those animals will continue to be chimpanzees.

Because they share with us 99 percent of their genetic material, chimpanzees can be infected with some human diseases that do not infect other animals. They are currently being used in research on the nature of hepatitis non-A non-B, for example, and they continue to play a major role in the development of vaccines against hepatitis B. . . .

Given the scientists' professed need for animals in research, let us turn aside from the sensitive ethical issue of whether chimpanzees *should* be used in medical research, and consider a more immediate issue: how are we treating the chimpanzees that are actually being used?

Horrifying Conditions in Primate Labs

I watched, with shock, anger and anguish, a videotape—made by an animal-rights group during a raid—revealing the conditions in a large biomedical research laboratory, under contract to the National Institutes of Health, in which various primates, including chimpanzees, are maintained. I was given permission to visit the facility.

It was a visit I shall never forget. Room after room was lined with small, bare cages, stacked one above the other, in which monkeys circled round and round and chimpanzees sat huddled, far gone in depression and despair.

Young chimpanzees, 3 or 4 years old, were crammed, two together, into tiny cages measuring 22 inches by 22 inches and only 24 inches high. They could hardly turn around. Not yet part of any experiment, they had been confined in these cages for more than three months.

The chimps had each other for comfort, but they would not remain together for long. Once they are infected, probably with hepatitis, they will be separated and placed in another cage. And there they will remain, living in conditions of severe sensory deprivation, for the next several years. During that time, they will become insane.

Active Primates

In the wild, primates are typically active animals. If they aren't searching for food, they may be fighting off intruders, playing with peers, investigating the world around them, breeding or sleeping. They have evolved physically to be ready for action and they are capable of engaging in acrobatic maneuvers with great finesse. These abilities are a part of their survival package. Their great investigatory and manipulative skills allow them to locate the very foods that sustain them. When held captive they maintain the potential and abilities that they were born with, but, without sufficient enrichment devices available inside their cages, they reside in a continuous state of unchallenged readiness. Like lack of social stimulation, lack of physical and mental stimulation leads to despair.

Peggy O'Neill, *Humane Innovations and Alternatives in Animal Experimentation,* 1987.

A juvenile female rocked from side to side, sealed off from the outside world behind the glass doors of her metal isolation chamber. She was in semidarkness. All she could hear was the incessant roar of air rushing through vents into her prison. . . .

I shall be haunted forever by her eyes, and by the eyes of the other infant chimpanzees I saw that day. Have you ever looked into the eyes of a person who, stressed beyond endurance, has given up, succumbed utterly to the crippling helplessness of despair? I once saw a little African boy, whose whole family had been killed during the fighting in Burundi. He too looked out at the world, unseeing, from dull, blank eyes.

Though this particular laboratory may be one of the worst, from what I have learned, most of the other biomedical animal-research facilities are not much better. Yet only when one has some understanding of the true nature of the chimpanzee can the cruelty of these captive conditions be fully understood.

Chimpanzees are very social by nature. Bonds between individuals, particularly between family members and close friends, can be affectionate, supportive, and can endure throughout their lives. The accidental separation of two friendly individuals may cause them intense distress. Indeed, the death of a mother may be such a psychological blow to her child that even if the child is 5 years old and no longer dependent on its mother's milk, it may pine away and die.

It is impossible to overemphasize the importance of friendly physical contact for the well-being of the chimpanzee. Again and again one can watch a frightened or tense individual relax if she is patted, kissed or embraced reassuringly by a companion. Social grooming, which provides hours of close contact, is undoubtedly the single most important social activity. . . .

Chimps are highly intelligent. They display cognitive abilities that were, until recently, thought to be unique to humans. They are capable of cross-model transfer of information—that is, they can identify by touch an object they previously have only seen, and vice versa. They are capable of reasoned thought, generalization, abstraction and symbolic representation. They have some concept of self. They have excellent memories and can, to some extent, plan for the future. They show a capacity for intentional communication that depends, in part, on their ability to understand the motives of the individuals with whom they are communicating.

Chimpanzees are capable of empathy and altruistic behavior. They show emotions that are undoubtedly similar, if not identical, to human emotions—joy, pleasure, contentment, anxiety, fear and rage. They even have a sense of humor.

The chimpanzee child and the human child are alike in many ways: in their capacity for endless romping and fun; their curiosity; their ability to learn by observation, imitation and practice; and, above all, in their need for reassurance and love. When young chimpanzees are brought up in a human home and treated like human children, they learn to eat at table, to help themselves to snacks from the refrigerator, to sort and put away cutlery, to brush their teeth, to play with dolls, to switch on the television and select a program that interests them and watch it. . . .

Ignored Emotional Needs

The chimpanzee facilities in most biomedical research laboratories allow for the expression of almost none of these activities and behaviors. They provide little—if anything—more than the warmth, food and water, and veterinary care required to sustain life. The psychological and emotional needs of these creatures are rarely catered to, and often not even acknowledged.

In most labs the chimpanzees are housed individually, one chimp to a cage, unless they are part of a breeding program. The standard size of each cage is about 25 feet square and about 6 feet high. In one facility, a cage described in the catalogue as "large," designed for a chimpanzee of up to 25 kilograms (55 pounds), measures 2 feet 6 inches by 3 feet 8 inches, with a height of 5 feet 4 inches. Federal requirements for cage size are dependent on body size; infant chimpanzees, who are the most active, are often imprisoned in the smallest cages.

An Unenforced Amendment

In 1985 Congress passed an amendment to the Animal Welfare Act which calls for "a physical environment adequate to promote the psychological well-being of primates." This amendment was added because as Senator Melcher described primate "cages are not much wider than the average shower stall and there is hardly enough room to allow the animal to stand erect." Intelligent, social primates are forced to spend their entire lives in such metal, or mesh-wire cages without the ability to touch, and often not even see, another primate. The above amendment is still not enforceable (three years after its passage) due to pressure from the Primate Centers. Frederick King, director of the Yerkes Center has stated that "to regulate something about their psychological well-being is patently absurd. How do we know when they [monkeys and apes] are happy or content? We think this is a bit of a mess" (Newsday 7/21/87). After decades of behavioral research using primates it seems absurd that we should not know something as basic as what conditions make them happy or content, let alone what conditions are adversary to them.

The Human/Animal Liberation Front, *The Regional Primate Research Centers: The Monkeys' Story,* 1988.

In most labs, the chimpanzees cannot even lie with their arms and legs outstretched. They are not let out to exercise. There is seldom anything for them to do other than eat, and then only when food is brought. The caretakers are usually too busy to pay much attention to individual chimpanzees. The cages are bleak and sterile, with bars above, bars below, bars on every side. There is no comfort in them, no bedding. The chimps, infected with human diseases, will often feel sick and miserable.

Scientists' Attitudes Toward Chimps

What of the human beings who administer these facilities—the caretakers, veterinarians and scientists who work at them? If they are decent, compassionate people, how can they condone, or even tolerate, the kind of conditions I have described?

They are, I believe, victims of a system that was set up long before the cognitive abilities and emotional needs of chimpanzees were understood. Newly employed staff members, equipped with a normal measure of compassion, may well be sickened by what they see. And, in fact, many of them do quit their jobs, unable to endure the suffering they see inflicted on the animals yet feeling powerless to help.

But others stay on and gradually come to accept the cruelty, believing (or forcing themselves to believe) that it is an inevitable part of the struggle to reduce human suffering. Some become hard and callous in the process, in Shakespeare's words, "all pity choked with custom of fell deeds." . . .

Many of the scientists believe that a bleak, sterile and restricting environment is necessary for their research. The cages must be small, the scientists maintain, because otherwise it is too difficult to treat the chimpanzees—to inject them, to draw their blood or to anesthetize them. Moreover, they are less likely to hurt themselves in small cages. . . .

And the chimpanzees must be kept in isolation, the scientists believe, to avoid the risk of cross-infection, particularly in hepatitis research.

Finally, of course, bigger cages, social groups and elaborate furnishings require more space, more caretakers—and more money. Perhaps, then, if we are to believe these researchers, it is not possible to improve conditions for chimpanzees imprisoned in biomedical research laboratories.

A Human Obligation

I believe not only that it *is* possible, but that improvements are absolutely necessary. If we do not do something to help these creatures, we make a mockery of the whole concept of justice. . . .

We take from them their freedom, their health and often their lives. Surely, the least we can do is try to provide them with some of the things that could make their imprisonment more bearable. . . .

Hunched and Miserable

I have had the privilege of working among wild, free chimpanzees for more than 26 years. I have gained a deep understanding of chimpanzee nature. Chimpanzees have given me so much in my life. The least I can do is to speak out for the hundreds of chimpanzees who, right now, sit hunched, miserable and without hope, staring out with dead eyes from their metal prisons. They cannot speak for themselves.

a critical thinking activity

The Ability To Empathize

The ability to empathize, to see a situation from another person's vantage point, is an important skill. When we empathize, we put ourselves in someone else's position. This helps us to look at a problem in a way that perhaps we have not considered before. The ability to understand an opponent's viewpoint is a difficult skill, one that is needed for a highly emotional and controversial subject like the benefits of animal experimentation.

Following are two excerpts. In the first excerpt, Jane McCabe describes her nine-year-old daughter's struggle with cystic fibrosis, an incurable childhood disease. McCabe tells how animal research has helped keep her daughter alive. In the second excerpt, Alex Pacheco gives a first-person account of the conditions he witnessed in a primate laboratory. He is horrified by the painful experiments these monkeys endure.

My daughter has cystic fibrosis. Her only hope for a normal life is that researchers, some of them using animals, will find a cure. . . .

How has research using animals helped those with CF? Three times a day my daughter uses enzymes from the pancreas of pigs to digest her food. She takes antibiotics tested on rats before they are tried on humans. As an adult, she will probably develop diabetes and need insulin—a drug developed by research on dogs and rabbits. If she ever needs a heart-lung transplant, one might be possible because of the cows that surgeons practiced on. . . .

I think the motivation of animal-rights activists is to cut down on the suffering in this world, but I have yet to hear them acknowledge that people—young and old—suffer too. Why is a laboratory rat's fate more poignant than that of an incurably ill child?

Jane McCabe, *Newsweek,* December 28, 1988

On 11 May 1981 I began work [at the Institute for Behavioral Research] and was given a tour. . . .

I saw filth caked on the wires of the cages, faeces piled in the bottom of the cages, urine and rust encrusting every surface. There, amid this rotting stench, sat sixteen crab-eating macaques and one rhesus monkey, their lives limited to metal boxes just 17 3/4 inches wide. . . .

[An old refrigerator] had been converted into a chamber containing a plexiglass immobilizing chair. A monkey would be placed in the chamber, and electrodes attached to his body. The monkey would be forced to try to squeeze a bottle of fluid with his surgically crippled arm in order to stop the painful electric shock that coursed through his body. The ceiling and walls of the chamber were covered with blood. I remembered Dr. Taub's assistant, John Kunz, telling me that some monkeys would break their arms in desperate attempts to escape the chair and the intense electric shocks.

Alex Pacheco in *In Defense of Animals,* 1985

The ability to empathize should be considered when weighing the possible benefits and harms of animal experimentation. While all of us can sympathize with the young mother in the above excerpt, we also do not want animals to suffer. Keeping these considerations in mind, read the following descriptions of experiments researchers wish to conduct. Assess the merit of each experiment *and mark a B by those you believe are beneficial and H by those in which the harm to the animal outweighs the benefit of the experiment.* If you are doing this activity as part of a class or group, discuss your answer with others.

1. Infect primates with the Simian Acquired Immune Deficiency Syndrome (SAIDS) so that the effectiveness of drugs which may cure AIDS in humans can be tested.

2. Have high school students dissect frogs so that they learn how the internal organs work.

3. Determine the toxicity of a new eyeshadow by putting it in liquid form and dripping it into rabbits' eyes.

4. In hopes of finding and testing effective therapies to treat Parkinson's disease, treat primates with a drug that will induce in their bodies the symptoms of the disease.

5. Use the internal organs of pigs to extract a compound that will be used in an antibody that may cure childhood leukemia.

6. To test a new, cheaper rabies vaccine that will be used to treat rabies-infected pets and farm animals, infect squirrels with rabies and test the vaccine on them.

7. Kill a baboon so that its heart may be transplanted into a human infant born with a heart defect. The chances of the experiment succeeding are low.

8. Treat mice with a newly-developed vaccine that clinical studies show may cure Lou Gehrig's disease.

9. To learn about the body's response to pain, send an electric shock through the tails of young rats and record their vocalizations.

Periodical Bibliography

The following articles have been selected to supplement the diverse views presented in this chapter.

The AV Magazine
"Chimpanzees: Primates Like Ourselves," January 1989.

Neal D. Barnard
"Beyond the Draize Test," *The Animals' Agenda*, December 1988.

Douglas M. Bowden
"Animals in Research," *Neuroscience Newsletter*, March/April 1988. Available from Society for Neuroscience, 11 Dupont Circle NW, Suite 500, Washington, DC 20036.

Geoffrey Cowley
"Of Pain and Progress," *Newsweek*, December 26, 1988.

Janis Wiley Driscoll and Patrick Bateson
"Animals in Behavioural Research," *Animal Behavior*, November/December 1988.

Jane Goodall, interviewed by Wayne Pacelle
"Spanning the Gap," *The Animals' Agenda*, October 1987.

Harper's Magazine
"Just Like Us? Toward a Notion of Animal Rights," August 1988.

Gary Indiana
"All Things Cruel and Profitable," *The Village Voice*, December 13, 1988.

Mark G. Judge
"Primates Get the Shaft," *The Progressive*, October 1986.

Ann Landers
"Should We Just Use Human Guinea Pigs?" *Chicago Tribune*, October 17, 1988.

John McArdle
"AV Fact Finding," *The AV Magazine*, October 1988.

Phil Maggitti
"Veterinarians: For or Against Animal Rights?" *The Animals' Agenda*, February 1989.

New England Journal of Medicine
"The Use of Animals in Research," April 10, 1986.

Science
"New Animal Regulations Causing Scientists Pain and Distress," August 8, 1986.

U.S. News & World Report
"Saving Creatures Great and Small," December 5, 1988.

Should Animals Be Used for Food?

Chapter Preface

Many farms today are run like mass-producing factories with animals as the product. While this has allowed farmers to vastly increase meat production, many people believe that animal welfare has been sacrificed.

In his book *In the Company of Animals,* James Serpell describes the life of a wild pig and contrasts it with the life of a pig raised on an efficient pork farm. The wild pigs are sociable, intelligent omnivores who spend much of their time foraging for plants. Serpell writes, "Foraging parties are noisy, maintaining a continual, conversational exchange of grunts, squeals, and chirps. At night these animals sleep *en masse* in large dens or nests." In contrast, Serpell states, domesticated animals suffer from having their natural instincts and way of life thwarted in today's factory farms. Domesticated pigs live in individual crates in climate-controlled buildings. They are fed a diet of pre-mixed feeds. Piglets are taken from their mothers as early as possible, so the sow can be bred again to produce more pigs.

The farming industry responds by arguing that modern farming methods give domesticated animals a better, more comfortable life. The American Farm Bureau Federation believes that climate-controlled buildings allow pigs to stay clean and comfortable without wallowing in mud. Feeds are carefully balanced to provide a nutritious, healthy diet. Regular veterinary care insures continued health. Housed in sheds, animals no longer have to suffer through blizzards, thunderstorms, and lightning strikes. Furthermore, farmers contend that the evolution of large-scale, intensive farming has been spurred by consumer demand. Were animals to be raised less intensively, consumers would have to be willing to pay significantly more for their food, a sacrifice the farming industry believes most people are unwilling to make.

Do farm animals suffer, or have modern methods improved animals' lives? This is a key issue in the animal rights debate. The authors in the following chapter consider whether farming is humane, and whether humans should use animals for food.

=====

"One of the best strongholds of animal welfare in our culture is the farmer."

=====

Modern Farming Is Humane

Animal Industry Foundation

The following viewpoint is an excerpt from a brochure published by the Animal Industry Foundation, an Arlington, Virginia group whose members are feed manufacturers. The Foundation disputes comparing a modern farm to a factory. It argues that farmers are and must be concerned with animal welfare in order to produce an abundance of healthful food for consumers.

As you read, consider the following questions:

1. What are the successes of American agriculture, according to the Animal Industry Foundation?
2. Why do the authors believe modern housing is beneficial for animals?

Animal Industry Foundation, "Animal Agriculture: Myths and Facts," 1988. Reprinted with permission. The Animal Industry Foundation's permission to reprint these excerpts does not constitute an endorsement of the anthology or the views otherwise contained therein.

In an increasingly urban society, our contact with animals, especially farm animals, is limited. While man and animal depend on each other, our modern culture separates us from other species more and more. As a result, our understanding of the needs and roles of domestic animals becomes weaker, and in some cases, distorted.

One of the best strongholds of animal welfare in our culture is the farmer. With the exception of zoos and animal parks, only the farmer enjoys close, daily contact with animals. As farmers tend livestock and poultry, guaranteeing their health and welfare, the animal provides an economic return to the farmer in the form of wholesome, high quality foods valued by the vast majority of consumers.

The consuming public today is generally unaware of farmers' relationship to their animals, and how meat, milk and eggs are produced on modern farms. The average consumer may not make the connection between attractively packaged meat, milk and eggs in the supermarket, and the process of getting these foods from the farm to the dinner table.

Farmers Care for Their Animals

The image of the family farm with its red barn, a few chickens in the yard, some pigs in the mud and cows in the field isn't accurate anymore. But neither is it the sterile, mechanized, emotionless "food factory" that some would have us believe. Today, U.S. animal agriculture is a dynamic, specialized endeavor, the envy of the rest of the world. Only in America can 3% feed 100% of the population as efficiently as we do. The key to this efficiency? The best cared for livestock and poultry in the world.

Modern farm animal production is no accident. Improved animal housing, handling practices, and healthy, nutritious feeds are the result of billions of dollars of private and government research into how to raise healthy animals. And as American animal agriculture grows and changes, there is a double constant: Farmers' concern for the welfare of the animal, and their dedication to providing the highest quality, safest food in the world.

Farmers have always enjoyed broad public support for their efforts to provide abundant, nutritious food. But today, groups which reject the harvesting of animals for food, and others, who because they don't have the facts or have bad information, are working to convince the public that farmers and ranchers no longer tend their animals as animals, but as food "machines."

It's time to set the record straight. . . .

MYTH: Farm animals deserve the same rights as you or I. All creatures deserve to share the planet equally with man.

FACT: To believe that man and all other animals exist with the same rights is anthropomorphism, or the "humanizing" of

107

animals. This is a belief held by some vegetarians and animal rights extremists, and is not accepted by the general population. There are theological, scientific and philosophical arguments for why man cares for animals so they may serve him. Certainly, man has the moral obligation to avoid cruelty in dealing with all animals in all situations.

MYTH: Farmers care less for their animals than they do for the money animals bring them. Agribusiness corporations mislead farmers into using production systems and drugs that mean profits at the cost of animal welfare.

FACT: Farmers and ranchers are neither cruel nor naive. One of the main reasons someone goes into farming or ranching is a desire to work with animals. A farmer would compromise his or her own welfare if animals were mistreated. Agriculture is very competitive in the U.S., a career which pays the farmer a slim profit on the animals he cares for. It is in the farmer's own best interest to see the animals in his charge treated humanely, guaranteeing him a healthy, high quality animal, a greater return on his investment, and a wholesome food product. No advertising campaign or salesman can convince a farmer to use a system or product that would harm an animal. Farmers are always looking for ways to improve their farms to ensure animal welfare and the economics of production.

Tender Loving Care

There is a movement in today's society which is concerned about animal rights. The man or woman who is engaged in farming doesn't think about his animals in exactly that way, but he or she knows that providing good nutritious feed, a clean, environmentally controlled building and tender loving care will produce healthier, happier animals, and that's exactly what everyone wants, especially the farmer!

Wisconsin Agri-Business Council, "No One Cares More than the Farmer!"

We must also understand the difference between what an animal may want and what it needs. Untended animals may overeat to the point of sickness or death, or drink until they are bloated. An animal may eat poisonous plants if in the open. An animal may "want" to do these things, but does it "need" to?

MYTH: Farming in the U.S. is controlled by large corporations which care about profits and not about animal welfare.

FACT: Of the 2.2 million farms in the U.S., 87% are owned by an individual or a married couple responsible for operating the farm. If partnerships—typically a parent and one or more children or other close relatives—are added to this total, 97% of U.S. farms are family-owned and operated, according to the U.S. Department of Agriculture's "1987 Fact Book of U.S. Agriculture." Even those farms which are legally corporations are generally family controlled, with USDA reporting only 7,000 non-family controlled corporate farms in the U.S.

MYTH: Farm animals are routinely raised on "factory farms," confined in "crowded, unventilated cages and sheds."

FACT: Animals are generally kept in barns and similar housing, with the exception of beef cattle, to protect the health and welfare of the animal. Housing protects animals from predators, disease, and bad weather or extreme climate. Housing also makes breeding and birth less stressful, protects young animals, and makes it easier for farmers to care for both healthy and sick animals.

Modern animal housing is well ventilated, warm, well-lit, clean and scientifically designed for the specific needs of the animal, such as the regular availability of fresh water and a nutritionally balanced feed. For instance, a hog barn wouldn't be used for cows, any more than an adult would sleep in a child's crib. Housing is designed to allow the farmer to provide the best animal care and control costs.

MYTH: Not only are all animals confined, most are held in crates and cages and not allowed to move at all.

FACT: Animal behavior is as varied as human behavior. In some cases, animals are restrained to avoid injuring themselves, other animals or the farmer. All forms of restraint are designed for the welfare of the animal as well as efficiency of production.

Farmers Keep Animals from Harm

Breeding sows are helped during breeding so they are not injured by the larger, heavier boar. When a sow is ready to farrow or give birth, she is placed for a short time in a stall to make her delivery easier, help with veterinary care if necessary, ensure she does not step on or roll over and crush her litter, while allowing her piglets to be near her. Pigs are naturally aggressive and curious, and what has been described as "manic" or abnormal behavior during this protective restraint is mostly normal activity and curiosity.

Dairy cows are milked in stalls, usually twice a day. This is so farmers can use modern milking equipment, and to protect the cow and the farmer. Placing the cows in these stalls during milking also facilitates medical treatment of an animal weighing more than 1,200 lbs. At other times, most dairy farmers will turn cows out into pasture or into large pens.

Laying hens are kept in cages to ensure adequate feed and water reaches every bird every day and to facilitate egg collection. It allows the farmer to care for more birds efficiently and produce the millions of eggs consumers value each year. Sorting the birds into small groups prevents naturally aggressive behavior, such as pecking and cannibalism. It takes greater amounts of land, labor and money to raise laying hens in open flocks because of exposure to bad weather, disease, predators, etc. Today, one egg farm may house 50,000-100,000 hens. If layers were not raised in a controlled environment, feeding, cleaning, preventing disease, treating sick birds, and locating where 50,000 birds laid 50,000 eggs each day would greatly increase the cost of eggs, and price a valuable food out of the diet of many consumers.

Veal Calves

Veal calves may be raised in stalls, hutches, pens or in small groups. The system used by an individual farmer varies by region and climate, type of calf, farmer preference and size of farm. One system cannot arbitrarily be said to be better than another in all situations.

Veal calves are generally kept in individual stalls to separate aggressive young bulls from each other, minimize or eliminate injury to the animals and the farmer, and to ease feeding and veterinary care.

Misleading and Malicious

The American public is being deceived by distorted, misleading and malicious reports that falsely accuse farmers of mistreating or abusing farm animals. . . .

Family farming and the way farm animals are raised have changed significantly in the past twenty years. Farmers now place their animals in an environment that encourages rapid growth and high production. Animals under stress do not gain weight rapidly, nor do they produce as many eggs or as much milk.

The illness or death of a farm animal has a direct impact on the farmer's pocketbook, and it is in his best interest to ensure that his animals are well cared for.

American Farm Bureau Federation, "Farm Animals."

In modern stall systems, calves can stand, lie down, see, touch and react to other calves in well-lit, sanitary barns. It is not true that veal calves are kept in "boxes" or perpetual darkness. Veal feed is a liquid milk "replacer" product that is specially formulated for baby calves. It is a fortified formula containing minerals, vitamins, and animal health products, including minimum recommended amounts of iron to ensure calf health. It is not true that calves are fed deficient diets to keep them anemic. The farmer would be compromising his own economic welfare if calves weren't kept healthy.

110

Beef cattle in large herds or feedlots are restrained generally when being given veterinary care. In cow/calf operations, housing allows for protection from predators and the elements, disease control and ease of handling.

Routine Handling Procedures

MYTH: Farm animals are routinely "mutilated" by beak trimming, tail docking, branding, dehorning, castration, and other practices to make it easier for the farmer.

FACT: To the inexperienced viewer, some routine farm animal handling practices necessary to the welfare and health of the animal and the insurance of quality food may appear brutal, just as some life-saving human surgical and medical practices may seem brutal to the casual observer. All of these practices are done in a professional manner to ensure the welfare of the animal.

Egg laying hens may have their beaks trimmed—not removed—to avoid injury to each other as a result of the bird's natural "pecking order." Claws may be trimmed to avoid injury during mating.

With hogs, piglets may have their needle teeth trimmed shortly after birth to avoid injury to the nursing sow and to litter mates. Tails may be docked or shortened to end a natural tendency toward tail biting that occurs in some swine herds.

Beef cattle, sheep and some dairy cattle may be dehorned when young to avoid injury to each other and to the rancher; castration may be necessary to avoid fighting and unnatural behaviors in young animals, and to insure quality meat. In sheep, tails may be docked to improve hygiene and prevent fly and parasite infestation.

Permanently identifying animals by ear-marking, tattooing, branding and other means is necessary to maintain accurate health records to prevent the spread of disease to animals and man. It also helps during marketing.

All of these practices are under regular review and new research is done to ensure their necessity and effectiveness, and to ensure the required results are achieved in the most humane, efficient manner.

Keeping Animals Healthy

MYTH: Farm animals in "confinement" are prone to disease, forcing farmers to routinely use antibiotics, hormones and drugs to keep them alive. This jeopardizes animal and human health.

FACT: Animal scientists, veterinarians and on-farm experience show animals kept in housing are no more likely to get sick than animals kept in the open. In fact, they're generally healthier because they are protected. However, farm animals do sometimes get sick. To prevent illness and to ensure that an animal remains healthy all of its life, farmers will take preventive measures, including the use of animal health products. These products are generally given to the animal in a scientifically formulated feed best suited to the animal's needs. This is the simplest way to make sure each animal gets the care indicated.

Animal health products include animal drugs and vaccines, in addition to vitamins, minerals and other nutrients the animal needs in a balanced diet. Not all animals are given the same treatment in all situations.

Animal drugs include antibiotics to prevent and treat animal disease, and most are not used in human medicine. There are antibiotics used in humans that are also used in animals. There is now an unresolved scientific debate over these uses. Since there is no conclusive scientific proof that the use of human antibiotics in animals—a practice going back 35 years—is a risk to human health, these products are used to prevent and treat illness in some animals, in addition to aiding growth.

"Unable to groom, stretch their legs, or even turn around, the victims of factory farms exist in a relentless state of distress."

Modern Farming Is Inhumane

Humane Farming Association

The Humane Farming Association is based in San Francisco. In 1988 it began an advertising campaign to publicize what it believed was the abuse many farm animals endure, particularly calves raised for veal. In the following viewpoint, the Association argues that small cages and wire floors are abusive to animals because they restrict an animal's freedom. Modern agriculture emphasizes profits over animal welfare, the Association believes, and the result is thousands of distressed, unhealthy animals.

As you read, consider the following questions:

1. Why do the authors contend that the use of antibiotics is more widespread now than it ever has been?
2. What is the life of a factory hen like, according to the Humane Farming Association?
3. How does the Association recommend consumers should respond to inhumane farming practices?

The Humane Farming Association, *Consumer Alert: The Dangers of Factory Farming,* 1985. Reprinted with permission.

Perhaps nowhere is the link between human health and animal welfare stronger than in the raising of animals for meat and dairy products. As traditional farming techniques give way to factory farming, human health and animal welfare are compromised.

Would you knowingly serve your family penicillin, tetracycline, or drug-resistant bacteria for dinner? Of course not. Unfortunately, these and countless other substances are now commonly found in America's meat supply.

This hazard is the direct result of the abuse of antibiotics and other chemicals used to counter the effects of livestock mismanagement and the disease-ridden conditions found on factory farms throughout the country.

Factory Farm Disease

Factory farm conditions result in severe physiological as well as behavioral animal afflictions. Anemia, influenza, intestinal diseases, mastitis, metritis, orthostasis, pneumonia, and scours are only the beginning of a long list of ailments plaguing factory farm animals.

By ignoring traditional animal husbandry methods such as exercise, fresh air, wholesome food, and proper veterinary care, factory farms are a breeding ground for countless infectious diseases. Factory farms attempt to counter the effects of grossly deficient husbandry, overcrowding, and intensive confinement by administering continuous doses of antibiotics and other drugs to the animals. This "cost effective" practice has a signficiant negative impact on the health of the consumer, as well as the animal.

The deprivation to which animals are subjected on factory farms has provoked concern among knowledgeable veterinarians, family farmers, and humanitarians for several years. Today, criticism of factory farm practices is widespread among human health care professionals as well.

Medical doctors now warn that the tragedy of factory farming reaches well beyond the farm animals themselves. According to a broad spectrum of scientists, the high level of contaminants in factory farm products now poses a serious danger to human health. Studies in the *New England Journal of Medicine* and research by the U.S. Centers for Disease Control, National Resources Defense Council, and the U.S. Food and Drug Administration all warn that the levels of antibiotics and other contaminants in commercially raised meat constitute a serious threat to the health of the consumer.

Almost 50% of all antibiotics manufactured in the United States are poured directly into animal feeds. This accounts for over $435 million each year for the pharmaceutical companies.

The most commonly used antibiotics are penicillin and tetracycline. The squandering of these important drugs in livestock production is wreaking havoc for physicians in the treatment of human illness. Widespread overuse of antibiotics is resulting in the evolution of new strains of virulent bacteria whose resistance to antibiotics poses a great threat to human health. Doctors are now reporting that, due to their uncontrolled use on factory farms, these formerly life-saving drugs are often rendered useless in combating human disease.

Dr. Jere Goyan, Dean of the School of Pharmacy at the University of California, San Francisco, tells us that the indiscriminate use of antibiotics in animal feed is leading to "a major national crisis in public health. Unless we take action now to curb the use of these drugs in the livestock industry, we will not be able to use them to treat human disease." Dr. Karim Ahmed, head scientist of the National Resources Defense Council, has long urged Congress to impose immediate controls on the use of antibiotics in animal feed. According to Dr. Ahmed, unless swift action is taken, "we are going to have an epidemic of untreatable stomach ailments, many of which will end in death."

Unprotected by Law

Billions of animals never see the light of day. For others, light is continuous. They exist standing in small stalls, tiny cages, or crowded pens, no bedding (straw), food piped in automatically, dust and ammonia in the air—eating, reproducing—nothing more. Their lives are characterized by immobility, crowding, stress and disease. There are no federal laws to protect them.

Eugenia L. Stubbs, *Manchester Union Leader,* May 25, 1987.

Unfortunately, the crisis has already begun. Scientists now calculate that the misuse of penicillin and tetracycline in animal feed is implicated in more than 2,000,000 cases of *Salmonella* poisoning each year, resulting in as many as 2,000 human deaths.

These illnesses and deaths need not occur. The routine use of antibiotics and other chemicals in animal feed is a dangerously irresponsible attempt to counter the harsh, disease-ridden conditions to which animals are subjected on factory farms.

Animal Factories vs. Family Farms

Factory farm equipment and drug companies tell us that farmers need intensive animal confinement facilities in order to make a large profit. In reality, it is the equipment companies and giant pharmaceutical corporations such as Lilly, Upjohn, American Cyanamid, and Pfizer (which collectively sell farmers over 15 million pounds of antibiotics each year) that profit most from factory farming.

Family farms are being squeezed out of business by their inability to raise the necessary capital to compete with huge factory farms. Traditional farming is labor intensive, but factory farming is capital intensive. Farmers who do manage to raise the money for confinement systems quickly discover that the small savings in labor costs are not enough to cover the increasingly expensive facilities, energy, caging, and drug costs.

The Stress Connection

Agribusiness companies will tell us that factory farm animals are "happy" and "as well cared for as your own pet dog or cat." Nothing could be further from the truth.

The life of a factory farm animal is characterized by acute deprivation, stress, and disease. Hundreds of millions of animals are forced to live in cages or crates just barely larger than their own bodies. While one species may be caged alone without any social contact, another species may be crowded so tightly together that they fall prey to stress-induced cannibalism. Cannibalism is particularly prevalent in the cramped confinement of hogs and laying hens. Unable to groom, stretch their legs, or even turn around, the victims of factory farms exist in a relentless state of distress.

"When animals are intensively confined and under stress, as they are on factory farms, their autoimmune systems are affected and they are prone to infectious diseases," reports veterinarian Dr. Bruce Feldmann. "When animals are raised with care and responsibility there is no need for continuous low-level antibiotic feed additives. It is as simple as that."

The public relations firms retained by agribusiness companies will publicly deny the existence of farm animal stress. Ironically, these PR campaigns are paid for out of the millions of dollars made selling drugs to treat stress and stress-induced diseases on factory farms.

If a kennel, stable, zoo, or other establishment treated animals in a manner common on factory farms, they could be fined or lose their license to operate. If a private citizen was discovered confining a dog or cat in a manner common on factory farms, he/she could be charged with cruelty to animals. There is an area, however, that society's laws protecting animals do not touch.

The powerful agribusiness and pharmaceutical lobbies have seen to it that *farm animals are explicitly excluded from the federal Animal Welfare Act*. There are virtually no laws which protect farm animals from even the most harsh and brutal treatment as long as it takes place in the name of production and profit. It is left *entirely* to the preference of the individual company how many egg-laying hens are stuffed into each little wire cage, or whether an artificially inseminated sow must spend her entire pregnancy chained to the floor of a cement-bottomed cage.

Factory Bacon

Of the 95 million hogs born each year in the U.S., 80% will spend their lives in an intensive confinement factory farm system. Piglets are commonly weaned as early as three weeks (an extremely stressful practice) and placed in bare wire, mesh "battery cages" or tiny cement pens.

When factory-farmed piglets reach the weight of 50 lbs. they are moved into small "finishing pens" providing each pig merely 6 square feet of space. The concrete slatted floors, with no straw or bedding, contribute to lameness and other injuries. The pens become extremely crowded and fouled as the animals grow rapidly to a market weight of 210-220 pounds. Stress runs high among these animals, who develop extreme behavioral "vices" such as tail-biting and cannibalism.

Wretched Existence

Modern animal husbandry has been swept by a passion for 'intensivism'; on this tide everything that resembles the methods of an earlier day has been carried away. Gone are the pastoral scenes in which animals wandered through green fields or flocks of chickens scratched contentedly for their food. In their place are factorylike buildings in which animals live out their wretched existences without ever feeling the earth beneath their feet, without knowing sunlight, or experiencing the simple pleasures of grazing for natural food—indeed, so confined or so intolerably crowded that movement of any kind is scarcely possible.

Rachel Carson, in *Factory Farming: The Experiment That Failed*, 1987.

The unnatural confinement of huge numbers of animals in cramped indoor facilities also poses grave environmental health hazards. Factory-farmed hogs are commonly confined directly over manure collection pits. The overpowering fumes from urine and feces cause respiratory diseases in factory farm workers as well as in the animals. The pork industry's own research documents that between 70% and 90% of the persons that work in such facilities "experience acute respiratory symptoms. 55% experience chronic bronchitis and at least 14 workers have died suddenly from acute respiratory distress and systemic toxicosis." Research by Eli Lilly Co. and Elanco Products Co. reported that 71% of factory-farmed hogs display symptoms of atrophic rhinitis and that 70% show symptoms of pneumonia.

The mistreatment of sows is also a major problem. At this moment there are well over a million pregnant sows individually locked in narrow "gestation crates." These tight-fitting metal crates allow the sows no freedom of bodily movement other than one half step forward and back. Often they are chained by a shoulder collar. These unfortunate animals suffer greatly from leg problems, obesity, and stress-induced diseases. The sows spend most of their distressed lives in confinement engaging in "bar biting," "head rocking," and other stereotyped "neurotic" activity.

Factory Eggs

The egg industry represents the most pervasive use of factory farming. Laying hens that are stuffed into small "battery cages" now produce over 95% of our eggs. The completely wire cages have a floor space commonly 12" by 18". In these cages, not one, but four, even five hens are confined. Fundamental behavioral needs such as stretching wings, perching, walking, scratching, and nest building are impossible.

Unsuited for wire cages, laying hens suffer extensive foot damage, feather loss, and other bodily injuries. These injuries are worsened by other agitated birds who peck at the injuries of cagemates. Competition for space within each cage is fierce. Unlike traditional free range or loose housing systems, birds low on the pecking order are helpless and cannot escape the pecking of the more aggressive, dominant cagemates. Cannibalism is widespread in egg factories. Rather than reducing stocking densities, egg factories attempt to control cannibalism by "debeaking," a painful procedure whereby the hen's beak is mutilated with a hot blade.

Feeding, watering, and egg collection are completely automated. Up to 250,000 birds will be confined in a *single building* on a factory farm. As few as three attendants will be responsible for this astounding quantity of chickens. Veterinary care is nonexistent. The individual hens are the least expensive and most easily replaced part of the egg factory system. The high disease and mortality rates are considered economically acceptable.

Veal Facts

From his first day to his last, the life of a "milk-fed" veal calf is one of deprivation, stress, and disease. In the name of "gourmet food," veal factories take newborn male calves from their mothers and chain them alone in crates measuring only 22" wide and 58" long. Here they will spend their entire lives.

• To prevent muscle development and speed weight gain, the calves are allowed absolutely no exercise.

• Chained in tiny crates, veal calves cannot turn around, groom, stretch their legs, or lie down in a natural position.

• To obtain the light colored meat sold as "premium" or "milk-

fed" veal, calves are kept anemic by withholding sufficient iron.
- Veal calves are kept in total darkness to reduce restlessness.
- One of the many drugs found in veal production is *chloramphenicol*. Chloramphenicol is a highly toxic drug. In minute quantities it can cause aplastic anemia and fatal bone marrow disease in susceptible persons. Though illegal, USDA warns that chloramphenicol is being used in veal calves and that "detection is extremely difficult."
- Serious leg injuries are caused by a complete lack of straw or other bedding covering the wood slatted floors.
- Respiratory and intestinal diseases run rampant among veal calves.
- Veal calves are denied all solid food.
- Veal calves are deprived of drinking water. In a futile attempt to quench their thirst, the calves gain weight quickly by drinking more of their milky liquid feed.

- Veal calves suffer from *chronic diarrhea* from being exclusively fed a liquid diet of growth stimulators, antibiotics, powdered skim milk, and mold inhibitors.

This is the terrible fate of one million calves every year in the United States.

Your personal boycott of veal and support of the Humane Farming Association will help end this cruelty and stop one of the most bizarre agricultural practices ever developed—the deliberate raising of sick animals.

Consumer awareness and *consumer pressure* are the most effective means we have in eliminating the health hazards posed by factory farming and alleviating needless animal suffering. Every effort should be made to avoid animal products that have been produced on factory farms. . . .

Vanishing with the Family Farm

The overcrowding and intensive confinement of animals on factory farms, coupled with the inhumane handling and transportation of livestock, constitute the most widespread abuses animals have ever faced. The most fundamental concepts of animal husbandry, such as proper veterinary care, adequate nutrition, even the freedom for animals to assume natural postures . . . are vanishing along with America's family farms.

*"A liberal meat supply has always been
associated with a happy and virile people."*

The Case for Eating Meat

John R. Romans, William J. Costello, Kevin W. Jones,
C. Wendell Carlson, and P. Thomas Ziegler

The authors of the following viewpoint argue that meat provides
an abundance of high-quality protein as well as several minerals.
Meat-eating has long been associated with a healthy population,
they contend. John R. Romans, William J. Costello, Kevin W. Jones,
and C. Wendell Carlson teach at South Dakota State University
in Brookings, South Dakota. Ziegler was professor emeritus of
animal husbandry at The Pennsylvania State University in University Park, Pennsylvania.

As you read, consider the following questions:

1. How do the authors believe the problem of cholesterol can
   be minimized?
2. What nutrients does meat provide, according to the
   authors?
3. What do the authors cite as the ultimate reason for eating
   meat?

John R. Romans, et al., *The Meat We Eat.* Danville, IL: The Interstate Printers &
Publishers, Inc., copyright © 1985. Used with permission.

Approximately two thirds of the world's agricultural land is permanent pasture, range, and meadow; of this, at least 60 percent is unsuitable for producing crops that would be consumed directly by humans. . . . Ruminants harbor microorganisms in the rumen portion of their four-compartment stomachs, which have the ability to utilize cellulose for energy and to synthesize essential nutrients, such as amino acids and certain vitamins. Furthermore, approximately 98 percent of the grain fed to animals in the United States consists of corn, sorghum, oats, and barley, none of which are major sources of human food in this country.

It is the function of these animals (cattle, sheep, goats, and deer) to utilize grasses and grains and convert them into a more suitable and concentrated food for humans as well as materials for clothing, pharmaceuticals, and many other valuable by-products.

Happy and Virile People

A liberal meat supply has always been associated with a happy and virile people and invariably has been the main food available to settlers of new and undeveloped territories. Statistics show that per capita meat consumption varies with meat production and decreases with density of population. Note that the United States is the number one meat producer, producing more than twice the amount of the world's second-place producer, the USSR. . . .

The peoples of the world as a whole are always hungry. They are hungry because of a lack of food or because of a lack of means to buy it. Under such conditions, likes and dislikes become secondary.

Those of us who dwell in a land of plenty, blessed by the elements developed through personal initiative under a system of free enterprise, have built for ourselves a rather selective standard of living. We are what we make ourselves, whether morally, spiritually, financially, or physically. These are voluntary, not decreed, acquirements.

Eating Habits

Broadly speaking, our eating habits are governed in a large measure by spendable income, concern for our personal well-being, and doctors' advice. Statistics continue to show that U.S. consumers spend only approximately 16 percent of their total disposable income on food (12 percent at home, 4 percent away from home). Of that food dollar, 50¢ is spent on food produced by animals, and of that, 80 percent, or 40¢, is spent for meat. . . .

Consumption will vary with income and comparative prices. Income also governs the consumer's selection of meat cuts. The old expression "no money, no meat" still holds. In most cases, those in the middle-income group are the heavy meat and potato consumers, particularly if their occupations require considerable physical exertion. Youths top the hamburger, hot dog, and pop-consuming group. Fortunately, they are also heavy milk and ice cream consumers.

Too few of us realize until too late that appetite is a poor governor for the operation of the intricate human engine. Opening the food throttle can result in many ailments and discomforts. Obesity and heart failure are blood relatives. The old saw that everybody loves a fat man is a hoax. Physical well-being can mean different things to different people.

Some of us are food faddists; we make food a religion. Others follow trends such as the order of the Slim Look or the Olympian. Then we have the Society of Suffering Distaffs who, by diet tricks or pills, take off 10 pounds in 20 days and recover it in 10. They are the Lost and Found. Let's be sensible and make *well-being* and *being well* a little more congruent. . . .

Indispensable Protein

The nutrient value of animal products is indisputable. Complete protein—the kind with sufficient quantities of the eight amino acids—is found only in animal products. The human body cannot manufacture these eight amino acids, so they must be supplied through proper diet.

American Farm Bureau Federation, "Farm Animals."

The trend in consumer preference for leaner meats continues. Unfortunately, the consumers are now bombarded from many sides with various admonitions concerning the composition of their diets, especially regarding the fat content. In the early 1950s, it was reported that the cholesterol level in the human circulatory system may be raised by the ingestion of certain fats. Cholesterol is found in the human blood stream and, when triggered by a factor yet unknown, may be deposited on the inside walls of arteries and veins, thereby hindering the free movement of blood to and from the heart.

Divided on the Diet-Heart Question

Yet, after 25 years of research costing several billion dollars, scientists are still divided on the diet-heart question. Some insist that diet manipulations to control levels of cholesterol and saturated fat intake are essential to control coronary heart disease. Animal fats are generally more highly saturated than vegetable fats; thus, these scientists condemn animal fat in the diet. Other scientists, by now the larger of the two opposing groups, cite evidence that factors other than diet, such as lack of exercise, high blood pressure, cigarette smoking, obesity, and heredity, have an equal or higher relationship to heart disease. Furthermore, cholesterol is manufactured by the human body itself and is essential in normal body functions. Fat does serve as a rich source of energy; so therefore, many of us rather sedentary American folks should not over-consume fat, for if we do, we will become obese. Other roles of fat in the human body are to serve as carriers of vitamins A, D, E, and K to protect body tissues and vital organs and to regulate body temperature. Thus fat is essential and by no means a nutrient to be avoided but rather to be consumed at proper levels.

The consumer demand for leaner meat has made certain demands on the producer, packer, and retailer. The producer must select and breed for quality meat animals that are more heavily muscled and that will reach a market weight at an earlier age without the extended feeding period. Progeny testing is essential in order to find the strains that efficiently produce more edible meat of acceptable quality and less waste fat. The packer must compensate these efforts by paying a premium for animals of superior meat type and quality and by discounting those that produce overdone carcasses and cuts and that require costly fat trimming. Packers are doing more further processing of carcasses and cuts, utilizing the latest techniques that have been developed to produce products uniform in size and quality. The retailer should in turn give the matters of trim and improved display conditions further consideration.

The consumer has recognized that fat in excess of 0.2 inch over the outside of a chop, steak, or roast is simply waste. However, this same consumer desires a tender, juicy, and flavorful meat cut. Marbling (fat within the muscle) is becoming less important to overall palatability as we continue to market younger animals. In fact, recent research has shown little relationship between marbling and tenderness in such animals. However, a certain minimum level of marbling is necessary to give meat its characteristic aroma, flavor, and juiciness. This minimum level is an amount of fat that would by no means cause a health hazard in the diet of any normal consumer.

Eating in Moderation

There should be no doubt in our minds that eating in moderation of those foods that furnish us a balanced diet is the answer to most of our overweight ills and that does not mean the exclusion of animal products.

Although the authors confess to being moderately heavy meat eaters, it is not to be concluded from what is to follow that meat is something magic. A mixed diet that includes sufficient grains and cereals, a liberal amount of vegetables, fresh fruit, milk, a savory serving of one of over a hundred possible tasty meat dishes, and as little of those complicated sweets that end up a meal as

124

possible is the sensible one. But even a sensible meal can be made destructive by over-eating. Over-work and over-distension of the digestive tract can be likened to an over-inflated tire run at high speed—it may result in a blowout. A quotation from *Exchange* is worth repeating at this point: "Some businessmen make more of a feature of their eating than of their business. Their business is merely an interval between meals. These men who hate to let business interfere with eating usually come to the day when their eating puts them out of business."

A Natural Food

The term *natural* takes on an added meaning to most consumers in the present day, since much has been made of *organic* or *natural* foods in the popular press. Yet, there is no official definition for *organic* or *natural* foods. The heading to this section does not imply any meaning other than the following: Lean muscle is composed of approximately 20 percent protein, 9 percent fat, 70 percent moisture, and 1 percent ash. An edible portion of meat with a fat covering of about 0.2 inch would be composed of 17 percent protein, 20 percent fat, 62 percent moisture, and 1 percent ash. The lean and fat tissues are very similar to human body tissue, and because of this, they are highly digestible and can be easily and rapidly assimilated by the human digestive tract. Milk and eggs are other foods of economic importance that have similar qualities. A chemical analysis may show that a food is rich in certain food elements, but these elements may not be very digestible, or the body may not be able to absorb and utilize them as efficiently as it would the same elements in another food. This is known as the biological value of a food nutrient.

The biological value of a food nutrient is determined under controlled conditions by accounting for the total nutrient intake in terms of what is retained in the body tissues versus that which is excreted in the feces and urine.

Meat proteins have a high biological value. Some products made from soybeans, which are now widely used as a meat extenders, lack the complete array of essential amino acids in the proper proportions alone, and thus blend well with meat proteins to raise the biological value of the final product. The concentrated nature of meat and its ability to be readily and almost wholly absorbed from the intestines makes it a highly desirable, if not essential, food for humans.

It Sticks to the Ribs

Experience is a great teacher. It has taught the soldier, the laborer, and the trainer of athletes that meat has something besides "fill-in value." Before scientists revealed its rather broad vitamin content and the high biological value of its proteins and fats, its merits were expounded by the expression "It sticks to the ribs." The 10 amino acids which are considered essential for human life are all found in meat. Its proteins have, by individual analyses for the amino acids, been found to be biologically complete.

The human requirements for energy secured through the medium of carbohydrates and fat can be supplied in large measure by the fat in meat, since fat has 2.25 times the energy value of carbohydrates.

Nutrient density is a measure of the concentration of a nutrient per calorie of food consumed. Selecting foods that are dense sources of nutrients assists one in obtaining needed daily vitamins, minerals, and protein while minimizing calorie intake. Lean meat is a dense source of protein.

With the exception of calcium, meat contains all the necessary minerals for human body metabolism. Add to this list of nutritive elements the daily discoveries, through extensive research, that meat is also rich in many of the vitamins so necessary to a normal, healthy body, and the completeness of meat as a food is rather evident. The meat diet of the hardy Eskimo attests to this fact.

The height and weight of humans are governed in large part by the available food supply. The human life span rises with a balanced diet and improved medical knowledge and facilities. The people of some nations consume rather low amounts of red meat and relatively high amounts of seafood. The importance of food overshadows every material need of our people. It is responsible for the world's number one business and is its prime political sedative.

The King of Foods

Brushing aside for the moment all that has been said, and forgetting high-sounding names, over-zealous scientists, and doctors' admonitions, let us revert to plain hungry mortals seated around the festive board. Instinctively we look for the platter of meat, which to most of us is not only the king but the whole royal family of appetite appeal. It transcends all other foods in aroma, causing a watering of the mouth and a conscious glow in the most bulbous organ of the gastro-intestinal tract. It is a psychological stimulus that causes a flow of saliva and gastric juice, preparing the food chamber for the royal guest. And it does not beguile us; it satisfies. It accomplishes this by supplying what it advertises to our nostrils before we consume it. As we crunch its juicy fibers between permanent or removable ivories, we receive our first pleasant realization of a previous longing sensation. As we swallow the tasty mass, we begin to radiate satisfaction in our eyes, in our speech, and in our actions. We become more amiable, more clear-minded, and more reasonable—certainly a most honorable tribute to any food product.

"The meat business depends on our repressing the unpleasant awareness that we are devouring dead bodies."

The Case for Vegetarianism

John Robbins

John Robbins is a psychotherapist in California who founded an environmental group called Concerned Citizens of Planet Earth. In the following viewpoint, Robbins argues that most Americans have been indoctrinated into believing that they must eat meat to be healthy. He points to studies showing that meat eaters die earlier than vegetarians. Eating this unhealthy food also requires putting thousands of animals to death. Robbins concludes that this myth of the healthiness of meat is maintained by slick advertisements from the meat industry.

As you read, consider the following questions:

1. What does Robbins find deceptive about advertising for meat products?
2. What studies does the author cite to support his argument that eating meat is unhealthy?
3. How much protein is necessary in the average person's daily diet, according to Robbins?

John Robbins, *Diet For a New America.* Walpole, NH: Stillpoint Publishing, 1987. Printed with permission of Stillpoint Publishing, a division of Stillpoint International, Inc.

Increasingly in the last few decades, the animals raised for meat, dairy products and eggs in the United States have been subjected to ever more deplorable conditions. Merely to keep the poor creatures alive under these circumstances, even more chemicals have had to be used, and increasingly, hormones, pesticides, antibiotics and countless other chemicals and drugs end up in foods derived from animals. The worst drug pushers don't work city streets—they operate today's "factory farms."

But that's just the half of it. The suffering these animals undergo has become so extreme that to partake of food from these creatures is to partake unknowingly of the abject misery that has been their lives. Millions upon millions of Americans are merrily eating away, unaware of the pain and disease they are taking into their bodies with every bite. We are ingesting nightmares for breakfast, lunch and dinner. . . .

From our earliest years in this culture we've been taught a cotton candy version of what happens to food animals. We have been taught to repress the bloody truth. We've worn our blinders for so long that it is hard to see them for what they are, particularly when our parents most likely wore them as well, and the culture as a whole takes such repression completely for granted.

I have seen egg cartons with pictures of smiling hens. The message is that these birds are pleased as punch with the whole situation, and lend their blessings and radiant happiness to our consumption of their eggs. Frankly, I have to wonder how the chickens would feel about this—the real life-birds who are crammed into wire cages, their beaks cut off so they won't kill each other in their panic at being unable to express any of their natural urges.

Happy To Be Eaten

In front of me right now is an advertisement from a local market which was dropped into my mail box this morning. It shows a cartoon drawing of a bull, winking at me with a big smile on his friendly face. Apparently he is an expert on beef, because he is shown playfully pointing with his tail to certain items of meat, happily beckoning me to try them. This and millions of other such advertisements hammer home the message over and over that bulls are delighted for us to eat bull flesh. I can't help but think that the correct term for this type of thing is "bull shit!"

I've seen ads and I'm sure you have too, in which animals are shown offering themselves to be eaten, virtually begging us to dine upon them. In one television commercial, cartoon hens, looking as happy and playful as the Rockettes, dance the can-can in a chorus line. What, you may wonder, are they so jubilant about? They're singing joyfully about how much we will enjoy their legs. . . .

The meat business depends on our repressing the unpleasant awareness that we are devouring dead bodies. Thus we have refined names like "sweatbreads" for what really are the innards of baby lambs and calves. We have names like "Rocky Mountain Oysters" for something we might not find quite so appealing if we knew what they really were—pig's testicles.

Our very language becomes an instrument of denial. When we look at the body of a dead cow, we call it a "side of beef." When we look at the body of a dead pig, we call it "ham," or "pork." We have been systematically trained not to see anything from the point of view of the animal, or even from a point of view which includes the animal's existence. . . .

Meat Eaters Die Earlier

After World War II, scientists began for the first time to compile comprehensive statistics correlating the diet-styles and health of all the populations in the world.

One fact that emerged consistently was the strong correlation between heavy flesh-eating and short life expectancy. The Eskimos, the Laplanders, the Greenlanders, and the Russian Kurgi tribes stood out as the populations with the highest animal flesh consumption in the world—and also as among the populations with the lowest life expectancies, often only about 30 years.

Far Healthier

A vegetarian diet not only spares animals suffering and death, but is far healthier than a diet high in animal flesh. The cholesterol and saturated fat found in meat, coupled with countless drugs, pesticides, and other chemical substances fed to farm animals, pose a serious threat to human health. Animal products are a major contributor to heart disease and cancer—the two biggest killers in the U.S. The wide variety of grains, beans, legumes, nuts, vegetables, and fruits makes a vegetarian diet delicious and satisfying.

Trans-Species Unlimited, "Meet Your Meat."

It was found, further, that this was not due to the severity of their climates alone. Other peoples, living in harsh conditions, but subsisting with little or no animal flesh, had some of the highest life expectancies in the world. World health statistics found, for example, that an unusually large number of the Russian Caucasians, the Yucatan Indians, the East Indian Todas and the Pakistan Hunzakuts have life expectancies of 90 to 100 years.

The United States has the most sophisticated medical technology in the world, and one of the most temperate climates. One of the highest consumers of meat and animal products in the world, it also has one of the lowest life expectancies of industrialized nations. . . .

Pushing Protein

I am sitting in elementary school. The teacher is bringing out a nice colored chart and telling all us kids how important it is to eat meat and drink our milk and get lots of protein. I'm listening to her, and looking at the chart which makes it all seem so simple. I believe my teacher, because I sense that she, herself, believes what she is saying. She is sincere. She is a grown-up. Besides, the chart is decorated and fun to look at. It must be true.

Protein, I hear, that's what's important. Protein. Lots of it. And you can only get good quality protein from meat and eggs and dairy products. That's why they make up two of the four "basic food groups" on the chart. . . .

Of course, just because the concept of the "basic four" food groups was promoted by the National Egg Board, the National Dairy Council, and the National Livestock and Meat Board, doesn't mean it is necessarily false. Just because there were hucksters in our classrooms doesn't mean the hucksters lied.

But it does mean their motives were a little less pure than we thought, and their "concern" for our education a little more self-interested than we knew. It might cast a shadow upon the wisdom of unquestioningly accepting the "truths" we were taught. It might mean, for example, that we should consult sources of information less biased than the Egg Board, or the Meat Board, or the others who applied so much political and economic pressure to get those nice pretty charts to say what they wanted them to say. . . .

I've found that not all authorities agree on a precise figure for our daily needs of protein, but their calculations do fall within a specific range. It is a range that runs from a low estimate of *two and a half percent* of our total daily calories up to a high estimate of over *eight percent*. The figures at the high end include built-in safety margins, and are not "minimum" allowances, but rather "recommended" allowances. . . .

If we ate nothing but wheat (which is 17% protein), or oatmeal (15%), or pumpkin (15%), we would easily have more than enough protein. If we ate nothing but cabbage (22%), we'd have over double the maximum we might need.

In fact, if we ate nothing but the lowly potato (11% protein) we would still be getting enough protein. This fact does not mean potatoes are a particularly high protein source. They are not. Almost all plant foods provide more. What it does show, however, is just how low our protein needs really are. . . .

For years it was thought that heart disease and strokes were simply misfortunes we had to somehow learn to accept. But over the last thirty years, this has changed. The most comprehensive research in medical history has discovered something of marvelous and far-reaching consequence: we are not helpless victims of atherosclerosis. It is a disease which, knowingly or unknowingly, we bring upon ourselves, and by the same token, can prevent. . . .

Some of the first evidence indicating that atherosclerosis was not simply a consequence of "growing old," but was rooted in our dietary intake of saturated fat and cholesterol, came inadvertently from the Korean War. Soldiers who had been killed were autopsied, and medical researchers were stunned by what they found. More than 77% of the American soldiers had blood vessels which were already narrowed by atherosclerotic deposits, while the arteries of the equally young soldiers of the opposing forces showed no similar damage.

"How's it prepared? First we chop off its head; then we rip its feathers off; then....

From the Spring, 1988 issue of *Conscience,* published by Canadian Vegans for Animal Rights.

At the time, it was thought that the pronounced differences in the conditions of the soldiers' arteries might be more a consequence of genetic predisposition than of their differing diet-styles. But this idea became quickly untenable when a large group of Korean soldiers were put on the U.S. Army diet. They rapidly developed significant increases in their blood cholesterol levels, an unmistakable sign of developing atherosclerosis. . . .

Stirred by the results of the Korean War autopsies, medical researchers undertook a major effort to learn more. From 1963 to 1965, a worldwide study of heart disease and stroke patterns was done, called the International Atherosclerotic Project. This truly mammoth undertaking involved examining the arteries of over 20,000 autopsied bodies throughout the world. The findings revealed an unmistakable pattern: people who lived in areas where consumption of saturated fat and cholesterol were high had markedly more atherosclerosis, more heart attacks, and more strokes.

It took a while for medical researchers to grasp the full implications of what was being learned, because the emerging truth required them to do a complete about-face from their well-entrenched assumptions.

Not Just a Theory

The meat, dairy and egg industries, meanwhile, were not exactly eager to support the researchers' new findings. They financed numerous studies which attempted to vindicate their products and discredit what they called the saturated fat and cholesterol "theory" of atherosclerosis. Some pointed out that animal foods were not the only products high in saturated fat, and attempted to point an accusing finger at plant sources. Directing attention to coconuts, palm kernel oil, and chocolate, which are all high in saturated fat, they loudly proclaimed that meat, dairy products and eggs should not be singled out and found guilty as the sole suppliers of saturated fats in our diets. But scientists who were not on the payroll of these industries, and who were perhaps a bit more impartial in their motivation, pointed out that coconuts, palm kernel oil and chocolate are the *only* plant foods significantly high in saturated fat. They also suggested that meat, eggs and dairy products probably make up a larger percentage of most people's diets than do coconuts, palm kernel oil, and chocolate. . . .

Cholesterol and Fat

In 1985, the Beef Council had the dubious distinction of being a repeat winner of the Harlan Page Hubbard Memorial Award for the year's most deceptive and misleading advertising. The award, named for a famous charlatan who glowingly advertised a worthless patent medicine, is given by a collection of consumer groups who are used to the distortions and exaggerations that typify Madison Avenue. But even to their weathered eyes the "beef gives strength" campaign took the cake for implying that beef is low in fat. The servings shown in the ads were only three ounces, when, according to USDA data, the average beef steak serving is double that. By not explaining that the serving shown in the ad is only half the size most people eat, the industry conveyed the impression that servings of beef are much lower in fat than they actually are. In announcing the award, Bonnie Liebman of the Center for Science in the Public Interest also pointed out that the technicians who did the laboratory analysis which produced the calorie and fat counts referred to in the ads used scalpels to remove every possible bit of fat from the meat samples. Thus the fat and calorie levels reported were not only for a serving size much smaller than viewers understood it to be, but also for a serving which had been trimmed of fat with a meticulousness no homemaker could possibly match. The industry ads also did not mention that cholesterol is found mostly in lean tissues, not in fat, and so no matter how meticulously you trim away the fat you cannot significantly reduce the level of cholesterol.

The industry ads have to go to such great lengths to give the impression their products are healthy because the truth is so incriminating. . . .

We know today how to prevent heart attacks and strokes. We know how to prevent the killers that account for more than half of the deaths in the United States every year. But most of us, thanks to the dedicated endeavors of the meat, dairy and egg industries, have not gotten the good news. We still think we must eat animal products in order to be healthy. We still think heart attacks and strokes are a regrettable but more or less inevitable byproduct that comes with living well and growing old. The heart attack has become so much a part of American life as to virtually be an institution. We take it for granted.

Few of us know that our passive attitude is perpetuated by the deliberate efforts of those who profit from our staying hooked on the foods that cause heart disease.

Making the Right Food Choice

As long as we remain passive we cannot make the real choices that empower us. Although there are people who do not want us to make such choices and are willing to do almost anything to confuse us, we now have for the first time in history, sufficient knowledge to take control over our bodies and our lives. Now we can make food choices which we know will dramatically improve the health of our cardiovascular system, prevent heart disease and strokes, and at the same time reduce the suffering in the world.

a critical thinking activity

Recognizing Deceptive Arguments

People who feel strongly about an issue use many techniques to persuade others to agree with them. Some of these techniques appeal to the intellect, some to the emotions. Many of them distract the reader or listener from the real issues.

Below are listed a few common examples of argumentation tactics. Most of them can be used either to advance an argument in an honest, reasonable way or to deceive or distract from the real issues. It is important for a critical reader to recognize these tactics in order to evaluate rationally an author's ideas.

a. *scare tactics*—the threat that if you don't do or don't believe this, something terrible will happen

b. *strawperson*—distorting or exaggerating an opponent's arguments to make one's own seem stronger

c. *bandwagon*—the idea that "everybody" does this or believes this

d. *slanters*—trying to persuade through inflammatory and exaggerated language instead of through reason

e. *generalizations*—using statistics or facts to generalize about a population, place, or thing

f. *personal attack*—criticizing an opponent personally instead of rationally debating his or her ideas

g. *categorical statements*—stating something in a way implying that there can be no argument

The following activity will allow you to sharpen your skills in recognizing deceptive reasoning. Some of the statements on the next page are taken from the viewpoints in this chapter. *Beside each one, mark the letter of the type of deceptive appeal being used. More than one type of tactic may be applicable. If you believe the statement is not any of the listed appeals, write N.*

134

1. Unless we stop the use of antibiotics on farm animals, we won't have enough antibiotics to cure sick people.

2. Most people don't believe the things animal extremists say.

3. Everyone who becomes a farmer loves animals.

4. Men who eat too much die young.

5. The completeness of meat as a food is obvious.

6. Animal rights activists would rather let people die of cancer than squash a mosquito.

7. There should be no doubt in our minds that eating meat in moderation is the answer for overweight people.

8. The American public is being deceived by distorted, misleading, and malicious reports that falsely accuse farmers of mistreating animals.

9. Millions of Americans are merrily eating away, unaware of the diseases they are taking in with every bite of meat.

10. The meat business depends on our repressing the unpleasant awareness that we are devouring dead bodies.

11. Farms are run by the greedy, who only care about making more money.

12. Most vegetarians are just following the latest fad.

13. For most of us, meat has the best aroma of all foods.

14. The worst drug pushers don't work city streets—they operate today's "factory farms."

15. The general population doesn't really care for meat.

16. The massive consumption of meat in this country will result in all of us dying before our time.

17. The minimal amount of fat in meat would in no way cause a health hazard to normal people.

18. The meat diet of the hardy Eskimo proves that eating meat will make you happy, virile, and bursting with good health.

Periodical Bibliography

The following articles have been selected to supplement the diverse views presented in this chapter.

Madonna Behen — "In Search of Leaner Beef," *Good Housekeeping,* May 1988.

George M. Briggs — "The Red Meat Controversy," *Science of Food and Agriculture,* March 1987. Available from CAST, 137 Lynn Ave., Ames, IA 50010-7120.

Gene Bylinsky — "Here Come the Bionic Piglets," *Fortune,* October 26, 1987.

Richard Conniff — "Superchicken: Whose Life Is It Anyway?" *Discover,* June 1988.

Jared Diamond — "The Worst Mistake in the History of the Human Race," *Discover,* May 1987.

Robert Epstein — "Psychic Numbing and the Psychology of Meat Eating," *Ahimsa,* January/March 1988. Available from The American Vegan Society, 501 Old Harding Highway, Malaga, NJ 08328.

Bill Gupton — "Guess What's Coming to Dinner?" *Utne Reader,* September/October 1988.

Gene Johnson — "Feeder-Pig Profit Factory," *Successful Farming,* February 1987.

Steve Lohr — "Swedish Farm Animals Get a Bill of Rights," *The New York Times,* October 25, 1988.

Wayne Pacelle — "Biomachines: Life on the Farm Ain't What It Used To Be," *Vegetarian Times,* January 1989.

Prevention — "Meat Eaters Top Cholesterol Charts," February 1988.

Lisa J. Raines — "The Mouse That Roared," *Issues in Science and Technology,* Summer 1988.

Jay Stuller — "Antibiotics: Snuffing Out Yesterday's Killers," *American Legion Magazine,* April 1988.

Claudia Wallis — "Should Animals Be Patented?" *Time,* May 4, 1987.

Does Wildlife Need To Be Protected?

ANIMAL RIGHTS

Chapter Preface

As the human population increases, more and more animal species are threatened by reduced land availability, pollution, and poachers. These and other factors have pushed many species of animals to the brink of extinction.

This devastation is particularly evident in Africa. David Western of the Elephant and Rhino Specialist Group at the International Union for Conservation of Nature and Natural Resources estimates that while there were 1.5 million elephants in Africa in 1978, there were only 700,000 in 1988. For black rhinos, the figures are just as grim. In 1970 there were 65,000 rhinos in Africa; today there are 4,000. And the mountain gorilla is perhaps most endangered: Only 400 remain in the wild.

Both conservation organizations and governments have responded to Africa's loss of wildlife through publicity campaigns and preservation programs. For example, the African Wildlife Federation declared 1988 the Year of the Elephant in an effort to heighten public awareness of the dwindling elephant population. Sixteen African governments have spent $45 million to support a system of parks and wildlife preserves. In addition, Rwanda has used tourist revenue to support its national park which encompasses the gorillas' habitat and to fund patrols that fight poaching of this endangered animal.

The loss of wildlife in Africa is representative of a phenomenon occurring throughout the world. As wildlife becomes more endangered, heated debate continues on how and whether humans can conserve animals. The viewpoints in the following chapter address these issues.

"Our species . . . is on the brink of causing, single-handedly, the worst mass extinction in 65 million years."

Endangered Species Should Be Saved

David Jablonski

David Jablonski is an associate professor of paleontology in the department of geophysical sciences at the University of Chicago. In the following viewpoint, he describes the current extinction of animals and plants as occurring far more rapidly than any previous extinction. After examining fossils from past extinctions, Jablonski concludes that humans must act to reverse the trend toward mass extinction.

As you read, consider the following questions:

1. What kinds of species may survive mass extinctions, according to the author?
2. What are the three lessons of the fossil record regarding extinction according to Jablonski?

David Jablonski, "Mass Extinctions: New Answers, New Questions" in *The Last Extinction*, edited by Les Kaufman and Kenneth Mallory. Cambridge, MA: The Massachusetts Institute of Technology Press, 1986. Copyright © 1986 by The Massachusetts Institute of Technology. All rights reserved.

Paleontologists have known for over a century that changes in the 4-billion-year history of life have not always been slow or steady. Major revolutions, such as the disappearance of the dinosaurs or of the ammonites, can be clearly seen in the fossil record. These events are termed mass extinctions. The geological and paleontological discoveries of the past five years have led to a new look at the phenomenon of mass extinction, both causes and consequences, and indeed a new look at the history of life on this planet. We certainly do not have the full story, but recent discoveries have set us on the track of a whole new set of problems and questions. . . .

Mass extinctions have plagued the Earth's biota repeatedly over at least the past 600 million years, the time interval since the origin of well-skeletonized organisms that make up the richest part of the fossil record. Geological, geochemical, and paleontological evidence suggests that one or more of these mass extinctions was either triggered or intensified by impacts of extraterrestrial objects. The role of these mass extinctions in shaping the history of life is still poorly understood, but new evidence suggests that they did not result simply from intensification of natural selection and other evolutionary processes that prevailed during the long time between mass extinctions. Instead, the rules of extinction and survival apparently change for a geologically brief period of time, removing many groups that are well adapted to the normal or "background" extinction processes that have prevailed over most of the Earth's history. The victims of mass extinction thus might easily include groups that were dominant during normal times, whereas survivors might include groups normally vulnerable to extinction.

Changing the Rules of Evolution

The history of life may thus be an alternation of normal and mass extinction rules, with a given group having radically different levels of vulnerability at different times in Earth history. This is a far cry from the more comfortable view that extinction serves to weed out the weak or the poorly adapted, making way for better-designed, more-advanced organisms. Particular groups of animals might rise to dominance, not because of any relative superiority but because they happen to weather a brief and unpredictable crisis. The great mammalian radiation, including our own lineage, may be the best example of all. Mammals may well owe their present dominance to a short-lived shift in the survival rules rather than to any innate superiority that mammals had over dinosaurs. . . .

The mass extinctions in the fossil record have compelling implications for the plight of today's wildlife and for the survival of the human species. The fossil record is telling us, first, that

DOONESBURY
by Garry Trudeau

major upheavals can and do occur and that such biological crises can be rapid, irreversible, and unpredictable. Once a species is extinct or a network of interacting species falls apart, it is gone forever.

A second message from the fossil record is that the tropics are the Earth's most vulnerable regions. This is bad news because the tropical forests are important for the well-being of us all. Incredibly rich centers of plant and animal life, tropical forests cover less than 7 percent of the Earth's land surface but harbor more than half of the world's species. . . .

Half a Million Species Lost

In his excellent book *The Primary Source,* Norman Myers estimates that the Earth is losing tropical forests at the rate of at least 200,000 square kilometers per year, mainly as a result of logging and the clearing of forest for agriculture. If this devastation continues, representing an annual loss of about 2 percent of the total tropical forest area, we will have lost at least half a million species, perhaps as many as a million in twenty years. As Myers has documented, this human-caused mass extinction will destroy a staggering wealth of biological resources. The tropics contain over 4000 species of edible fruits and vegetables, and fewer than fifty of these are being used on a large scale today. The other 3950 species could certainly help relieve hunger in the coming decades but only if those species survive to be cultivated. . . .

In more general terms, the fossil record shows us that, when the rate of extinction strongly outpaces the evolution of new species, as it is doing with a vengeance today, the stage is set for the kinds of extreme changes that I labeled mass extinctions at the beginning of this chapter. Destruction and extinction may be rapid, but recovery is painfully slow. The reefs at the end of the Cretaceous were not unusual in this regard: They were extinguished in only tens to thousands of years, but they took 10 million years to become reestablished. The appearance of tropical reefs required the evolution of new kinds of reef builders, because the Cretaceous builders, the rudist clams, were gone. Perhaps just as chilling is what we have learned about the likely survivors of these crises: not the most highly evolved life forms nor the most useful to our own species, but the most widespread ecological generalists. The survivors would be the weeds and the cockroaches, not the medicinal or nutritional plants.

Our species, then, is on the brink of causing, single-handedly, the worst mass extinction in 65 million years. The very species that provide, or might provide, a rich harvest of medicines, foods, fuels, raw materials, and even climate regulation are being driven into extinction, forever beyond our reach. It is up to us, as beneficiaries of the last major mass extinction, to reverse this trend.

2

"Extinction is an inevitable fact of evolution, and it is needed for progress."

Endangered Species Should Not Be Saved

Norman D. Levine

Norman D. Levine is professor emeritus at the College of Veterinary Medicine and Agricultural Experiment Station at the University of Illinois in Urbana. In the following viewpoint, Levine argues that extinction is one phase of the process of evolution. Those animals who cannot adapt to changing habitats cannot be saved, he argues, and an effort to prevent extinction is neither realistic nor feasible.

As you read, consider the following questions:

1. What does Levine argue is the purpose of extinction?
2. How have humans changed animal habitats, according to the author?
3. Why does Levine believe it is futile to try and save endangered species?

Norman D. Levine, "Evolution and Extinction," *BioScience* 39: 38, January 1989.

Evolution is the formation of new species from pre-existing ones by a process of improved adaptation to the environment. Evolution began long ago and is still going on. During evolution those species better adapted to the environment replaced the less well adapted. It is this process, repeated year after year for millenia, that has produced the present mixture of wild species. Perhaps 95% of the species that once existed no longer exist.

Man's activities have eliminated many wild species. The dodo is gone, and so is the passenger pigeon. The whooping crane, the California condor, and many other species are on the way out. The bison is still with us because it is protected, and small herds are raised in semicaptivity. The Pacific salmon remains because we provide fish ladders around our dams so it can reach its breeding places. The mountain goat survives because it lives in inaccessible places. But some thousands of other animal species, to say nothing of plants, are extinct or soon will be.

Stopping the Clock

Some nature lovers weep at this passing and collect money to save species. They make lists of animals and plants that are in danger of extinction and sponsor legislation to save them.

I don't. What the species preservers are trying to do is to stop the clock. It cannot and should not be done.

Extinction is an inevitable fact of evolution, and it is needed for progress. New species continually arise, and they are better adapted to their environment than those that have died out.

Extinction comes from failure to adapt to a changing environment. The passenger pigeon did not disappear because of hunting alone, but because its food trees were destroyed by land clearing and farming. The prairie chicken cannot find enough of the proper food and nesting places in the cultivated fields that once were prairie.

Introducing Species

And you cannot necessarily introduce a new species, even by breeding it in tremendous numbers and putting it out into the wild. Thousands of pheasants were bred and set out year after year in southern Illinois, but in the spring of each year there were none left. Another bird, the capercaillie, is a fine, large game bird in Scandinavia, but every attempt to introduce it into the United States has failed. An introduced species cannot survive unless it is preadapted to its new environment.

A few introduced species are preadapted, and some make spectacular gains. The United States has received the English sparrow, the starling, and the house mouse from Europe, and also the gypsy moth, the European corn borer, the Mediterranean fruit fly, and the Japanese beetle. The United States gave Europe the gray squirrel and the muskrat, among others. The rabbit took over in Australia, at least for a time.

The rabbit and the squirrel were successful on new continents because their requirements are not as narrow as those of other species that failed. Today, adjustment to manmade environments may be just as difficult as adjustment to new continents. The rabbit and the squirrel have succeeded in adjusting to the backyard habitat, but most wild animals have disappeared.

Do We Need Them?

About 1,260,000 species of animals have been named, and perhaps 72,000 are threatened with extinction. But would the world be a better place if dinosaurs and trilobites and dodos still existed? Do we really need snail darters and condors and black lion tamarins?

Let us not be disturbed at the loss of some species. Extinction is not evil; it is normal and necessary.

Norman D. Levine, *BioScience*, May 1986.

Manmade environments are artificial. People replace mixed grasses, shrubs, and trees with rows of clean-cultivated corn, soybeans, wheat, oats, alfalfa, or lespedeza. Variety has turned into uniform monotony, and the number of species of small vertebrates and invertebrates that can find the proper food to survive has become markedly reduced. But some species have multiplied in these environments and have assumed economic importance; the European corn borer in this country is an example.

Would it improve Earth if even half of the species that have died out were to return? A few starving, shipwrecked sailors might be better off if the dodo were to return, but I would not be. The smallpox virus has been eliminated, except for a few strains in medical laboratories. Should it be brought back? Should we bring panthers back into the eastern states? Think of all the horses that the automobile and tractors have replaced, and of all the streets and roads that have been paved and the wild animals and plants killed as a consequence. Before people arrived in America about 10,000 years ago, the animal-plant situation was quite different. What should we do? Should we all commit suicide?

Evolution Cannot Be Stopped

Evolution exists, and it goes on continually. People are here because of it, but people may be replaced someday. It is neither possible nor desirable to stop it, and that is what we are trying to do when we try to preserve species on their way out. It can be done, I think, but should we do it to them all? Or to just a few, as we are doing now?

"Beyond their educational dimension, and despite their inability to save everything, zoos can at least save something."

Zoos Are Necessary for Animal Conservation

Jon R. Luoma

Some of the larger zoos in the US have established captive breeding programs. In the following viewpoint, Jon R. Luoma supports these programs. According to Luoma, captive breeding shows why zoos are necessary: Zoos can conserve animals endangered by the loss of habitat. A writer on environmental issues, Luoma has written *A Crowded Ark* and *Troubled Skies, Troubled Waters: The Story of Acid Rain.*

As you read, consider the following questions:

1. Why are zoos criticized, according to the author?
2. What does Luoma believe is the crucial issue in wildlife conservation?
3. Why does Luoma argue it is better to preserve a species in zoos than to allow the species to become extinct?

I visited a small group of environmentalists in St. Paul. Someone asked what subject I was working on. I might as well have announced that I was going to write a book about proctology. When I said I was going to write a book about zoos, but not a denunciation of same, there was a puzzled silence.

"I don't like zoos," one woman finally said quietly. As we talked, it turned out that her experience with zoos had been acquired in the 1950s and earlier and that she had never visited the local zoological gardens. But the response is similar to one I ran into repeatedly in the following months and years. Most mainstream environmentalists—or conservationists, for those who prefer the more traditional term—who learned I was working on such a project—and worse, that I had positive feelings about zoos—limited themselves to polite silence. A few acknowledged, if somewhat grudgingly, that for some species zoos might be the only hope, but they didn't like them anyway. A few, ticked off, listed all the bad things they had ever heard about zoos. . . .

Zoos' Critics

Certainly, there are those whom the zoo world will never please, and zoo people doubtless would waste their collective breath trying to change them. Notably, Michael Fox, an official of the Humane Society of the United States (an organization that has, incidentally, gone on record in support of good zoos), commented, in a 1986 issue of *The Animals' Agenda,* an animal rights magazine, "With such high-tech innovations as operant training devices, behavioral monitoring, ova transplantation, and genetic engineering, the contemporary zoo is fast becoming emblematic of capitalist industrial technology."

Fox continued with the statement that zoos were providing animals to "lucrative game ranches in Texas" for trophy hunters to shoot; that he had divined that the animals were troubled because he had tried during a visit to the National Zoo to look into the animals' eyes and they did not look back; and that if zoo visitors were made aware of the suffering of the animals, "then this zoo, like all zoos, would be demolished and the animals liberated by a compassionate humanity." Where he would propose to liberate the hippos, lions, and pandas in a world of devastated habitat, Fox didn't say.

But more sensible voices have expressed concerns about zoos. Norman Myers, a noted ecologist and author, once wrote quite correctly, in *The Sinking Ark,* that zoo scientists simply have too little knowledge to breed successfully many of the endangered animal species. He noted that the cheetah, penguin, and hummingbird—and he might have added the giant panda—have been difficult or outright impossible to breed. He remarked that zoos are not only far more expensive places to maintain wildlife than natural habitats, but that natural habitats preserve much more than a single species. . . .

An Animal out of Context

In a brief 1985 editorial in *BioScience,* zoologist Eric Pianka of the University of Texas wrote, "Like all biologists, I *love* zoos, but they aren't enough." In the process of explaining why they aren't enough, Pianka may have hit upon the key reason why so many ecologically oriented people are dubious about zoos altogether. He said that a zoo animal

> is totally out of context. Just as a word taken out of a paragraph loses much of its meaning and information content, an animal extracted from the wild no longer has a natural environment. Any given word is a subject, object, noun, verb, modifier, etc., with complex relationships to other words in the paragraph in which it resides; similarly, any wild organism is either a producer or a consumer and has its enemies, predators, potential competitors, and for many, its prey. Individuals also possess meaningful relationships to other members of their own populations, such as their own offspring, potential mates, neighbors on adjacent territories, kin, and so forth. . . . For the population biologist, an animal in a zoo has been stripped of most of what is interesting about it; it is like an isolated word out of context.

There have been harsher criticisms. In one of the most ringing condemnations, *Not Man Apart,* a publication of the Friends of the Earth, printed in 1985 an article by David Phillips and Sandra Kaiser entitled "Are Zoos an Excuse for Habitat Destruction?" One of the three internal boldface heads of the article was "The Captive Breeding Boondoggle." The authors wrote,

> The altruistic roles of zoos, the ones that are paraded in front of wealthy foundations and the public, are those of educator and nurturer of endangered species. But those roles are being increasingly challenged as it becomes apparent that the full measure of a specie includes the ecosystem that molds it. More and more people are coming to believe that animals have a right to exist in their own natural habitats, instead of being shown off for the amusement of humans.
>
> The overall effect of the zoos' attempts to be arks for endangered species may be to accelerate the loss of habitat. Zoos are giving a false impression that species can be saved, even if the wild is destroyed.

The authors also noted that zoos had reintroduced few endangered species to the wild. . . .

No, tragically, zoos cannot save entire ecosystems or even significant pieces of ecosystems. No, unfortunately, zoos have reintroduced few endangered species, in part because the habitat problems that caused them to become endangered in the first place have not been resolved.

Yes, saving habitat is *the* critical issue. During my dozens, probably hundreds, of interviews and conversations with zoo biologists and administrators, that very theme recurred constantly. No professional biologist, and no reasonably astute amateur, would ever suggest otherwise. The best places to preserve species are intact wild ecosystems, with emphasis on *intact*.

Saving Wild Animals

But what happens when the wild habitat is lost? Is it reasonable for the ark to stay afloat? Is it reasonable for zoos to provide a buffer, a fallback, for those species—the Siberian and Sumatran tigers, the black rhino, the orangutan, and the others—that survive in the wild, but only tenuously? Some have argued that it isn't, that it is somehow nobler for a species to "die with dignity" in the wild than live through generations in captivity. But since no one can see fifty, one hundred, or two hundred years into the future does it not seem stunningly arrogant for a human being to suggest that an entire evolutionary line be allowed to terminate at the hand of humans when there is any reason, however slim, to hope that somehow, someday, that species might thrive again in the wild with the help of humankind?

A Response to the Purists

For those who feel that we should be purist and remove all zoos from our civilisation, let me state a few brutal facts. The human population of Africa is doubling with every generation. This means that in 60 years' time, when our children have reached retiring age, the wild animals of Africa will have only a quarter of the space they now enjoy. And so it will go on until Africa, like Europe, will have nearly eliminated all its large fauna. Similar trends will occur elsewhere in the world. The wild places everywhere will, by then, have shrunk to the size of, dare I say it, large zoos. In a few centuries, wild animals will survive only in zoos, because that is all the space they will have left, anywhere. So perhaps we should start now to plan our 'ideal zoos' rather than be emotional about the concept of captivity.

Desmond Morris, *BBC Wildlife,* December 1987.

Is there a danger that zoos can create a sense of complacency, the sense that "the zoos are saving the tamarin, so it must be okay to destroy the Atlantic coast forest"? Perhaps. It is no better an argument for shutting down zoo-based propagation programs than that a hospital should be shut down because it encourages people to avoid preventive medicine. But it is a danger the zoo world should take seriously, considering the propaganda skills of those who would commercially drain, fill, torch, inundate, stripmine, and otherwise desolate natural landscapes without regard for their biological importance. Yet the hard fact is that the planet already is losing plant and animal diversity—and habitat—at a staggering rate. Virtually none of it can be attributed to the deleterious effects of zoos, but rather to the human birth rate, hunger, poor land use, and bad politics. . . .

Educating the Urban Public

As . . . William Conway, [of the New York Zoological Society has said,]

> Our urban populations have expanded so rapidly that whole generations are growing up without any natural contact with wild creatures; a new public opinion concerning wildlife and wild environment is arising unfettered by fact and unguided by experience. Except at the zoo, the opportunities to know or even become interested in living wild creatures are largely vicarious ones for many city dwellers. Yet it is the Bronx bus driver and the corner pharmacist whose votes will determine the fate of the Adirondack wilderness, the Everglades, of Yellowstone Park. You must give your visitors a new intellectual reference point, meaningful and esthetically compelling; a view of another sensory and social world; a feeling of personal interest in diminishing wild creatures and collective responsibility for their future which is so closely linked to that of man. Zoos must be natural history and conservation centers of the future.

Beyond their educational dimension, and despite their inability to save everything, zoos can at least save something.

Preserving Part of Nature

Says Conway, "To put it baldly, what zoos will end up doing is preserving those animals that mean a great deal to people for esthetic and emotional reasons. We're not even talking about preserving ecologically important species—if it's very rare it no longer has ecological value by definition. Zoos have no business suggesting they're going to preserve all of nature. I don't know of a single credible zoo director who would suggest it. The vast majority of the organisms on earth are far smaller than my little fingernail—virtually none will be present in a zoo's collection. Take it a step further: the biomass of termites of Africa is far greater than the biomass of elephants. Take it a step further: the biomass of plant life is many times that of all the animal life. No, zoos can't preserve plants and all those millions of creepy-crawlies. But at zoological gardens, if we can overcome our problems, we have the charge of preserving that very small portion of life that is at the tip of the iceberg—that which has inspired man, his attitudes, and his poetry. Of course it's not enough. *Of course* it's not preserving the diversity of life on earth. But at least we're making a stab at it."

150

"Because what zoos teach us is false and dangerous, both humans and animals will be better off when they are abolished."

Zoos Are Unnecessary for Animal Conservation

Dale Jamieson

Dale Jamieson is a philosophy professor and an associate at the Center for the Study of Values and Public Policy at the University of Colorado in Boulder. In the following viewpoint, he criticizes zoos and argues that they cannot save endangered species. Jamieson maintains that captive breeding programs are limited by a restricted gene pool and cannot produce the kinds of healthy, adapted animals that are born in the wild. Rather than breed weak animals, he believes, some species should be allowed to become extinct while humans learn to live in harmony with other animals, rather than dominating them and putting them on display.

As you read, consider the following questions:

1. What lessons do zoos teach people about animals, according to Jamieson?
2. In the author's opinion, what are the hazards of captive breeding programs?
3. How does the author believe zoos harm animals and conservation?

Dale Jamieson, "Against Zoos," in *In Defense of Animals*, edited by Peter Singer. New York: Basil Blackwell, 1985. Copyright © Peter Singer. Reprinted with permission of Basil Blackwell.

Before we consider the reasons that are usually given for the survival of zoos, we should see that there is a moral presumption against keeping wild animals in captivity. What this involves, after all, is taking animals out of their native habitats, transporting them great distances and keeping them in alien environments in which their liberty is severely restricted. It is surely true that in being taken from the wild and confined in zoos, animals are deprived of a great many goods. For the most part they are prevented from gathering their own food, developing their own social orders and generally behaving in ways that are natural to them. These activities all require significantly more liberty than most animals are permitted in zoos. If we are justified in keeping animals in zoos, it must be because there are some important benefits that can be obtained only by doing so. . . .

What might some of these important benefits be? Four are commonly cited: amusement, education, opportunities for scientific research, and help in preserving species. . . .

Most curators and administrators reject the idea that the primary purpose of zoos is to provide entertainment. Indeed, many agree that the pleasure we take in viewing wild animals is not in itself a good enough reason to keep them in captivity. Some curators see baby elephant walks, for example, as a necessary evil, or defend such amusements because of their role in educating people, especially children, about animals. It is sometimes said that people must be interested in what they are seeing if they are to be educated about it, and entertainments keep people interested, thus making education possible.

Zoos Are Not Educational

This brings us to a second reason for having zoos: their role in education. . . . Despite the pious platitudes that are often uttered about the educational efforts of zoos, however, there is little evidence that zoos are very successful in educating people about animals. Stephen Kellert's paper 'Zoological Parks in American Society', delivered at the annual meeting of the American Association of Zoological Parks and Aquariums in 1979, indicates that zoogoers are much less knowledgeable about animals than backpackers, hunters, fishermen and others who claim an interest in animals, and only slightly more knowledgeable than those who claim no interest in animals at all. Even more disturbing, zoo-goers express the usual prejudices about animals; 73 per cent say they dislike rattlesnakes, 52 per cent vultures and only 4 per cent elephants. One reason why some zoos have not done a better job in educating people is that many of them make no real effort at education. In the case of others the problem is an apathetic and unappreciative public. . . .

[Edward G.] Ludwig's study [of the Buffalo, New York Zoo] indicated that most animals are viewed only briefly as people move quickly past cages. The typical zoo-goer stops only to watch baby animals or those who are begging, feeding or making sounds. Ludwig reported that the most common expressions used to describe animals are 'cute', 'funny-looking', 'lazy', 'dirty', 'weird' and 'strange'.

Of course, it is undeniable that some education occurs in some zoos. But this very fact raises other issues. What is it that we want people to learn from visiting zoos? Facts about the physiology and behaviour of various animals? Attitudes towards the survival of endangered species? Compassion for the fate of all animals? To what degree does education require keeping wild animals in captivity? Couldn't most of the educational benefits of zoos be obtained by presenting films, slides, lectures and so forth? Indeed, couldn't most of the important educational objectives better be achieved by exhibiting empty cages with explanations of why they are empty?

A Better Investment

Many zoos talk about conservation, but often they are only just *talking* about it. Even if they *do* breed rare animals there are very many problems involved in returning them to the wild.

Wouldn't the money and expert knowledge be better spent in conserving animals in the wild? This would not only be better for the animals, it would be better for us—we might begin to understand that human beings share the earth with many thousands of other species who have just as much right to live their own lives as we have.

Tess Lemmon, *Greenscene,* no. 2.

A third reason for having zoos is that they support scientific research. . . .

Research that is conducted in zoos can be divided into two categories: studies in behaviour and studies in anatomy and pathology.

Behavioural research conducted on zoo animals is very controversial. Some have argued that nothing can be learned by studying animals that are kept in the unnatural conditions that obtain in most zoos. Others have argued that captive animals are more interesting research subjects than are wild animals: since captive animals are free from predation, they exhibit a wider range of physical and behavioural traits than animals in the wild, thus permitting researchers to view the full range of their genetic possibilities. Both of these positions are surely extreme. Conditions in some zoos are natural enough to permit some interesting research possibilities. But the claim that captive animals are more interesting research subjects than those in the wild is not very plausible. Environments trigger behaviours. No doubt a predation-free environment triggers behaviours different from those of an animal's natural habitat, but there is no reason to believe that better, fuller or more accurate data can be obtained in predation-free environments than in natural habitats. . . .

In assessing the significance of research as a reason for having zoos, it is important to remember that very few zoos do any research at all. Whatever benefits result from zoo research could just as well be obtained by having a few zoos instead of the hundreds which now exist. The most this argument could establish is that we are justified in having a few very good zoos. It does not provide a defence of the vast majority of zoos which now exist.

Preservation of Species

A fourth reason for having zoos is that they preserve species that would otherwise become extinct. As the destruction of habitat accelerates and as breeding programmes become increasingly successful, this rationale for zoos gains in popularity. There is some reason for questioning the commitment of zoos to preservation: it can be argued that they continue to remove more animals from the wild than they return. Still, zoo breeding programmes have had some notable successes: without them the Pére David Deer, the Mongolian Wild Horse and the European Bison would all now be extinct. Recently, however, some problems have begun to be noticed.

A 1979 study by Katherine Ralls, Kristin Brugger and Jonathan Ballou, which was reported in *Science*, convincingly argues that lack of genetic diversity among captive animals is a serious problem for zoo breeding programmes. In some species the infant mortality rate among inbred animals is six or seven times that among non-inbred animals. In other species the infant mortality rate among inbred animals is 100 per cent. What is most disturbing is that zoo curators have been largely unaware of the problems caused by inbreeding because adequate breeding and health records have not been kept. It is hard to believe that zoos are serious about their role in preserving endangered species when all too often they do not take even this minimal step.

In addition to these problems, the lack of genetic diversity among captive animals also means that surviving members of endangered species have traits very different from their conspecifics in the wild. This should make us wonder what is really being preserved in zoos. Are captive Mongolian Wild Horses really Mongolian Wild Horses in any but the thinnest biological sense?

"It's Bob, all right...but look at those vacuous eyes, that stupid grin on his face —he's been domesticated, I tell you."

There is another problem with zoo breeding programmes: they create many unwanted animals. In some species (lions, tigers and zebras, for example) a few males can service an entire herd. Extra males are unnecessary to the programme and are a financial burden. Some of these animals are sold and wind up in the hands of individuals and institutions which lack proper facilities. Others are shot and killed by Great White Hunters in private hunting camps. In order to avoid these problems, some zoos have been considering proposals to 'recycle' excess animals: a euphemism for killing them and feeding their bodies to other zoo animals.

Many people are surprised when they hear of zoos killing animals. They should not be. Zoos have limited capacities. They want to maintain diverse collections. This can be done only by careful management of their 'stock'.

Even if breeding programmes were run in the best possible way, there are limits to what can be done to save endangered species. For many large mammals a breeding herd of at least a hundred animals, half of them born in captivity, is required if they are to survive in zoos. As of 1971 only eight mammal species satisfied these conditions. Paul and Anne Ehrlich estimate in their book *Extinction* that under the best possible conditions American zoos could preserve only about a hundred species of mammals—and only at a very high price: maintaining a breeding herd of herbivores costs between $75,000 and $250,000 per year.

Animal Extinction

There are further questions one might ask about preserving endangered species in zoos. Is it really better to confine a few hapless Mountain Gorillas in a zoo than to permit the species to become extinct? To most environmentalists the answer is obvious: the species must be preserved at all costs. But this smacks of sacrificing the lower-case gorilla for the upper-case Gorilla. In doing this, aren't we using animals as mere vehicles for their genes? Aren't we preserving genetic material at the expense of the animals themselves? If it is true that we are inevitably moving towards a world in which Mountain Gorillas can survive only in zoos, then we must ask whether it is really better for them to live in artificial environments of our design than not to be born at all.

Even if all of these difficulties are overlooked, the importance of preserving endangered species does not provide much support for the existing system of zoos. Most zoos do very little breeding or breed only species which are not endangered. Many of the major breeding programmes are run in special facilities which have been established for that purpose. They are often located in remote places, far from the attention of zoo-goers. (For example, the Bronx Zoo operates its Rare Animal Survival Center on St. Catherine's Island off the coast of Georgia, and the National Zoo runs it Conservation and Research Center in the Shenandoah Valley of Virginia.) If our main concern is to do what we can to preserve endangered species, we should support such large-scale breeding centres rather than conventional zoos, most of which have neither the staff nor the facilities to run successful breeding programmes. . . .

Captivity does not just deny animals liberty but is often detrimental to them in other respects as well. The history of chimpanzees in the zoos of Europe and America is a good example.

Chimpanzees first entered the zoo world in about 1640 when a Dutch prince, Frederick Henry of Nassau, obtained one for his castle menagerie. The chimpanzee didn't last very long. In 1835 the London Zoo obtained its first chimpanzee; he died immediately. Another was obtained in 1845; she lived six months. All through the nineteenth and early twentieth centuries zoos obtained chimpanzees who promptly died within nine months. It wasn't until the 1930s that it was discovered that chimpanzees are extremely vulnerable to human respiratory diseases, and that special steps must be taken to protect them. But for nearly a century zoos removed them from the wild and subjected them to almost certain death. Problems remain today. When chimpanzees are taken from the wild the usual procedure is to shoot the mother and kidnap the child. The rule of thumb among trappers is that ten chimpanzees die for every one that is delivered alive to the United States or Europe. On arrival many of these animals are confined under abysmal conditions. . . .

A False Lesson

Zoos teach us a false sense of our place in the natural order. The means of confinement mark a difference between humans and animals. They are there at our pleasure, to be used for our purposes. Morality and perhaps our very survival require that we learn to live as one species among many rather than as one species over many. To do this, we must forget what we learn at zoos. Because what zoos teach us is false and dangerous, both humans and animals will be better off when they are abolished.

157

"*Hunters and fishermen are paying, as they have for many years, almost all of the bills for practical wildlife conservation.*"

Hunting Helps Animal Conservation

Archery World

Governmental efforts to conserve US wildlife populations began in the early part of the twentieth century. State agencies were established to manage animal populations. These agencies, funded in part by hunting licenses and fees, established hunting seasons and limits on the number of animals killed. In the following viewpoint, *Archery World* magazine argues that this system saved many animals from extinction. Hunting is a necessary conservation tool, according to the author. *Archery World* is a monthly magazine for bow and arrow hunters.

As you read, consider the following questions:

1. How does the author distinguish conservation from preservation?
2. What programs do hunters' fees support, according to the author?
3. How does *Archery World* believe hunting is misunderstood, and why is this misunderstanding dangerous?

"The Hunter's Story," published in *Archery World*, now *Bowhunting World*. Reprinted with permission.

There are more than 20 million sport hunters in the United States. And they have one of the greatest—*but least understood*—stories ever told: the work they have done and the dollars they have contributed to ensure the healthy existence of our nation's wildlife species. It is known and proven that sport hunting has never caused the endangering of any wildlife species on our land. But it is not commonly known that sport hunters lead the fight to eliminate market hunting, to organize and fund state conservation departments, to restrict themselves with season and bag limits and a highly-developed code of ethics, to sponsor research into wildlife management, to develop wildlife refuges.

Conservation vs. Preservation

Sport hunters were among the first to realize that conservation cannot be mistaken for total preservation, to realize that wildlife cannot be stockpiled. They realized that nature constantly grows and changes, and wildlife goes or grows with habitat changes. The overmature forest doesn't support game, the overbrowsing of habitat ruins the habitat and attendant wildlife populations for years, the overpopulation of game in any given area leads to increased incidence of disease, starvation. We have replaced natural predators, yet predation is needed to cull and crop wildlife populations to keep them healthy. This is done by managed sport hunting. . . .

To understand the present, you must know what it was like in the past. Around the turn of the century, most authorities did not have much hope for larger forms of wildlife surviving beyond the 1920s. This view could not foresee the development of scientific wildlife management programs in the 1930s, programs which have expanded through the years. But here are some of the results of those programs, which were stirred by the sporting hunters' concern for wildlife populations:

• Beaver: *1900*—Eliminated from states of the Mississippi Valley and all eastern states except Maine; common only in Alaska and a few localities of the Pacific Northwest and Rockies. *Today:* Common to abundant in nearly all states except Hawaii. . . .

• As recently as 1900, the total whitetail deer population of North America was estimated at about 500,000, following a study by the U.S. Biological Survey. Nearly every state in the nation had closed its deer hunting season. Massachusetts counted about 200 on Cape Cod; New York claimed about 7,000 in the Adirondacks and Pennsylvania had a small herd centered in Potter County. In Delaware and New Jersey, deer were considered practically gone.

In contrast, by the early 1960s every state in the country allowed some form of deer hunting. The deer population of the U.S. is now estimated at around 16 million head. In many states, the expanding herds have created traffic hazards and caused crop damage. In

1972, the total legal deer harvest in the U.S. was reported at 2.1 million, more than four times the entire deer population of North America at the turn of the century.

• Since 1920, deer populations in the national forests have increased 500 percent according to the Bureau of Sport Fisheries and Wildlife. National forests are hunted regularly.

• Wild turkey: *1930*—Common in only a few southern states, eliminated from most. *1952*—About 97,000. *Today:* Restored to 43 states, including establishment in several outside original range of species. Population over one million; more than 30 states offer spring and/or fall hunting.

• Trumpeter swan: *1935*—73 survivors south of Canada on one wildlife refuge. *Today:* Thriving populations on two national parks and several national wildlife refuges. Removed from endangered status in the late 1960s.

• Wood duck: *1915*—Greatly reduced in numbers and considered a candidate for early extinction. *Today:* The most common breeding waterfowl in eastern U.S.

• Egrets and herons: *1910*—Several species on the brink of extinction because of slaughter on their nesting grounds by feather collectors to supply the millinery trade. *Today:* Most species common to abundant over most of the U.S.

Controlled Harvest

Most present deer management systems call for the controlled harvest of a certain percentage of the female, or doe, segment of the population. This, in turn, provides the tool used to raise, lower or maintain population numbers. By maintaining deer numbers at or just below the carrying capacity of the range, biologists are able to manage for a healthy herd and, consequently, better reproduction rates. The end result is more deer available each year for the hunters to harvest.

Since the ultimate responsibility is not to exceed carrying capacity, biologists must rely on sportsmen to harvest the required number of deer each year.

Dick Thomas, *Deer & Deer Hunting,* March 1989.

Since 1938, state fish and wildlife agencies have used sportsmen's license fees and special taxes under the Federal Aid in Fish and Wildlife Restoration Acts to:

• Acquire, develop or manage 2,900 wildlife refuges and management areas totalling nearly 40 million acres. These lands protect vital habitat of a wide range of wildlife and are heavily used by bird watchers, nature students and other outdoor enthusiasts.

• Construct or restore more than 300 lakes for fish and wildlife with a total surface acreage of 35,000.

• Acquire or develop more than 3,000 public access areas that open nearly a million otherwise inaccessible acres and 2,000 miles of stream to outdoor use.

• Livetrap and transplant to unoccupied habitat more than 50,000 deer, 16,000 antelope, 2,000 elk, 1,000 mountain sheep, 18,000 fur animals, 20,000 wild turkeys, 22,000 waterfowl, and 130,000 quail.

• Conduct extensive research on wildlife habitat needs, diseases, population trends, predator-prey relationships, and wildlife crop-damage abatement.

• Assist hundreds of thousands of landowners with wildlife habitat improvement projects.

• Conduct public conservation education programs for school teachers and students and promote understanding of wildlife needs and habits through articles and television shows.

• Protect both hunted and non-hunted wildlife by apprehending conservation law violators. Many state conservation law enforcement officers also enforce laws against polluters, whose activities impose serious threats to wildlife and its habits. But, as in all resource management efforts, public support is essential.

A Bit of Irony

In one of our sadder ironies, the bald eagle won out over the wild turkey in the voting long ago for selection of our national bird. Now eagles are in danger, but wild turkeys are not. The eagle has been totally protected from everything but pesticides and insecticides which now cause it to produce weak-shelled eggs. The wild turkey, which is a regularly hunted bird, is thriving. . . .

Some Americans' sense of responsibility for wildlife has been mistakenly channeled into a denunciation of gunning or archery. Not realizing that hunting and the hunter's money play vital parts in modern game management, not recognizing that properly managed hunting exerts no detrimental effect on wild populations, sincere people have been convinced that hunting is a destroyer of wildlife. Sport hunting is being denounced as a primitive blood sport, outmoded by the "progress of civilization," whatever concepts those words evoke.

Real Dangers to Wildlife

The great danger in this polarization of sentiments is the responsibility that people of equally good intentions will fail to unite against the real dangers of wildlife because they are diverted by the perils that they imagine are posed by the sport hunter. Most wildlife work in the U.S. is supported by the hunter's dollar. Arguments over hunting threaten the flow of these dollars, dollars which are badly needed if wildlife, both hunted and non-hunted, is to survive.

Many wildlife forms are facing extinction, both in our country and in the rest of the world. Mankind's destruction and pollution of wild environments are the dominant reasons. Research can provide facts, but only united public opinion can provide the understanding needed to work out the people problems.

Harvesting Only the Surplus

Some people oppose hunting because they feel that wildlife should be preserved and allowed to increase. This is not possible because wildlife is a resource which cannot be stockpiled.

And, if hunters are not allowed to cleanly harvest any annual overabundance of game, nature often takes over in a cruel and harsh way. . . .

Hunting is a useful part of today's wise game management practices, and by teaming habitat improvement with carefully regulated shooting seasons and bag limits, our professional conservationists make sure that hunters harvest only the surplus of game populations.

National Shooting Sports Foundation Inc., *The Hunter and Conservation*, May 1985.

Whenever local habitat conditions change, the species composition of the local wildlife populations also changes. Some species may be eliminated, others decline, and still others increase. If changes remove any of its essential habitat requirements, a species cannot continue to live in the affected area. If habitat of the kind it needs is reduced to remnants, the species will become endangered. If it is eliminated everywhere, the animals will become extinct. In the absence of adequate habitat, protection of individual animals is meaningless in terms of perpetuating wild populations. . . .

Remember, more than 2,000 acres of wildlife habitat per day are disappearing under the inroads of urban development, highways, dredging, draining, etc.

• Potentially, a deer population can more than double every second year. One doe can produce 15 or more fawns in an average life span of eight years. If all her young and theirs survive to the same age and breed as successfully, they would number 150 or more before her death. Many animals—songbirds, rabbits, squirrels, quail and ducks, for example—can increase at even greater rates.

• In recent years, the dove has become the most popular game bird in America. Despite an annual harvest of about 20,000,000 the basic breeding flock of doves has increased over the past two decades.

Obviously, when a population of a particular species begins to multiply, something has to give—and it does. Each piece of land has a limit on the number of animals of any one species it can support. Wildlife biologists call this "carrying capacity". It is the capability of an area to provide a species' food, water, shelter and other needs in a given season. Once carrying capacity is reached, the surplus animals must move elsewhere or die. If suitable under-stocked habitat is not available within their range of mobility, the surplus animals are doomed.

The higher the reproductive rate of a species, the higher its natural mortality rate. In the wild, animals that produce many young have short lives and lose most of their young in the first year.

Natural mortality rates are surprising:

• In bobwhite quail and doves, 75 to 80 percent of the population dies annually whether the birds are hunted or not.

• Research shows that a good deer herd in a well-balanced habitat can withstand an annual harvest of about 40 percent without ill effect on future populations. Yet in most states hunters rarely take more than 15 percent. But wildlife cannot be stockpiled.

Protected Game

Animals classed as game under state and federal laws may be hunted, but they are not without protection. They may be taken by hunters only under regulations that prescribe calendar dates, hunting hours, bag limits and methods of taking. Under certain circumstances, hunting seasons for some game species may be closed completely. All game species are protected by law while they are nesting and raising their young. These regulations, based on careful research, are designed to assure the carry-over to the next breeding season of enough animals to repopulate the available habitat.

By teaming habitat improvement with carefully regulated shooting seasons and bag limits, our professional conservationists make sure that hunters harvest only the surplus of game populations.

In fact, of all the wild birds and mammals in North America, the hunted species are among the most secure—not necessarily because they are hunted but because they are under management's attention. Since the advent of modern management, hunting has not contributed to the extinction of a single species.

Even without direct land purchase, unhunted or endangered species have benefitted greatly from improvements aimed at game animals. Woody cover established for winter protection of pheasants in northern states has provided nesting and escape cover for songbirds. Fencing livestock off big game ranges has greatly improved ground cover for small birds and animals. A waterfowl management area often harbors species such as the killdeer, longbilled curlew, glossy ibis, common egret, great blue heron, white pelican, ground squirrel, weasel, mink, otter, striped skunk, badger, muskrat and beaver.

Federal aid funds through the Pittman-Robertson program have financed research into the life history and needs of many nongame species, including those threatened with extinction.

An Intricate Web

The environment does not belong to man alone nor to the particular group of species he favors most; the environment is for all living things, and all are interconnected like a massive, intricate web. The maintenance of an environment that can serve the most complex web of life is not just an ethical imperative, it is vital to the everyday business of saving ruffed grouse and mule deer and woodcocks—and maybe ourselves.

Very few states had any real semblance of wildlife administration at the turn of the century, except for a small number of game wardens. Today, every state in the union has a well-organized agency, almost entirely financed by sportsmen, for the protection and management of wildlife. The wildlife conservation programs of state fish and game departments add up to a vast undertaking, one involving thousands of people working for the well-being of hundreds of species of birds, animals and fish, game and nongame species alike, on millions of acres of land and water.

This costs a tremendous amount of money, hundreds of millions of dollars every year.

Here, once again, the hunter enters the picture, because, unlike other state governmental agencies, fish and game departments receive little support from taxes paid by the general public. Instead, virtually all their operating funds come from the outdoor fraternity of hunters and fishermen.

Hunters Pay the Bills

This means that hunters and fishermen are paying, as they have for many years, almost all of the bills for practical wildlife conservation and paying them not just for their own benefit, but for the benefit of all Americans. Local sportsmen's groups and individuals have consistently worked with owners of large tracts of private land to open more acreage for a wide range of outdoor recreational uses of all types.

The nation's lumber industry provides a good example of the benefits of this hunter-landowner cooperation. Today, hunting is permitted on more than 95 percent of the roughly 70 million acres of woodland managed by the forest products industry.

These efforts and successes do not benefit the sportsman alone. Each is a contribution to the total outdoor scene of America which benefits every citizen.

Of some 13.5 million acres preserved for migratory bird habitat in the United States, 8.25 million acres (61%) are preserved as a direct result of hunting-oriented programs. This basic fact sums up the critical role that America's duck and goose hunters play in the conservation of both waterfowl and a host of other wetland species, from marsh wren to osprey.

Maintaining Natural Habitats

Of these 8.25 million hunter-financed acres, 5.2 million are owned or controlled by waterfowl hunting clubs. These private wetlands and marsh areas are not only managed to provide prime waterfowl habitat; they are also kept out of the hands of those who would drain, dredge or "develop" these irreplaceable natural habitats.

"Hunters have a stranglehold on wildlife management."

Hunting Hinders Animal Conservation

Wayne Pacelle

In the following viewpoint, Wayne Pacelle argues that hunters exert too much influence on wildlife conservation efforts. Pacelle describes fish and wildlife agencies' policies that are designed to conserve game birds. These policies, he writes, show that conservation agencies manage populations for the benefit of hunters only, rather than working to preserve animals for everyone's benefit. Pacelle is the associate editor of *Animals' Agenda,* a monthly magazine that supports animal rights.

As you read, consider the following questions:

1. Why does Pacelle believe it is harmful that hunters influence wildlife conservation efforts?
2. What factors have contributed to the low duck population, according to Pacelle?
3. Why does the author criticize programs that stock pheasants?

Wayne Pacelle, "Flying the Unfriendly Skies," *The Animals' Agenda,* November 1988. Reprinted with permission from The Animals' Agenda, 456 Monroe Turnpike, Monroe, CT 06468.

These days, the skies over 36 states are no place for mourning doves, the most populous of dove species. Hunters in those states legally shoot and take home about 50 million of the birds each year, making them, numerically, the most significant "game" species in the U.S. What's more, some studies indicate that hunters cripple but don't retrieve an additional 20 to 25 percent of that total. Finally, there is an undetermined but significant illegal kill. In all, the death toll is staggering, and the bulk of it occurs in the span of a single month.

No Exemptions from the Kill

One might think the doves' reputation as gentle and inoffensive creatures would exempt them from this onslaught. But the birds have no such luck. To wildlife managers and hunters, the birds' abundance, prolific breeding abilities, and desirability as a "game" species are the primary considerations, not their reputation. Says Dave Dolton, the mourning dove specialist for the U.S. Fish and Wildlife Service (FWS), "the birds harvested we believe would have died naturally anyway. Our focus on management is providing an opportunity for the harvest of a renewable resource, like you are harvesting crops and trees."

According to the most recent annual survey figures, some states have bumper "harvests": 3.1 million doves in South Carolina, 3.7 million in Alabama, and 5.4 million in Texas. On the other hand, a belt of northern states—running from Iowa and Minnesota in the Midwest through Michigan and New York to Massachusetts and Maine in the East—protect the birds from hunters. In those states, mourning dove populations have never rivalled those of southeastern or grain belt states, and the tradition of dove hunting never became established.

Yet some wildlife agencies in those northern states seem intent on starting that tradition and creating a demand for dove hunting. In Michigan, for instance, despite a public outcry, the Department of Natural Resources' (DNR) wildlife board voted unanimously to inaugurate a dove hunting season. As a response, the Michigan Humane Society (MHS) filed a lawsuit, charging that the legislature was the only body endowed with the authority to make or change law. The MHS's suit succeeded, and the hunt was blocked. The DNR appealed the decision, however, claiming that it, as the expert agency, should have ultimate authoritiy on wildlife management decisions. The conflict begs the question, who controls America's wildlife anyway?

A Monopoly on Wildlife

Robert Blohm, a survey biologist with the FWS maintains, "Whether you work for the Federal government or the state government, hunters are the constituency." These words echo through the corridors of wildlife management agencies throughout the country. Confirms Dale Sheffer, the director of the Bureau of Game Management of Pennsylvania, a state with more hunters than the standing army of the U.S., "The hunters are the constituency, they buy the hunting licenses."

According to the 1985 National Survey of Hunting, Fishing and Wildlife-Associated Recreation, approximately 16 million hunters in the U.S. annually pay for state hunting licenses. A sizeable percentage of those people pay additional state and Federal fees, such as "duck stamps" and "pheasant tags." Beholden to their constituents, most state wildlife agencies devote more than 95 percent of their expenditures to projects, administration, and law enforcement closely related to "game" species management. For as much attention as they get, the non-game animals, who comprise the vast majority of each state's faunal species, might as well be extinct. . . .

Crushing Devastation

Every large mammalian species in the eastern part of America has been destroyed by modern man—except those he has chosen to protect for his own selfish purposes. . . . Nor have our depredations been limited to the bigger beasts. Large or small, all suffered crushing devastation if any profit was to be gained thereby; or if they seemed to pose even the threat of competition with our rapacious appetites. Meat, hides, and fur were the initial rewards. . . . Today a new motivation overrides those older ones: the slaughter keeps its bloody pace, largely in the name of recreation for mankind.

Farley Mowat, *Sea of Slaughter,* 1984.

Hunting opponents charge that these structures have to change. Jennifer Lewis, senior wildlife scientist for the Humane Society of the U.S. (HSUS), concludes, "Hunters have a stranglehold on wildlife management at the state level because they pay into the existing structure and because they dominate state game boards, which are the bodies that set policies. Until non-consumptive wildlife enthusiasts can change the funding sources for wildlife management and sit on wildlife boards, the problems are going to continue."

Ducks Unlimited

Of the U.S.'s five million migratory bird hunters, mourning dove hunters are the most numerous at 2.7 million. Bullet for bullet however, the waterfowl hunters (primarily duck hunters) may wield more influence than any other breed of hunters. Numbering only 1.5 million, they pump out the cash in order to kill the ducks. Besides expenditures on state hunting licenses and on a variety of consumable goods, waterfowl hunters are obligated to purchase a Federal "duck stamp." About 40 states also require the purchase of a state "duck stamp." What's more, they fund one of the most powerful hunter-advocacy groups in the U.S., Ducks Unlimited (DU). . . .

Despite a dramatic decline in the number of ducks since the 1950s, the FWS continues to allow liberal "harvest" frameworks. According to the FWS's 1988 Supplemental Environmental Impact Statement on the Sport Hunting of Migratory Birds (SEIS '88), "Total ducks, mallards and pintails reached all-time lows in 1985 and have not recovered significantly since. Black ducks have declined steadily since 1955 [60 percent] and are now at an all-time low. Some species considered to be lightly utilized and capable of sustaining greater harvest (e.g., blue-winged teal) have also declined in recent years." Scaup, canvasback, and several other species are also at their lowest levels in years.

Undoubtedly, habitat elimination and deterioration partly explain the dive in duck populations. But excessive hunting is also a culprit. Take the case of the black duck, once the most numerically significant waterfowl species shot in the Atlantic flyway. Even as far back as 1976, Walter Crissey, a senior scientist with the FWS and ten-year director of its Migratory Bird Population Station, concluded in an extensive report on the black duck: "It seems to me that all of the available information favor the hypothesis that over-harvest has been the most likely cause of the decline." Yet the FWS has not once closed the season on black ducks, and has often liberalized the bag limits on the bird during the last ten years. As expected, the situation is getting even blacker for the black duck.

Ironically, the FWS's actions would never indicate that the agency is, in fact, aware of the population problems. Over the years, the FWS has concocted several regulatory devices designed to maximize the duck kill, including such things as zones and bonus birds and special and split seasons. For instance, special seasons—which allow bonus shooting opportunities—on blue-winged teal have been made available to some states in September. The FWS opened these seasons because the ducks migrate in advance of the regular season opening for duck hunting, and because the FWS determined that the "resource" had been "underutilized." Scaup and sea ducks also suffered from the dreaded "underutilization," and FWS rectified that situation by opening special seasons on them. . . .

Illegal Kills

Though the FWS upper echelon does not like to talk about illegal kill, it is an epidemic. Said Dave Hall, a 27-year veteran of the FWS and special agent for its law enforcement division in Louisiana, "From some of the cases we made it looks that the guys who hunt illegally are taking four times more than the guys who hunt legally." Illegal kill is indeed a monumental problem in Louisiana, where ducks from both the Mississippi and Central flyways converge to winter. *The St. Paul Press Dispatch's* Dennis Anderson reported,

> During the state's most recent 10-day September teal season, FWS special agent Bill Mellor . . . on one day tagged [arrested] seven hunters in possession of 192 ducks, including pintails and mottled ducks, which are protected during the teal season. The daily Louisiana duck limit is up to five, depending on the 'point value' assigned the species of ducks in a hunter's bag . . . Mellor found the daily limits grossly exceeded again on Dec. 26, 1987 when he and other agents tagged three hunters with 71 ducks. Two weeks later, on January 9, 1988, Mellor and his colleagues tagged another three hunters with 168 ducks.

Night hunting is common in many regions of the South, especially for wood ducks. Dan Tabberer, a former FWS biologist documented that 79 percent of wood ducks return to their roosts after sunset, when shooting hours are closed. Yet, Anderson

"Why don't they thin their own damned herd?"

reports, "Roost shooters just fire at the birds as fast as they can, trying to drop as many as they can. Then they grab what birds they can find. The birds they can't find in the dark they leave behind."

According to Hall, "It [illegal kill] is not just in Louisiana, it's every place I've ever worked." Indeed, in Wisconsin, Dr. Robert Jackson watched 500 hunters from spy blinds and recorded that one in five hunters violated a game law while being watched. Subsequent to that, he interviewed hunters in their homes and asked the question, "Have you ever violated game laws?" About 85 percent admitted they had.

Excessive Hunting

Despite the gravity of the problem, "Not one study," according to Anderson, "has been commissioned by the Fish and Wildlife Service to chronicle the problem's severity and integrate it into the nation's waterfowl management plan." That is the case even though Hall maintains, "Our brood stock is continually being reduced through the years. In my opinion, it has definitely had something to do with overharvest." . . .

The fact remains, while there may be multiple causes for the population decline, hunting is the only management "tool" that the FWS has at its disposal. Yet, the agency fails to restrict the use of that "tool" and publicly attributes the problems almost solely to habitat deterioration. John Grandy, vice president of wildlife and environment for the HSUS, believes that the FWS decision-makers do understand the role that excessive hunting has played, but ignore that factor in setting regulations because of political pressure. He claims, "What is keeping the hunting season open is state fish and game agencies fearing that if hunters don't hunt for two years, they'll never hunt again." The bottom line is, if fewer hunting licenses are purchased, less money is available to pay for the projects and salaries of wildlife managers.

Stocking Birds

As Grandy's comment suggests, state agencies sometimes seem more zealous than hunters in pushing for waterfowl hunting. For other "game" bird species—especially those exclusively managed by the states—wildlife agencies don't just cater to hunting demand, they create it.

To an increasing extent, wildlife managers are pouring money into programs to establish populations of upland "game" birds, such as turkeys, quail, pheasants, and partridge. Ostensibly, it's being done to return once-resident birds to the forests. The primary reason is, they stock them to shoot them.

Absent for some time from much of their original range, wild turkeys are trapped and stocked all across the U.S. Promoting turkey hunting as a sporting challenge, states proudly point out that kill numbers increase every year in most states. And they're intent on maintaining that trend. As stated in Utah's latest turkey report, "Since gobblers are difficult to bag in the fall, it has become a widely accepted management practice to hunt them when they are most vulnerable, during the spring rutting season." In fact, that report offers instructions on how to hunt turkeys, saying "be ready for a quick shot, preferably at the head." Nearly all states have both fall and spring turkey hunting seasons—head shooting and all.

Pheasants

In terms of state dollars spent and birds killed, the turkey programs can't compare with the pheasant programs. Not indigenous to the U.S., pheasants were introduced from Asia around the turn of the century, and established themselves as self-propagating populations in many regions. In the late 1960s though, for reasons that remain unclear, pheasant populations declined throughout the U.S. Since that time, many states have been propagating, planting, and promoting the birds, who have been referred to as a "sportsman's delight" because of their elaborate plumage. . . .

Even if pheasants are intentionally released, they don't do well in the wild. Said Game Commission executive director Peter Duncan in an article in *Pennsylvania Game News* (September 1983), "Farm-raised pheasants are anything but wild, and are so susceptible to predation and other mortality that they have almost no chance of surviving in the wild." Another article on pheasants in *Pennsylvania Game News* (November 1983) reported that "Research has shown that only one out of four birds stocked in the fall ends up in the hunter's bag. The other three, or 75 percent, succumb to predation, starvation or just an inability to survive in the wild." Comments from several game managers confirm that hunters kill fewer than half of released pheasants, although the percentage varies depending on the time of the birds' release. Only a limited percentage survive until the next hunting season, a time that hardly seems worth the wait.

Not making much biological sense, pheasant stocking does not make much economic sense either. Connecticut's pheasant biologist Mark Clavette reported that in 1986 the program cost $239,784, or about $6.85 a bird. He pointed out that a $5 pheasant tag—which pheasant hunters must purchase—entitles a hunter to kill up to 10 pheasants, and that those tags brought the state only $8,500. . . .

Perhaps the programs will pay for themselves in time as the states gradually increase demand for the activity. The most serious issue though remains: should the states be involved in the shooting preserve business?

> *"The ordeal of falling prey to a trapper is no more brutal than any other death in the wild."*

Fur Trapping Is Justified

Steven M. Geary

Steven M. Geary has a master's degree in history and a law degree. He has consulted with state conservation departments and published articles in outdoor journals. In the following viewpoint, he argues that furtrapping is necessary to control the populations of muskrats, beavers, and other animals. Geary writes that new, more humane traps have been developed which spare animals excessive pain.

As you read, consider the following questions:

1. Why does the author believe fur clothing is actually inexpensive compared to synthetic clothing?
2. How do leghold traps affect animals, according to Geary?
3. What does Geary mean when he discusses the Bambi syndrome?

From *Fur Trapping in North America* by Steven M. Geary. Reprinted by permission of A.S. Barnes, San Diego 92123.

Those persons seeking to rationalize trapping should have no great difficulty succeeding. Furbearers are simply a renewable part of our natural resources. The main product of the harvest of surplus furbearers is beautiful fur clothing. As a renewable resource, however, fur clothing costs very little when compared to such nonrenewable resources as fossil fuels. Comparable synthetics used for clothing are very costly, whether they come from nonrenewable fossil fuels such as coal or oil or such energy-intensive resources as cellulose or wood fiber.

Destructive Furbearers

Furbearers can be viewed negatively. They can be extremely destructive when their numbers are not controlled. Peak populations of muskrats and beavers can be destructive to fruit trees and other forestry resources. Muskrats can cause great losses by riddling pond dams and irrigation channel walls. Weasel, coyote, and fox prey on domestic fowl when the furbearers' numbers get too high. Despite record high prices for wool and lamb, several states have had declines in sheep ranching as a result of the great losses sustained from predation. The State of Wyoming alone reported a predator loss of over 100,000 sheep valued at $2.2 million in 1972, a year in which inflation had not yet devastated the dollar. In brief, not harvesting excess furbearers results in wasted pelts, domestic animal loss, and other damages.

Despite these facts, trapping has always been subject to criticism. One criticism is that wild fur harvests could not begin to approach the human needs for warm clothing. This contention avoids the obvious, the fur harvest frees up a proportionate amount of resources that otherwise would have gone into clothing production. More important, furbearers that exist in harvestable numbers are a resource that cannot be stockpiled. The land will support only a certain number of furbearers (termed the land's "carrying capacity") and the animals in excess of that carrying capacity succumb to predation, disease, starvation, or cold. One dramatic example of damage both to habitat and the furbearer itself, which can result from overpopulation, is the so-called "eat out" by muskrats. When muskrat populations peak, the animals routinely destroy their entire habitat, which results in a long-term decline in habitat for other animals, as well as the number of muskrats. Animals lost to disease, starvation, predation, and other causes are a waste in the sense that they are lost for human use. It is simply poor management of a resource to support total protection when the resource is cyclical and incapable of being stockpiled.

The primary objection to trapping, however, is the emotional charge of cruelty. When the entire list of criticisms is carefully reviewed, this well-intentioned—if poorly reasoned—sentiment is all the antitrappers will have to say. Everything else is merely designed to "make weight."

The cruelty objection is not well-founded. The antitrapper will often display some hideous, jagged-toothed trap and offer it as evidence of the inhumanity of traps, when in fact such relics are outdated curiosities which never had much use and which, in any event, have been illegal for decades. Other evidence of cruelty will be the occasional horror scene of a maimed or otherwise suffering furbearer struggling pitifully or dangling from a poorly constructed snare. These scenes are not in any way typical, but are unusual. At worst, they are the work of a tiny percentage of trappers who are irresponsible. Trappers take no pleasure in the pain or suffering of furbearers. On the contrary, they make every effort to keep the time spent by animals in the traps at a minimum and the actual loss of life as humane as possible.

Ecologically Sound

Trapping with steel traps has been used for centuries to harvest wildlife and to reduce animal damage. Today, trapping remains an effective, economical, and ecologically sound method of harvesting or controlling certain species of wildlife.

The Wildlife Society, "Conservation Policies of the Wildlife Society," 1985.

Trappers—and the term here includes trappers' associations and suppliers—have gone to great lengths to design humane traps. The conibear, or body-gripping trap, is one example of a humane trap that captures the animal and kills it quickly with very little suffering. The conibear has an obvious limiting factor, however, in that the occasional nontarget animal who wanders into it does so only once in a lifetime. The use of the conibear is necessarily limited to small sizes or sets where domestic animals are not present, such as in the water or in very high places. The live trap also has its place, as the captured animal presumably experiences no suffering with the possible exception of some degree of exposure prior to a quick end from a bullet. These live traps, unfortunately, are very bulky and for that reason are not suited for use in large numbers or in remote places.

The Leghold Trap

Use of the killer-type traps and live traps having thus been more or less restricted, all that remains for harvest of the fur resource is the steel leghold trap. Consequently, this trap has become the target of the antitrappers. The horror stories connected with these traps are either mostly nonsense or the result of irresponsible, illegal behavior. The suffering of animals in leghold traps has been greatly exaggerated, since the clamping effect of a properly matched trap does no damage. The author has personally released, uninjured, a nontarget squirrel and even a mouse from leghold traps. The clamping effect of the trap quickly results in numbness, and the trap and drag merely restrict the animal's movements. A properly constructed drowning set dispatches the animal very quickly. Dry land sets that use the leghold trap do not cause great suffering either. . . . The author has witnessed animals actually sleeping in leghold traps. As a further example of the lengths to which trappers have gone to make the leghold trap as painless as possible, there is now available a trap with so-called offset jaws that do not match perfectly, which results in less pressure on the foot. An obvious limiting factor is that the trap must hold fast enough to prevent escape.

The Bambi Syndrome

The problem then is one of overcoming the emotionalism attached to the perceived suffering of the furbearers. The habit of giving humanlike characteristics to animals—variously called the Bambi syndrome or anthropomorphism—does not vanish in face of the facts. It should be remembered that brutality is the way of wild animals, that such wild animals very rarely die painlessly or peacefully. The ordeal of falling prey to a trapper is no more brutal than any other death in the wild, where nature is neither kind nor cruel but rather is indifferent.

Trapping, in brief, is merely a management tool for a resource, just as surely as the ax is a management tool for a different resource. Through the intelligent use of the resource, we approach a maximum sustained yield without damage to any species of animal. Without the management tool, the resource is simply wasted.

"*Fur coats are products of agony.*"

Fur Trapping Is Not Justified

The Humane Society of the United States

The Humane Society of the United States, one of the largest animal welfare agencies in the US, works on a variety of animal welfare issues to promote compassionate treatment of animals. In the following viewpoint, The Humane Society calls furtrapping a barbaric and unnecessary practice. The Society concludes that the suffering trapped animals endure cannot be justified.

As you read, consider the following questions:

1. Why does The Humane Society argue that fur coats are unnecessary?
2. How does the fur industry try to justify their business, according to the Society?
3. How do leghold traps affect animals, according to the author?

The Humane Society of the United States, "Close-Up Report: Fur Shame," October 1988. Reprinted with permission from The Humane Society of the United States.

What do you think would happen if, every time a woman wore a fur coat in public, no one thought she looked beautiful? What if, whenever she walked down the street, she got disapproving glances instead of admiring looks? What if, whenever this woman asked acquaintances how they liked her new fur, they averted their eyes, shook their heads, and said nothing? What if someone finally said, "How can a coat made of animals who suffered and died be beautiful?"

Do you think this woman would wear her fur coat in public again? Would she ever buy another fur coat?

Products of Agony

Fur coats are products of agony. Millions of sentient mammals—who have highly evolved central nervous systems and thus suffer and feel pain just as humans do—are brutally raised or trapped and killed each year for fur garments that, with the current availability of many warm alternatives, are mere extravagances in our advanced, civilized society.

You should be ashamed to wear fur. This is the message The Humane Society of the United States (HSUS) will be communicating to consumers this 1988-89 winter season, as we launch our biggest anti-fur campaign yet.

Our goal: to make the wearing of fur garments socially unacceptable. Our strategy: when consumers stop buying, the animals will stop dying. . . .

"Our aim is to make the wearing of fur garments as controversial as smoking in public now is," says HSUS President John Hoyt. "Slowly but surely, the wearing of fur garments will become socially unacceptable, as it already has in parts of Europe. People who continue to wear fur garments will be distinguished not by their fashion sense, but by their lack of sensitivity. Eventually, the killing of animals for their fur will become unthinkable, and the practice of wearing fur garments will go the way of the cave man—extinct."

The HSUS campaign is energized by wildly successful drives in Europe in which consumers were also targeted. [Since 1983] Dutch activists have cut consumer purchases of fur garments by 90 percent! In Switzerland, where winters are cold, consumer fur purchases are down 75 percent after a major anti-fur blitz. Things are now heating up in England, where polls show that 74 percent of the public opposes the wearing of fur.

Public Opinion

The United States is next. Several public-opinion polls have shown that a majority of Americans oppose killing animals for their fur. One major marketing study, for example, confirmed that killing animals "for fun and fashion is not acceptable." From two-thirds to three-quarters of those polled were opposed to "hunting animals for sport, hunting animals for their skins or pelts, raising animals for their skins or pelts."

Ironically, a Gallup poll commissioned by the fur industry itself found that when pollsters linked the fur coat issue to the issue

Fougasse poster for the Universities Federation for Animal Welfare.

of animal welfare, fur-coat owners and non-fur-coat owners alike "became supportive of the concern for animal life vs. clothing for fashion."

What do surveys like this mean? Obviously, they show that Americans care deeply about animals and are horrified by animal cruelty. We can only conclude, therefore, that fur sales are currently high because many consumers have been taken in by the clever deceptions of the fur industry. People are simply not aware of the terrible suffering on which the fur trade is based. . . .

Fur Myths

Few industries strive as hard as the fur industry to control the release of information about itself. Small wonder!

Perhaps the most successful myth the fur industry has perpetuated about itself is that fur coats originating from animals raised on "ranches" are a humane alternative to those from animals who were trapped in the wild. This is simply not the case. In fact, fur ranching is just as cruel as trapping.

An Assault upon Earth's Creatures

One of the most widespread assaults upon the Earth and her creatures is the practice of trapping. Fur trappers kill whatever animals bring in the dollars, not the often-hyped "damaging" predators or overpopulated species. Regulation by state game departments masquerades as "scientific management," when in reality there are no reliable population figures available, no significant studies of the impact of trapping on target species, and virtually no enforcement of trapping regulations in the field due to the scattered and widespread nature of this destructive activity.

Dave Foreman, *Ecodefense: A Field Guide To Monkey Wrenching,* 1985.

Did you know that:

• 5.2 million wild animals were killed for their fur on American fur ranches in 1986.

• There are no laws or government regulations to protect ranch-raised animals.

To complement the myth that ranched furbearers are raised and killed humanely, the fur industry invented another myth: that the United States produces many more ranch-raised pelts than pelts from animals who were trapped. The fur industry alternately claims that ranched animals supply 60 percent of the U.S. fur trade, or that "three-quarters of the fur produced in North America is raised on family farms."

In reality, however, only 23 percent of all pelts produced in the United States in 1986 were from ranched animals. A whopping 17 million animals—including wolves, foxes, coyotes, raccoons, bobcats, beavers, muskrats, badgers, otters, opossums, and minks—were trapped in the United States in 1986, accounting for 77 percent of all pelts produced in this country that year.

To combat long-standing criticism of trapping cruelties, however, the U.S. fur trade is cleverly giving fur from animals trapped in the United States a low profile by selling it abroad. In fact, the United States is the world's largest exporter of pelts—virtually all of them from trapped animals. American dressed fur exports were 90 percent trapped fur in 1986 and 86 percent in 1987! Only the higher-priced trapped furs, such as fisher and lynx cat (bobcat), tend to be promoted on the American retail market. In an attempt to assuage the American conscience and, thus, sell lots of coats, the American fur trade imports huge amounts of foreign-produced ranch-raised fur, mostly mink, and sells it to Americans.

A clever deception indeed.

The Leghold Trap

Did you know that:

• Most of the 17 million wild animals trapped for their fur in the United States in 1986 were caught in the infamous leghold trap, an instrument so torturous it has been banned in more than 65 countries. The tremendous force with which the trap slams down on the paw or leg of an animal can be likened to a car door being slammed on a child's hand, crushing it, for up to two weeks.

• In their frantic attempts to stop their pain and escape, animals frequently bite off their own trapped limbs.

• Several other popular traps are equally cruel. The Conibear, a whole-body trap, was judged to bring agonizing and prolonged pain to 40 percent of the animals it catches. The neck snare, a trap made of wire, inflicts prolonged agony by slowly strangling its victims over a period of hours or days—especially when large animals are caught.

• States that have laws regarding the placement and handling of traps vary widely in how often they require traps to be checked. Some states have no checking requirement. Trapped animals left for more than a day are likely to die from exhaustion, dehydration, starvation, freezing, and/or predation. There have been many documented reports of animals being found alive after nearly two weeks in a trap.

• There are no laws or government regulations regarding how trapped animals may be killed. Consequently, they are killed in whatever way is most convenient for the trapper and does not damage the pelt.

Killing Methods

• Popular killing methods include: beating an animal with a blunt instrument or holding on to the animal's rear legs while slamming its head against a tree or rock.

• Another method is to stand on the animal's chest, thus slowly suffocating the creature or crushing its heart.

• Animals who are trapped in or near water, such as beavers and muskrats, are drowned. This is quite an ordeal since beavers can hold their breath for 20 minutes.

• Commercial trapping of animals for their fur is encouraged and widely practiced in our national wildlife "refuges" and parks.

• Other major government subsidies to the fur industry include the cost of maintaining state trapping authorities that promote trapping to gain license revenue; and the Animal Damage Control branch of the U.S. Department of Agriculture (USDA), whose 51,000 traps send up to 90,000 furbearing mammals to the U.S. fur trade each year! The USDA also spends millions of taxpayer dollars each year promoting American fur overseas.

Accidental Trapping

• In addition to the 17 million wild animals trapped for their fur each year in the United States, an estimated 5 million so-called "trash animals"—including domestic animals and unwanted wild species—are accidentally trapped and thrown away. Included in this figure are thousands of endangered or threatened species such as bald eagles and grizzly bears.

All this agony, all this waste—for what? *You should be ashamed to wear fur!*

Recognizing Statements That Are Provable

From various sources of information we are constantly confronted with statements and generalizations about social and moral problems. In order to think clearly about these problems, it is useful if one can make a basic distinction between statements for which evidence can be found and other statements which cannot be verified or proved because evidence is not available, or the issue is so controversial that it cannot be definitely proved.

Readers should be aware that magazines, newspapers and other sources often contain statements of a controversial nature. The following activity is designed to allow experimentation with statements that are provable and those that are not.

The following statements are taken from the viewpoints in this chapter. Consider each statement carefully. *Mark P for any statement you believe is provable. Mark U for any statement you feel is unprovable because of the lack of evidence. Mark C for any statements you think are too controversial to be proved to everyone's satisfaction.*

If you are doing this activity as a member of a class or group, compare your answers with those of other class or group members. Be able to defend your answers. You may discover that others will come to different conclusions than you. Listening to the reasons others present for their answers may give you valuable insights in recognizing statements that are provable.

P = provable
U = unprovable
C = too controversial

1. The trumpeter swan, which in 1935 numbered 73 on a wildlife refuge in Canada, now thrives in two national parks and several wildlife refuges.

2. Our species is on the brink of causing, single-handedly, the worst mass extinction in 65 million years.

3. Millions of sentient mammals—who have highly evolved central nervous systems and thus suffer and feel pain just as humans do—are brutally killed each year for fur.

4. Most wildlife work in the US is supported by the hunter's dollar.

5. Due to predation and exposure to the elements, wild animals rarely die painlessly or peacefully.

6. Hunters cripple but don't retrieve 20 to 25 percent of the more than 50 million birds they shoot each year.

7. In Switzerland, consumer fur purchases are down 75 percent after a major anti-fur blitz.

8. Not harvesting excess furbearers results in wasted pelts, domestic animal loss, and other damages.

9. Zoos teach us a false sense of our place in the natural order.

10. If fewer hunting licenses are purchased, less money is available to pay for the projects and salaries of wildlife managers.

11. Over eight million acres are preserved as a direct result of hunting-oriented programs.

12. Using empty animal cages to explain extinction and the need for wildlife preservation is more useful and humane than the current practice of trapping the animals and exhibiting them in zoo cages.

13. In 1972, the total legal deer harvest in the US was reported at 2.1 million, more than four times the entire deer population of North America in 1900.

14. Total ducks, mallards, and pintails reached all-time lows in 1985 and have not recovered significantly since.

15. The rule of thumb among trappers is that ten chimpanzees die for every one that is delivered alive to a zoo.

Periodical Bibliography

The following articles have been selected to supplement the diverse views presented in this chapter.

Andrew Davis	"The Slaughter of Dolphins," *The Nation*, November 14, 1988.
Field & Stream	"Are We Managing the Outdoors to Death?" February 1987.
Michael W. Fox	"The Captive Panther," *The Animals' Agenda*, September/October 1988.
John W. Grandy	"Fur: Making the Right Choice," *The Animals' Agenda*, November 1988.
Melissa Greene	"No Rms, Jungle Vu," *The Atlantic Monthly*, December 1987.
Don L. Johnson	"The Battle for Hunting Rights," *Outdoor Life*, March 1987.
David M. Kennedy	"What's New at the Zoo?" *Technology Review*, April 1987.
Norman D. Levine	"Preservation Versus Elimination," *Bioscience*, May 1986.
Landon Lockett	"Whales off the Faeroe Islands," *Newsweek*, November 23, 1987.
Jim Mason	"An Interview with Paul Watson of the Sea Shepherd," *The Animals' Agenda*, November 1988.
Norman Myers	"Extinction Rates Past and Present," *Bioscience*, January 1989.
Leslie Roberts	"Hard Choices Ahead on Biodiversity," *Science*, September 30, 1988.
Michael Satchell	"Refuge Hunting: Perverse Use or Logical Harvest?" *U.S. News & World Report*, January 12, 1987.
Jean Seligman	"How To Handle an Elephant," *Newsweek*, November 14, 1988.
Erich Wiedemann	"Is Saving the Seals Killing the Eskimos?" *World Press Review*, July 1987.

How Can the Animal Rights Movement Improve Animal Welfare?

Chapter Preface

The animal rights movement has received a lot of media attention for illegally breaking into research laboratories to steal animals and, in some cases, destroy property. A primary question facing the animal rights movement today is whether such tactics are necessary to promote animal welfare.

The biomedical research community has been the most affected by these raids, and it has argued that it is unnecessary for activists to break the law. Researchers and many others believe that laboratory animals are already adequately protected by US law. The Animal Welfare Act of 1966 set standards for the care of laboratory animals and empowers the US Department of Agriculture to inspect research laboratories. In addition, the 1985 amendment to the act requires institutions to establish their own committees which conduct periodic inspections. Furthermore, the National Institutes of Health, the primary source of funds for medical research in the US, sets guidelines that researchers must follow to receive the Institutes's grants.

Activists defend their illegal raids by arguing that the legal safeguards mentioned above have not protected animal welfare. They maintain that the Department of Agriculture has not had the resources to conduct frequent, rigorous inspections. Furthermore, the Animal Welfare Act does not cover rats or mice, which constitute ninety percent of the laboratory animals used in the US. One of the most vocal US animal rights organizations, People for the Ethical Treatment of Animals, argues that raids on laboratories have played an essential role in bringing abuses to public attention. A commonly-cited example is a 1984 raid on the University of Pennsylvania's Head Injury Lab, which had been inspected by the Department of Agriculture just one week earlier. The protesters found and stole a videotape from the lab that showed researchers handling baboons carelessly, failing to anesthetize them, and making fun of their suffering. As a result of the publicity from the raid, the lab was closed. Activists point to such incidents as ultimate proof that legal means have not been adequate to protect animals. These incidents, say the activists, show that breaking the law is the only way to bring the plight of these animals to public attention and improve animal welfare.

While illegal raids have received the most attention for the animal rights movement, there are a variety of other methods the movement has advocated. Several strategies are debated in this chapter.

"Lab offenders now face a growing crew of humane crusaders who are pressing for . . . alternatives which make sense."

The Animal Rights Movement Promotes Animal Welfare

Belton P. Mouras

The author of the following viewpoint, Belton P. Mouras, writes that activists who have broken into labs have unveiled some of the researchers' brutal practices. These activities had been hidden from the public under the guise of scientific research. He argues that, by exposing such cruelty, the animal rights movement effectively works for the humane treatment of animals. Mouras is the founder and president of the Animal Protection Institute of America, an animal rights group in Sacramento, California.

As you read, consider the following questions:

1. What is the typical response of researchers whose labs have been broken into by animal liberationists, according to the author?
2. What is Mouras's description of an animal rights protector? How does it differ from Donald Kennedy's, the author of the opposing viewpoint?
3. In the author's opinion, what was the significance of the break-in at Edward Taub's laboratory in Silver Springs, Maryland?

Belton P. Mouras, "Lifting the Curtain on Animal Labs." Reprinted from USA TODAY MAGAZINE, March 1988. Copyright 1988 by the Society for the Advancement of Education.

The commando-style raiders who hit what they called the "Frankenstein Room" at Toronto's Hospital for Sick Children in 1981 swept up 21 mutilated animals, including devocalized dogs, cats with their ears cut off, and a pig seared from burnings. It was a crack in the door, a brief glimpse (and they nearly all have been brief) into the kind of labyrinth which—often for fear of a volatile reaction in the outside world—is more apt to keep its operations mysterious and out of sight than to describe in detail what happens, for the public nearly always grows alarmed when the door cracks.

Several years after the raid at Toronto, a hospital spokesman "wasn't quite sure" what had happened as a result or whether all had gone on much the same, once the excitement died. Just hearing the question raised seemed precarious to the hospital. Quite differently from nearly all other enterprises in the world—including many a scientific quest after the most elusive of goals—the laboratories, both the raided and the unraided, are content to have their operations almost totally ignored. No attention is good attention.

More than a P.R. Problem

In February, 1986, the University of Florida at Gainesville assumed a defensive posture, wanting to say absolutely as little as possible about proposed experiments which were bringing complaints from as far away as Mexico. Gainesville's problem occurred when word leaked out in advance about an experiment where 22 dogs were to have fluids injected to bring them within an inch of drowning and another proposed experiment would have put 60 cats in a tortuous simulation that outraged every cat-lover who heard about it. The plan, reported Fawn Germer in the Jacksonville *Times-Union and Journal,* was to suspend the cats for periods up to three months by their hind-quarters in order to make some findings on "weightlessness." . . .

"We've got a heck of a P.R. problem on our hands," lamented University of Florida Vice-Pres. Al Alsobrook. The scheme of the university, which emerged from the news accounts, was to retreat until "the public outrage is tempered," then see if the experiments could be started up again. Mistaking public attacks on the wisdom, the fairness, the morality—and the blinding cruelty—of misconceived, misrun, and unnecessary animal experiments is the commonest blunder of the lab defenders. "P.R. problem" is the least of it. The real questions are: by what right and to what purpose? . . .

The ugliest of disclosures about the goings-on in laboratories are followed by protestations that they aren't typical, don't reflect the experimental community as a whole (this is true, they don't), and, most importantly, that comparatively arbitrary experiments by the psychologists or the product testers shouldn't be confused with the absolutely necessary experiments related to the search for cures for cancer, heart disease, AIDS, and all the principal afflictions of earthlings.

Making Progress

I think there are signs that we are making some progress. . . . We have been able to stop a lot of laboratory experiments that were never stopped before. For years the research community has been its own judge and jury.

Cleveland Amory, *Animal Press*, January 1989.

While there are animal defenders who oppose all studies with animals (some are humane, some are merely anti-science), the real focus of a battle which has reached the uplift stage now after a century of confrontations—and 90 years of not getting anywhere—is "the discovery and rediscovery of the obvious." Claiming deep purpose, some science-connected animal abusers have been witless, some have been reckless, and there is a suspicion that some are actually sadists, finding an outlet. . . .

For several years now, opponents on both sides have been reaching out to the law to drive their arguments home. If the laboratory people were anxious to trip up the raiders who came by night and stole the evidence of their tortures, some of the animal defenders were interested in showing there are legal limits to the mistreatment of animals. Given general exemptions from cruelty statutes, the labs—indulging in extraordinary slashing, bruising, cutting, and burning—were much heckled, but little prosecuted. It changed with the incident at Silver Springs, Md., where an undercover inquiry blew up into the most profound crisis the labs have faced.

The Silver Springs Incident

At Silver Springs, in a behavioral lab where the behaviors included monkeys losing limbs, Alex Pacheco—a dedicated animal worker—did a four-month undercover check on the lab while working there. The usual mystery with which such behavioral labs operate was shattered. Convicted of cruelty (the conviction was later overturned on technical grounds), lab director Dr. Edward Taub became the focal point for an argument which now rages in all directions. The custody of monkeys themselves—the organization I head paid for temporary cages for them when the lab was struggling to get them back—is still being fought over.

Pacheco ramrodded the fast-rising PETA (People for the Ethical Treatment of Animals) into a potent demonstrator against abuses in the lab and also joined the humane mainstream, working with many existing organizations to try to break the potency and the mystery of labs which believe they have a right to work behind an impenetrable curtain where the public can't judge their actions and effects. Hundreds of thousands of persons became clamoring advocates of holding the labs accountable, before and after the probe at Silver Springs which led to a Congressional investigation and has given real propulsion to putting experimentation in the open.

The Humane Movement

The next year or two are apt to decide whether the tawdriest and most ghoulish of the experiments will disappear or whether the old secrecy barriers will continue to protect against a sea of outrage. Inside the animal welfare groups which press this cause, the "anti-science" groups were dismissed, half a century ago, as faddists and fanatics. They have been largely succeeded by scientifically oriented crusaders—often with skilled behavioral psychologists, biologists, and veterinarians on their staff or among their advisors. Lab offenders now face a growing crew of humane crusaders who are pressing for adoption of experimental alternatives which make sense instead of worn-out processes and traditions which treat animals as objects and leave an incriminating trail of blood and pain.

In 1968, I founded the Animal Protection Institute (API) and it has grown, after many controversies, to more than 200,000 members today—roughly 20 times the size of the "great confederation" of humane workers I thought might be achieved. That spiral came about because many Americans were becoming concerned. Over and over, the API members—who "select priorities" each year among all the raging animal problems of the world—have chosen abuse of lab animals as the number-one raging problem. This should be a sign to the laboratories of the fury they have engendered.

The Animal Defender

If I were drawing a portrait of an imaginary, composite animal defender from my organization and others, I would have to describe someone who has utterly strong feelings about saving sick children, sick adults, sick anybody, but extends those strong feelings and wants to save animals, too; who deplores destroying an animal's body and soul and is apt to be far more enraged with arbitrary behavioral experiments (which tear the animal apart as thoroughly as any other) than with direct medical experiments; who *does* want an emphatic national push on solutions for major illnesses, but can see the contradictions in multiplying experiments that create more suffering than their findings will ever relieve; who believes that leaders of the laboratories deserve public scorn, and betray a national trust, when they duck the search for alternatives.

Besieging the universities which turn out our newest scientists to imbue them, within the curriculum itself, with a feeling for "ethics in experimentation," the animal crusaders want the National Institutes of Health (NIH) and lab operators everywhere to realize that they are betraying the animals, the public which supplies their funds (the NIH distributes taxpayer money— sometimes for primate torture), and the cause of scientific enlightenment itself when they resist needed change.

Pro-Animal, Not Anti-Science

A lot of me-too exists in lab work—tired experiments not leading to the new *or* the special *or* the life-saving. It is perfectly fair, of course, to demand of the animal protectors: "Can't you concede that modern science, medical and otherwise, holds the promise of delivering animals from suffering, not just condemning them to it? Isn't it true that a struggle with disease will help us all?" My composite protectionist doesn't disagree with this and is surprised instead that his pro-animal stance is confused with old charges of being anti-science. A horde of animal workers, simply because they feel so deeply, have been careful to verse themselves in what computer modeling and other alternatives to animal testing can do and what they can't do.

"There is another agenda working here [in the animal rights movement]—one that has less to do with animals than it has to do with the control of science."

The Animal Rights Movement Undermines Animal Welfare

Donald Kennedy

Before becoming president of Stanford University in Stanford, California, Donald Kennedy was a biologist and served as commissioner at the US Food and Drug Administration. In the following viewpoint, Kennedy argues that animal rights activists are deceptive. While they claim they seek humane housing for lab animals, their goals are far more radical: They work to eliminate all research. He cites examples where activists have actually opposed improvements in housing for laboratory animals and concludes that such activities hinder better conditions for animals.

As you read, consider the following questions:

1. What does the author believe is the underlying agenda of animal rights groups?
2. What are the three problems researchers must face to defuse the threat posed by animal rights groups, according to Kennedy?
3. Why does Kennedy argue that the public is ignorant of science?

Donald Kennedy, "The Anti-Scientific Method," *The Wall Street Journal,* October 29, 1987. Reprinted with permission of The Wall Street Journal © 1987 Dow Jones & Company, Inc. All rights reserved.

American science faces a worrisome new threat. It stems from a shift in the attitudes of the public at large. Its genesis is ignorance and fear of science itself, and of the institutions in which it is done.

All over the U.S., for example, facilities for research on and housing of experimental animals are being blocked or picketed or invaded by members of the "animal rights movement." That movement is rather difficult to define; it surely contains some quite reasonable elements, but it also contains some respected groups that have shifted in recent years to a more militant posture, and it contains some other groups that openly advocate breaking into research facilities, theft of materials, and "liberation" of animals.

Moderate to Radical

Those of us who had close experience with the "student movement" of the late 1960s recognize at least one similarity: It is a great convenience for any anti-establishment coalition to have a range of elements, from moderate to radical. In that way the credibility of reasonable assertions can be maintained even against a background of violent action. Thus we hear again: "Of course, we wouldn't contemplate actions of that kind; but you must understand that some of the people in this movement are very frustrated, and we can't make guarantees about what they might do." In quite different circles, this is called maintaining deniability.

Indeed, the disparity between assertion and action goes much further than this.

For example, proponents of the animal rights movement often start an action by saying that their chief concern is with animals that have been, or might be, used as pets. In Massachusetts and California, among other places, they pushed hard for pound laws that would prohibit the taking of pound animals for medical research, thus requiring that they be put to death instead. Some said that was all they wanted; that it would be enough. Some universities and states have engaged in what a colleague of mine calls "prudential acquiescence," and caved in. But after its passage in Massachusetts, the pound law's advocates immediately initiated new legislation aimed at much more severe research restrictions. So much for "enough."

Thwarting Humane Housing

Animal rights advocates assert that they are interested in more humane care for research animals. Stanford spent $13 million on a state-of-the-art animal research facility, and at the beginning of summer [1987] had committed an even larger sum for a second one that would bring almost all of the university's scattered animal quarters into one set of superb quarters. At Stanford, various mammals—mostly genetic strains of several rodent species—are essential for research on the immune system, cancer genetics, developmental biology, and various inherited diseases of

194

childhood. To the university's surprise, the building permit was opposed before the Santa Clara County Board of Supervisors by a coalition headed by the Palo Alto Humane Society.

The movement says it wants better housing and treatment for lab animals yet does its best to prevent construction of facilities that will provide them—not only at Stanford, but at the University of California and elsewhere. Especially when they sound moderate, you want to watch what they do, not what they say.

False Advocates

The use of animal subjects in research should be encouraged rather than discouraged in order to increase human safety and well-being. Those who claim to speak for animal rights quite obviously weigh the balance *against* the relief of human misery and even animal suffering. They do not seem to care about human suffering *or* animal suffering. Rabies killed many more pets than humans, and based on animal research a vaccination for feline leukemia has been developed. Moreover, such extremists really are not promoting animal rights. The most basic of rights is the right to life, and yet they do not demand legislation for compulsory spaying of pets but simply endorse the useless killing of unwanted pets.

Dennis M. Feeney, *American Psychologist*, June 1987.

Indeed, most of the movement's more moderate assertions focus on the wrongness of doing injury or inflicting pain; they usually avoid direct assaults on science itself. But when in front of an audience they believe will be receptive, proponents do not hesitate to label all of biomedical research as a failed enterprise, dedicated primarily to aiding the careers and satisfying the personal curiosity of the practitioners.

Victorian England

The situation is strikingly reminiscent of that in Victorian England, where the antivivisection movement achieved great strength by raising moral outrage over individual acts while decrying, at the same time, the progress of science itself. Like the contemporary opponents of medical research who charge it with failing to cure cancer, the Victorian antivivisectionists displayed an affection for quack remedies: An important organization of that period published a pamphlet on the use of cinnamon in the treatment of cancer. It puts one in mind of Laetrile.

A safe conclusion from these clear differences between assertion and action is that there is another agenda working here—one that has less to do with animals than it has to do with the control of science and the institutions in which it is done. Support for that view comes from the ease with which this and other causes against science can be brought together.

The coalition of objectors brought together to block Stanford's new facility marched under the animal rights banner. But many of the objections at the hearing were to possible environmental hazards. It was therefore no surprise to see many of the same players in support of an initiative—this time under the leadership of the Santa Clara Toxics Coalition—objecting to the permit for constructing a biology building. The hazards of recombinant DNA were touched on in the opposition to the animal facility; they were center stage in the dispute over the biology building.

A similar convergence has occurred elsewhere between the movement to block recombinant DNA research—already successful in halting a number of university experiments that have passed the standards of the federal Recombinant Advisory Committee—and the objectors to research using fetal tissues.

Now, there are ethical and/or health issues associated with each of these propositions. Some are concerned that, despite our reassuring experience with contained recombinant DNA research, genetically engineered organisms might escape and cause harm. And there are concerns that intervention into the process of evolution, especially if it involves human genes, may be tinkering with nature in a hubristic way.

Mistrusting Science

Whatever the nub of that somewhat mysterious worry, it is surely very different from those that have to do with the ethics of animal research or the morality of employing for scientific purposes the tissues of fetuses. What links these objections is a vague and alarming mistrust of science, indeed of the elitism of expertise.

Its impact on Stanford's own region should be a source of deep distress. The Bay Area owes much of its economic strength and its future potential to the activity of three great research universities. Yet each of the three now finds itself blocked on major projects by local coalitions, deeply suspicious of science and prepared to join together any set of concerns that promises to add political strength to their efforts. At Stanford, imposed building delays on the two projects I've mentioned will cost us more than $2 million. I am told that combined costs at Berkeley and at the University of California at San Francisco will run in the millions. And we are, after all, just one regional reflection of an issue that is national in character.

Diagnosing the Problem

What can be done? As usual, diagnosis is a lot easier than treatment. But I think we can recognize three key problems.

The first is that with respect to all of the concerns raised by the objectors to science, it is easy to assemble the constituency of the disaffected, but much harder to gather the (largely future) beneficiaries of the research. Animal lovers come together more easily than the parents of cystic fibrosis children, who are busy caring for their youngsters and supporting research efforts. They are strong advocates, but only after they have come to recognize the threat.

The second is that the current trend finds objectors aiming at local political processes. If it is believed that there are risks, their locus of action will be local—whereas the benefits are likelier to be regional or even national in character.

Helping Animals

In California we are facing increasingly fanatical and dangerous activists. These activists eschew logic and humanitarian values for the sake of a deeply-felt belief that animal research, no matter what its purpose or benefit, violates the "rights" of animals and must be stopped. . . .

It is helpful to reflect on how animal research helps other animals. We fulfill a dual responsibility to our fellow human beings, and to the animals veterinarians are trained to treat, by actively supporting the responsible use of animals in research.

Sandra Bressler, *California Veterinarian,* September/October 1987.

The third is that the general public is understandably confused by claims and counterclaims regarding scientific issues. If two apparently well-credentialed people can be brought to testify on opposite sides in a hearing, it is far too easy for people to call the outcome a tie, without applying other standards to the merits of the argument. Part of that has to do with the tyranny of expert knowledge. But unfortunately, part of it relates to the disappointing level of scientific literacy displayed by the lay public. If a substantial proportion of our adult population believes in astrology and the efficacy of pyramids in promoting health, why should we expect thoughtful analyses of problems like these?

The Solution

But there is the outline of a program here. First, we need to get the beneficiaries of research—patients and loved ones—to be effective players in getting these matters decided politically. Wherever that has been done it has improved matters—notably in documenting the value of biomedical research against the claims of the animal rights movement.

Next, we need some bold experiments in regionalizing some of these local political decisions. The Bay Area is too unified and too important a region, and its universities are too important to it, to

197

let those institutions become the victims of "not in my backyard" local politics. Broadening the regional framework for that decision would allow a more realistic comparison of cost and benefits for the whole area.

I think it would be salutary if the officers of the Palo Alto Humane Society had to meet the gay voters of San Francisco at a hearing to determine whether a Stanford facility important in AIDS research will be built. We know how to construct port authorities and air-pollution control districts, and we ought to be able to do this.

Improving Science Education

But in the long run it is the third problem we have to solve, and I'm afraid that will be a long haul. It starts with the admission that we haven't done as well as we should in science education. We need to produce a generation of voters with at least enough knowledge to avoid being bamboozled by foolishness.

"*Legislative or voluntary control systems . . . provide a forum in which some of the essential questions, including moral ones, can be asked by researchers themselves.*"

The Animal Rights Movement Should Use the Political Process

Judith Hampson

Great Britain updated its 1876 Cruelty to Animals Act in 1986 with a new law, the Scientific Procedures Act. In the following viewpoint, Judith Hampson argues that this new law provides a better system of control over animal research experiments. She writes that the law's passage proves that animal rights groups can get effective change by lobbying legislatures. A consultant on laboratory animal welfare, Hampson was formerly Chief Animal Experimentation Research Officer at the Royal Society for the Prevention of Cruelty to Animals in England.

As you read, consider the following questions:

1. What were the successes of the campaign to "put animals into politics," according to the author?
2. What mechanisms in the new law does Hampson describe? Why does she believe they will reduce animal abuse?
3. How do British legislative efforts compare with US legislative efforts, according to Hampson?

Judith Hampson, "Legislation: A Practical Solution" in *Vivisection in Historical Perspective*, edited by Nicolaas A. Rupke. London: Croom Helm Ltd, 1987. Reprinted with permission.

The United Kingdom has begun to phase out its 1876 Cruelty to Animals Act, the oldest piece of legislation on any statute book designed to regulate animal experimentation. Its replacement in May 1986 by the Animals (Scientific Procedures) Act was an historic event, not only because it represented the culmination of 110 years of effort by animal welfarists to reform a law which had remained unamended for over a century, but because the new law represents a radical departure from the one that it replaces. It is an enabling piece of legislation, proscribing almost nothing but attempting to control and regulate almost everything. Both its weaknesses and its strengths lie in its very flexibility.

The passage of this Act far from being hailed as a success by the animal welfare movement as a whole, has again opened up bitter divisions which have dogged the anti-vivisection movement for over a century. . . .

Three Key Events

In 1975 the debate entered the arena of public controversy. Three events were crucial in this: the publication and widespread public acclaim of the book *Victims of Science* by Richard Ryder, then Chairman of the RSPCA [Royal Society for the Prevention of Cruelty to Animals], the story of ICI's smoking beagles in the popular newspaper, the *Sunday People*, and the conviction and sentencing to imprisonment of the two ringleaders of the newly-formed Animal Liberation Front, Ronnie Lee and Clifford Goodman. Each received three-year sentences for damage inflicted to an animal breeding unit and to sealing boats and other property.

Since this time, the topic of animal experimentation has hardly been out of the public eye. During the same period a campaign was launched, spearheaded by Lord Houghton, to 'put animals into politics'. This campaign, which followed the Animal Welfare Year of 1976, succeeded in obtaining animal welfare commitments in the 1979 election manifestos of all three major UK political parties. The Conservative Party which was elected to government had pledged to replace the 1876 Cruelty to Animals Act with a piece of modern legislation to control animal experimentation. It was this promise which resulted in the Animals (Scientific Procedures) Act which received its Royal Assent on 20 May 1986. . . .

Once the government indicated its clear intention to legislate, animal protectionists faced a clear challenge, whether to accept the compromises which a government bill would inevitably contain or whether to remain true to their stronger policies to the extent of opposing new legislation for which the movement had campaigned for so long.

The first White Paper of 1983 was outrightly condemned by most groups. The RSPCA criticised it on the grounds that it failed adequately to meet any of its central priorities: promotion of 'alternatives', elimination of pain and suffering, elimination of 'trivial' research, and public accountability. The main anti-vivisection groups went further; they formed a coalition calling itself 'Mobilisation Against the Government White Paper'. Finding themselves unable to compromise, particularly on the issue of pain which they felt could not be regulated by the law, these anti-vivisectionists chose to focus their campaign on gaining public support for the prohibition of certain kinds of experimentation. These included the LD50 and Draize tests, weapons research, tests on cosmetics and most behavioural research.

The Need for Compromise

To many who had campaigned long and hard for new legislation over the years, this strategy seemed to be missing the point. The RSPCA pointed out that pain was the central issue and could not be avoided simply by ignoring it, now that new legislation was becoming a reality. Moreover, the areas of research targeted by Mobilisation, even if it were possible to attain prohibition of them (which seemed hardly practical), accounted for only about 11 per cent of the total number of animals used. Was the animal protection movement now to turn its back on the other 89 per cent in order to feel it had kept its hands clean of compromise? Almost despairingly, Lord Houghton, who had worked for so long to get laboratory animals into the political arena, found himself accusing his erstwhile supporters of being afraid now to go through the open door on which they had been knocking for so long. . . .

The Lawful Path

It is only by the moderate and lawful path of legislative process and humane education, coupled with constant vigilance and unyielding determination, that the animal rights movement will attain the worthwhile goals we pursue.

Thomas G. Bickleman, *The AV Magazine*, December 1988.

The new British law represents perhaps the most pragmatic attempt yet enacted in any legislation to deal with the very real ethical dilemmas and practical difficulties raised by animal experimentation. As stated above, it is an enabling piece of legislation which proscribes practically nothing but seeks to control everything through a dual licensing system operated by a strong administrative machinery.

The system requires two licences to cover every scientific procedure. The personal licence testifies to the competence of the licensee, who accepts responsibility for the animals (s)he uses and for implementing the conditions attached to the licence. The project licence, which might be held by an individual researcher working alone or by a project leader in charge of a large programme of research, specifies the project in detail, including the species and number of animals to be used, the techniques to be applied and the permitted level of severity under this project licence.

The system enables the administrative authority (which in the UK is the Home Office) for the first time to have real control over what is done in a specific piece of scientific work. The project will be scrutinised by the Home Office Inspectorate before a licence is granted. They must assure themselves that there is no alternative means available of carrying out the work, and that the degree of severity likely to be attained is fully justified in terms of the aims and objectives of the research. The Home Secretary has finally accepted responsibility for *justifying* what is licensed, a responsibility which, for many years, he has been loath to accept but one for which moderate reformers have continued to press. This means that scientific work, for the first time, becomes truly publicly accountable through the parliamentary process. . . .

A Well Thought Out System

In order to understand how the machinery of the new legislation will work in practice it is necessary to read the new Act in conjunction with the lengthy Guidance Note on the Operation of the New Legislation, issued by the Home Office. This document reflects the government's recognition that no law, however good in practice, will work unless a well-thought-out system is put in place to implement it.

As part of this system the law charges three people with statutory responsibility for day-to-day care of the animals. One of these persons is the holder of the registration certificate for the premises, one is a senior animal technician or curator who is in charge of the animals on a daily basis, and the other is a veterinarian, either employed by the laboratory or available to be called in whenever the need arises. . . .

The Volatile US Situation

The situation in the United States is extremely volatile. Over the last five years, exposés by animal rights activists, resulting from meticulous underground investigations and illegal break-ins, have highlighted glaring inadequacies in the current system of control. These dramatic examples have been impossible to ignore by regulatory and funding agencies. The result has been recent amendments to the law itself and an overhaul of the controls exercised by granting bodies.

The main legislation relating to animal experimentation is the Animal Welfare Act, originally the Laboratory Animal Welfare Act, passed in 1966 and amended in 1970, 1976 and 1985. The existence of this law is largely the result of a case involving a stolen dog which was taken across state lines for sale to a laboratory. This history has meant that the legislation relates primarily to supply, husbandry and transport of animals. Until recently it has exerted very little control over their actual use in experimental procedures. Moreover, rats, mice and birds, species making up more than 80 per cent of animals used in the USA, are excluded from its provisions because of inadequate resources for enforcement of the law. The general feeling in America has been that there should be as little as possible bureaucratic interference with free scientific enquiry. American researchers have, on the whole, tended to regard the system of control applied in the United Kingdom as draconian. . . .

Practical Possibilities

Political action will always be concerned with practical possibilities. Animal welfarists must come to terms with this fact. We do animals a disservice when we place our sacred principles regarding rights above achieving some progress in alleviating their suffering.

Clive Hollands, in *In Defense of Animals,* 1985.

The new [National Institutes of Health] *Guide* [for the Care and Use of Laboratory Animals], which applies to all registered facilities, contains more detailed recommendations on care and treatment of animals, including provision for veterinary care, anaesthesia, analgesia, post-operative nursing, humane euthanasia and factors affecting environmental health. Multiple survival surgery is discouraged. Institutions are to designate clear lines of authority and responsibility, naming two officials, one with overall responsibility for research programmes, the other to be a veterinarian. Institutional care and use committees are to be involved with all aspects of the research programme, including review of applications for funding and approval of those sections relating to animal care and use. Funding will be dependent upon this documentation. Detailed information on each research programme is to be filed with the NIH Office for Protection from Research Risks.

Animal protection groups continue to complain that the changes offer too little and come too late. They are likely to continue to press for tougher legislative changes. . . .

Ethical Dilemmas and Practical Realities

Vivisection is a moral and social problem of the first order of magnitude and one which does not exclusively concern the expert. Certainly the rights and wrongs of using animals in research, and the practical realities of what constraints must be placed upon the activity, are societal issues. They cannot be the sole province of the scientific community. Almost every activity in which modern society indulges, from exploring the depths of the oceans and the vastness of space, to the development of new industrial products and cosmetics, or the search for a cure for AIDS, is dependent to a greater or lesser degree on the use of laboratory animals. These animals are a shield with which we defend ourselves. Whether this is regarded as a matter of considerable moral signficance, or merely a regrettable necessity, depends upon whether one considers animals to be worthy objects of our moral concern, or merely tools for our use and manipulation.

While few scientists today would openly declare that science should be pursued unhindered by any moral or legal restraints, the research community still maintains that the pursuit of knowledge is paramount. Obligations to treat animals as humanely as possible are generally recognised, but the extent to which those obligations are acted upon is variable, and very few indeed are the researchers who address the question of whether they have a right to use animals at all, or even to make them suffer. There exists a significant difference in degree of sensitivity between researchers who expect to carry out their practices unhindered (e.g. in the US) and those who have become accustomed over many years to a fairly elaborate system of constraints (e.g. in the UK).

In this can be seen the beginnings of a practical solution to the ethical dilemma. While legislative or voluntary control systems do not address themselves to the fundamental question of whether or not it is morally justifiable to experiment on animals, they do change the moral climate. Moreover, they can provide a forum in which some of the essential questions, including moral ones, can be asked by researchers themselves. . . .

Legislating a Chain of Responsibility

After years of debate over how best to control and scrutinise the purposes for which research is carried out, and how to reduce animal suffering, it was concluded by those who had thought long and hard about these issues, notably Lord Houghton, that such an administrative system was the only way to achieve the desired ends. Houghton has emphasised that such subjective issues as 'justifiable' purposes and 'permissible' levels of suffering could not be tied down in the statute law, but must be subjected to the judgement of reasonable men and women.

"We need to build a strong effective movement based on economic sabotage against large centres of animal abuse."

The Animal Rights Movement Should Use Economic Sabotage

Animal Liberation Front

The Animal Liberation Front includes people who break into academic and commercial laboratories, take the animals, and sometimes vandalize property. Due to the illegality of their actions, they remain anonymous. This Front originated in Great Britain and has been most active there, although several activists in other countries use the British groups' tactics as a model. In the following viewpoint, members of the Front trace the growth and successes of their movement. Their ultimate justification for using illegal means is that legislation and legal protest cannot free animals from abuse, while breaking into laboratories can.

As you read, consider the following questions:

1. What was the effect of carrying out raids during the day, according to the authors?
2. Why do the authors believe lobbying is ineffective?
3. What is the authors' attitude toward the use of violence?

Animal Liberation Front, *Against All Odds: Animal Liberation 1972-1986.* London: ARC Print, 1986. Reprinted with permission.

Right from those days in the last century when vivisection began there have been, from time to time, people who have taken direct action against it. Now and again one hears tales of the rescue of animals from laboratories by intrepid individuals many decades ago—but these were isolated incidents and did not form part of a campaign. The current campaign of direct action against vivisection has its origin only as far back as the early 1970's.

It was only in 1972 that a few people involved in the HSA [Hunt Saboteurs Association] decided to embark on a campaign of direct action against vehicles and other property used by the hunt. In order to do this, a group called the Band of Mercy was formed and proceeded to carry out raids on fox hunt kennels in the South of England.

In the autumn of 1973 members of the Band of Mercy decided that their campaign should expand to include all forms of animal abuse and during November two arson attacks were carried out (causing over 45,000 British pounds of damage) on a laboratory being built for the Hoechst drug company at Milton Keynes. . . .

The Birth of ALF

In June 1976 the ALF [Animal Liberation Front] was born with the remnants of the Band of Mercy and a couple of dozen new activists coming together to create the new organisation. . . .

The handful of "veterans" of the Band of Mercy blinked in surprise at this new phenomena. Up until this time there had been virtually no support for their activities from the rest of the animal protection movement and two Band of Mercy members had been thrown off the HSA committee (they were later reinstated) when it was suspected they were involved in "illegal activities".

The ALF took up where the Band of Mercy left off, and carried out ten raids against vivisection targets in the remainder of 1976. Action was mainly against the property of animal suppliers. . . .

In 1977 the ALF carried out 14 raids against vivisection and liberated over 200 animals from laboratory suppliers.

The hardest hitting ALF raid so far was carried out when activists broke into the Condiltox lab in North London and caused 80,000 British pounds of damage. Quite soon afterwards the lab went out of business.

An American group calling themselves "Undersea Railroad" released two porpoises from a Hawaii research lab at about the same time.

By this time there was considerably more support for the ALF amongst other animal protection groups, especially from the HSA and the BUAV [British Union for the Abolition of Vivisection] but the National Anti-Vivisection Society continued to condemn the activists in its publications.

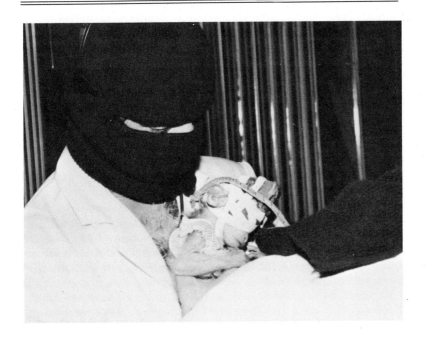

A member of the Animal Liberation Front holds Britches, a five-week-old monkey who was taken from the psychology laboratory at the University of California at Riverside in April 1985. Britches had been the subject of sight deprivation experiments.

In late 1977 and early 1978 the authorities struck a telling blow against the ALF with the imprisonment of half a dozen of the most active members. For a while this had a crippling effect on the organisation with several other good activists being "frightened off" and it was not until well into 1979 that a recovery began to be made.

Even then it was action abroad rather than in England which was getting the attention. The American ALF carried out their first raid in March, posing as lab workers to rescue five animals from New York University Medical Center, and on Christmas night the newly formed Dutch ALF rescued 12 beagles from a laboratory at Zeist. . . .

1982: A Landmark Year

There was a further increase in anti-vivisection raids in 1982 and in many ways the year was a landmark for animal liberation action.

ALF activists decided . . . to carry out large scale raids in the daytime. The first of these occurred in February when activists smashed their way into Safepharm labs near Derby and were photographed by the press and filmed by T.V. rescuing rabbits. Several activists, identified by the police from press photos, received suspended sentences for their part in the raid.

The Safepharm action turned out to be a curtain-raiser for what was to follow just a week later. In a large scale daylight raid, codenamed "Operation Valentine" (the date was 14 February), dozens of activists stormed the Life Science Research labs at Stock, Essex, while a demo went on outside. A variety of animals were rescued, 76,000 British pounds of damage was caused and 60 people arrested. Eight activists were later sent to prison for their part in the raid.

Operation Valentine attracted a great deal of publicity, caused considerable loss to Life Science (40 of their employees were laid off) and won many new recruits for direct action—but it was to be the last large scale ALF daylight raid. In retrospect there seemed to be no advantage in carrying out such an action in daylight, the extra publicity being outweighed by the greater risk of arrest, and it was evident that, when serious damage occurred, it was much more difficult for activists to pretend that they were just part of the peaceful demonstration—indeed, in the "Valentine" case, several of the peaceful demonstrators ended up charged with conspiracy.

So it was back to "Creeping about in the night"—but such "creeping" rescued 12 beagles from Boots' Laboratories near Nottingham and closed down Leicester University Psychology Department's animal laboratory after a rescue and damage raid later in the year. . . .

In May [1983] the American ALF raided a research lab at the University of Pennsylvania, causing considerable damage and taking away videos made by the vivisectors themselves. From these films "Unnecessary Fuss" was made, which revealed the full horror of head injury experiments on monkeys and the callous attitude of the vivisectors. This evidence was later instrumental in causing the laboratory to close down. . . .

Thousands of Rescued Animals

In the 12 years since organised direct action against vivisection began nearly 6,000 animals have been rescued from laboratories and suppliers, and several million pounds worth of damage done in the 400-plus raids which have taken place. Direct action has also played a major part in forcing the closure of several vivisection establishments and has, without doubt, been influential in reducing the official figures for animal experiments in the UK; these were previously on the increase all the time, but have gone down by about two million in recent years.

The price for all this has been paid by the two dozen or so activists who have been imprisoned for anti-vivisection actions and by many others who have been fined or faced other penalties. A large number of ALF people have not been brought before the courts through clever detective work but have got into trouble because of their own admissions to the police. . . .

The Real Extremists

People involved in direct action are not 'terrorists, vandals or criminals' in the moral sense, they are ordinary people who dislike injustices perpetrated on animals enough to want to do something practical about it. . . .

It must be remembered that these actions are taken because the real extremists, the real vandals who partake in such violent actions as pouring chemicals into rabbit eyes, forcing farm animals into tiny cages and stalls where they can barely move only to later suffer indescribable fear and pain at the abattoir, or mutilating animals for their fur, are free to inflict this enormous and unnecessary suffering under the protection of our legal system.

Tom Perry, *Animal Liberation: The Magazine,* Autumn 1987.

The attitude of the national anti-vivisection societies [NAVS] to the activists has been fickle to say the least. The NAVS now speak out less than previously against direct action but Animal Aid are not so supportive as they used to be, seeming to dislike damage to property. The BUAV claim to support the activists, but in reality they have only courted favour with the activists in an attempt to woo them into supporting the doomed parliamentary strategy. . . .

The Futility of Politics

The problem with the national societies is that, in general, they will only voice support for direct action when it serves their own purposes, in other words only when it can be used as a boost to the political campaign. Real support would be shown if they were prepared to take actions which made it more likely that more people would get involved in direct action. The national societies dislike in particular the recent change in attitude of the ALF, which is becoming increasingly outspoken in its rejection of political campaigning and its belief that the movement will have to bring the vivisection industry to its knees by economic sabotage rather than lobbying parliament. Anarchist ideas about people changing things themselves, rather than by means of politicians, and the historic failure of political campaigning have both encouraged the rapid growth of this point of view. . . .

The direct action movement is starved of funds, mainly because these are all in the hands of the national societies, and lack of money without doubt reduces the amount of effective action. But the main problem is not lack of finance, but lack of initiative. Unless there are hundreds if not thousands, of groups all over the country (and in all other countries) organising and carrying out their own activities, we will never put an end to vivisection or any other form of animal persecution.

All of the actions [between 1972 and 1984] have been organised and carried out by ordinary people with enough determination and common sense to see the whole thing through. It is well within the means of virtually everyone in the movement to become involved in direct action. But we have to be resolute if animal torture is ever to be ended. . . .

The State's Tactics

To defend its power and influence the British State has many tactics, developed over hundreds of years. Its opponents are urged to participate in endless rounds of parliamentary campaigns and to operate within a self-regulated boundary of ineffective and tiresome protest. In the animal rights movement we have consistently been urged to play the parliamentary game, gearing our campaigns towards the next election. However no serious political party has ever had a manifesto commitment to abolish vivisection and so each successive parliament is another disaster for animals in laboratories. This 'wait and see' policy, building up hopes only to see them dashed again is often enough to see the energy of a campaign worn down.

The traditional anti-vivisection societies responded to the emergence of the animal rights movement, born as it was out of the direct action of the Hunt Saboteurs and the Animal Liberation Front, by creating new, 'radical' versions of their old, failed, campaign tactics. 'Putting Animals into Politics', the 'General Election Co-ordinating Committee on Animal Protection' and 'Mobilisation for Laboratory Animals' were all formed and rapidly funded by reformist anti-vivisection groups as a direct response to the growing support for militancy amongst the grass roots of local animal rights groups. . . .

Despite the fact that the Government was committed to expanding the scope of the vivisection industry, the Mobilisations sponsor groups chose to demand the loyalty of the animal rights movement to a parliamentary approach, at a time when we were achieving successes by the use of direct action.

The Importance of Class

The parliamentary campaign is doomed to failure because, despite our democratic traditions, we live in a political system were M.P.s [Members of Parliament] have a greater allegiance to their social class than to the wishes of the electorate they have to face once every four years.

If vivisection was against the interests of the ruling class they could abolish it very quickly, either by the use of their legislative powers, or more simply by decisions made at Board meetings. Commercial forms of animal abuse such as vivisection and factory farming are in the financial interests of the ruling class, and bloodsports are an essential part of their social fabric. The parliamentary campaign is in fact asking us to petition the ruling class to act against their own best interest.

We do not take direct action out of choice, we do so out of the realisation that if it were possible for parliamentary campaigns to bring about the end of vivisection they would have done so by now. . . .

The early success of the Animal Liberation Front was in its ability to cause economic damage to centres of animal abuse whilst at the same time gaining widespread attention and sympathy from the media and the public. The image often given was that of a masked figure rescuing beagles from horrific experiments in laboratories, and chickens from despicable conditions in battery cages. The activist was seen as a person who cared more about the abuse of animals than their own individual liberty.

A Moral Thing To Do

It seems to me perfectly natural and a very moral thing for people to intervene directly to save animals from persecution. Of course, this would often mean breaking the law, but those laws had been made by a selfish and arrogant human species without taking the interests of animals into consideration.

Ronald Lee, quoted in *New Times*, no. 9, March 1987.

This image began to change when it was recognised that the ALF were becoming effective, and were bent on causing as much damage to animal abuse centres as possible. The media, being as much a part of the State as the police and big business, turned against the ALF tending only to report those actions that they could portray in a bad light. . . .

Economic Sabotage Is Essential

The issue of violence, which is largely a media creation, must not be allowed to become embroiled in the movement—individual acts of violence will not stop animal abuse, no more than asking politely will. We have been shown that political campaigning is a waste of time, there is too much vested interest for the politician to legislate against animal abuse. . . . Therefore we need to build a strong effective movement based on economic sabotage against large centres of animal abuse. Although small scale actions are important it is ultimately the centres of animal abuse, e.g. laboratories that have to be targets. There are few large laboratories in this country but, with carefully planned raids, many of these places could be put out of action for many months, resulting in large scale disruption and uncertainty for those who control vivisection, millions of pounds of lost revenue and the saving of many thousands of animals' lives.

"The struggle for animal rights has only just begun. And so has the use of our most powerful weapon. Civil disobedience."

The Animal Rights Movement Should Use Civil Disobedience

Tom Regan

A philosophy professor at North Carolina State University in Raleigh, Tom Regan is one of the best-known animal rights advocates in the US. In the following viewpoint, he describes his experience at a sit-in, protesting federal funding for a laboratory which had been accused of abusing animals. Regan argues that such acts of civil disobedience send the public a powerful message: A dedicated group of people is willing to risk arrest to try to stop cruelty toward animals.

As you read, consider the following questions:

1. What lessons did Regan learn from protesting at the National Institutes of Health?
2. Why does Regan oppose the use of violence during protests?
3. How can the animal rights movement gain the sympathy of the public, according to the author?

Tom Regan, *The Struggle for Animal Rights*. Clarks Summit, PA: International Society for Animal Rights, Inc., 1987. Reprinted with permission.

My debts to Gandhi are great. The influence of his thought and the example of his life helped change my life—and continue to do so even now, as I struggle to become the person I aspire to be. Were he alive today, I would be counted among his followers. Perhaps I am.

My dedication to his ideals began with my decision to become a vegetarian. It has taken me a step further, then another, then another. . . .

The NIH Protest

The nonviolent occupation of the administrative offices on the ninth floor of Building #39 on the campus of the National Institutes of Health was back in June of 1985. What prompted this classic sit-in was the NIH's refusal to stop the funding of the Head Injury Laboratory at the University of Pennsylvania. This is the lab whose notion of "research" has been captured for everyone to see on the film, "Unnecessary Fuss." What one sees there gives both science and humanity a bad name. Even so, NIH had decided to ride out the storm of protest. The lab stayed in business.

I was one of the 101 civil disobedients who took part in the NIH sit-in. We stayed four days. When it was over, none of us had been arrested and the decision had been made to suspend NIH's funding of the Penn lab, pending a further investigation. In time all funds were stopped and the lab closed down. It had taken more than 13 months of serious activism and a decision on the part of more than 100 law-abiding citizens to risk arrest. All for a small victory. All to get *one lab* closed—and even then to lose the monkeys to the scientific bureaucracy. They remain in some lab somewhere, for some purpose or other—probably lost forever.

All that effort, time, money and anxiety: Was it worth it? I don't know if there is any way to prove what the right answer is. I think perhaps the best we can do is to ask the people who participated in this piece of history what they thought and felt as they marched out of Building #39, singing the Anthem of the Animal Rights Movement.

> We speak for the animals,
> Their pain and ours are one.
> We'll fight for the animals,
> Until their rights are won.

We all had tears in our eyes. Tears of relief and pride, of hope and compassion, of love and friendship. We had joined in making a public statement about the rights of animals. We had risked arrest. Each of us had proven our willingness to suffer for those who had no choice in the matter. If there had been a mountain in our way that day, we would have moved it!

Was it worth it? I think the answer is a resounding "Yes!" On that day we showed the world that the Animal Rights Movement *means business.* The battle lines were never more clearly drawn. *Our* civil war was formally declared. In a civil way.

That war must continue. And it will. The struggle for animal rights has only just begun. And so has the use of our most powerful weapon. Civil disobedience. Gandhi would be proud of us.

But a note of caution: Civil disobedience is a fragile weapon. When used in the wrong setting or by violent people pretending to be nonviolent, its sharp moral edge is dulled and can be broken. . . .

Wisely Choosing Civil Disobedience

I'm a strong supporter of civil disobedience (CD). I engage in it myself. But it has to be chosen wisely. It can't fill the whole movement. I mean, the movement has to be far more than that, it has to be more diverse than that. Basically, what CD does is gain publicity, it's a publicity ploy. . . .

I'm a Gandhian. That's how I got into the movement, from Gandhi. Any movement for social justice has to have civil disobedience. Gandhi was a master at this. But it wasn't a buckshot approach to civil obedience. That does nothing.

A Mass Movement

As more and more money gets rechannelled into the hands of those who are truly committed to the animal rights movement as a *liberation* movement, we will see ever more significant victories for animals and ever decreasing suffering and slaughter. We will begin to see the visible signs of a mass movement in the mainstream media—with thousands, then millions of ordinary people marching to a different drummer than the old guard animal welfare bureaucrats, people out in the streets, *demanding* an end to animal exploitation and slaughter, blockading laboratories, disrupting slaughterhouse operations, hunts, and rodeos. When that day comes, the goal of animal liberation in the truest and fullest sense of the word will begin to become a reality.

George P. Cave, *Between the Species,* November 1988.

So when I say I'm an advocate of it, I'm an advocate of it wisely chosen and expertly executed. It's got to be a *winnable* issue. That's what we risk people getting arrested for. If we just go out and protest that something is going on in a particular laboratory and get arrested, we get some publicity but we haven't changed a thing because there is no focus.

Civil disobedience should be that toward which we work in a campaign, but it shouldn't be the thing that fills the campaign. In other words, it should be, again, very Gandhian. What we try to do is cooperate with the opposition, "We don't want to do this, we want to find some way to get what we want without resorting to this," etc. And then—when all else fails—*then* we resort to civil disobedience. It should be the last choice, not the first choice, in a campaign. But we've got to have a campaign. You see, we have to have some strategy, we have to have some vision, some focus. We have to know what we want. . . .

Getting More than Publicity

But the buckshot approach to civil disobedience for the sake of publicity plays into the hands of the media. The public's perception of the movement is the media's perception of the movement. So if we're just out there protesting, protesting, protesting, and a bunch of people get arrested, it may actually look like "those animal radical crazies," and that's what the public sees.

The NIH civil disobedience should be the recipe for how to use CD. And I can't think of any other CD cases like that one that have been really effective on the research establishment and public opinion regarding the animal rights movement.

For civil disobedience to succeed as something other than a publicity ploy, we have to get the sympathy, empathy and moral backing of the public on our side. The people who are watching will finally have to say, "You know, I think these people are right." And that, again, is what Martin Luther King Jr. was great at, and Gandhi was especially good at it. Finally, the politicians, the people in power, the public at large believe the protesters are right. *Then* we're talking, *then* we have power. . . .

Against Vandalism

I'm against vandalizing for lots of reasons, not the least of which is that it's bad strategy. What happens when you vandalize a lab is that *it* becomes the story. The story is not what was in that lab or what the animals were, it becomes "these vandals went in and stole animals". So it plays right into the hands of the research establishment. When we left NIH, we ran the sweepers, we washed the windows, we cleaned up, we polished. We made it as clean as it could be. All the signs were taken down, no spray paint, none of that stuff. It would just be detrimental. We were what I called Norman Rockwell radicals. We were middle America in a sit-in, and that's very important to appear that way and to be that way.

However, what I think is right strategy and right psychology is for the people who liberate animals to come forth and identify themselves as the people who did it. And this is what is really hard to do and a lot of people are going to turn off on me right there.

But the reason it's right strategically and right psychologically is because what it says is that they were confident enough when they broke in, that what they were going to reveal was going to be so powerful in terms of turning public opinion that the public

216

is going to sympathize with them. When they come forward and say, "We're the ones who did this," now it's real civil disobedience. They've come back and are saying, "Punish us." Here's this devastatingly horrible stuff that the system denies, covers up, and here they are, risking arrest, trial and imprisonment, but that's the price I think those kind of activists have to face.

Willing To Go to Jail

If they're really going to perform the most important function for the movement, that is, to continue to sustain the story, that's why it's right strategy. As it is now, there's a break in, some stuff comes out, it gets dispersed, it gets forgotten. Now what sustains the story? What sustains the story is someone is getting punished. The story stays alive. It's right strategy. And what it says to the public is, "You cannot trust the government. You cannot trust the researchers. Here we are, up against the system. What the research establishment is doing to animals is so wrong, we're willing to go to jail over it."

"The main purpose of having public membership on committees is to bring an outside and different perspective to the review."

The Animal Rights Movement Should Use Ethics Committees

Steven M. Niemi and W. Jean Dodds

In the following viewpoint, Steven M. Niemi and W. Jean Dodds write that animal welfare advocates and people who are not scientists should join local ethics committees which approve or disapprove researchers' projects using animals. By adding a new perspective, these advocates will help committees weigh the benefits and drawbacks of proposed research and come to a just compromise, they argue. Niemi is director of Veterinary Services at the EG&G Mason Research Institute in Worcester, Massachusetts. W. Jean Dodds is the chief of the hematology laboratory in the New York Department of Health and the president of Scientists' Center for Animal Welfare in Washington, DC.

As you read, consider the following questions:

1. Why do the authors advocate a moderate position toward animal research? What do they consider moderate?
2. How will animal welfare advocates help committees reach decisions, according to the authors?
3. Why do Niemi and Dodds believe it is valid to have a person on the committee who is not a scientist?

Steven M. Niemi and W. Jean Dodds, "Animals in Research." Reprinted with permission from *National Forum: The Phi Kappa Phi Journal,* Winter 1986.

There is no contemporary issue in science and technology that has generated more controversy and misunderstanding than the debate over the use of laboratory animals. Animal protectionists claim that most (or all) use of animals in research, education, or testing is not only immoral but also unnecessary today because alternative technologies that utilize computers and cell culture provide adequate replacements. . . .

From the other side of the debate, biomedical scientists, educators, and administrators counter that animals continue to provide irreplaceable subjects and materials for research, education, and testing. They contend that we simply do not understand nature adequately to rely on nonanimal systems to evaluate new drugs, probe disease mechanisms, and estimate personal and environmental health risks from industrial chemicals to which we are all exposed in increasing quantities. Furthermore, any limitation on animal experimentation is often predicted to have immediate and grave consequences for the health and well-being of both people and animals.

Finding Middle Ground

The public is often presented with only these more extreme views from both sides. The diatribes result in further bewilderment and serve no constructive purpose. To be certain, there are individuals with moderate voices from both sides who recognize the need for animals in these scientific and regulatory endeavors but in fewer numbers and in conjunction with nonanimal technologies. As laboratory animal veterinarians, we are most comfortable in the middle ground of the debate, since we are committed to both animal welfare and the betterment of humans and animals. . . .

Presently, there are two major trends in laboratory animal use. These are (1) the increasing use of laboratory animals to provide biological materials for *in vitro* research and testing and (2) the inclusion of public (lay) members as advocates for the animal in the review of laboratory animal use at the local level. Both trends are becoming socially as well as scientifically acceptable, and these practices will alter the use of laboratory animals in a positive manner. . . .

The New Dialogue

[A] major development involves the increased role and input of animal-welfare advocates and activists in the process of overseeing laboratory animal use. The value of having such advocates and activists has been difficult to define and assess in terms of the precise role and intent of such oversight. The impetus has arisen mainly as a response to the perceived callousness of the biomedical scientific community, the intransigence of the regulatory bodies responsible for safety testing, and the often-exaggerated claims by antivivisectionsists and other vocal factions of the animal protectionist movement of abuse and neglect of research animals. In addition, the USDA, [US Department of Agriculture], which is the primary agency responsible for enforcing the Animal Welfare Act (the main piece of legislation protecting research animals from neglect and abuse), has been grossly underfunded and inadequately staffed to carry out its regulatory mandate effectively. This problem has further heightened public concern for improper laboratory animal husbandry.

Although not without tremendous acrimony in some cases, the public as well as the parties involved have responded to these perceptions and circumstances by supporting greater control and oversight of animal research. This change has been implemented by creation or strengthening of institutional animal care and use committees, whereby membership is extended to nonscientists and animal welfare proponents. In addition, animal advocacy groups are supplementing the federal monitoring of research animal use. These groups are serving in an inspection capacity in several states, including Massachusetts. Animal advocates also are increasing their involvement in encouraging and funding research on animal replacements. They are also sponsoring public forums on alternative research and the regulation of research animal uses.

A National Forum

I have watched the development of the various committees formed overseas and in the Australian States to provide a meeting place for all elements in the debate. . . . A national council, . . . while it may have representation of welfare organisations must include working farmers and others directly interested in the welfare of farm animals.

Bill Gee, *Animal Liberation, The Magazine,* October 1985.

This union (willing or otherwise) of former antagonists should be applauded and encouraged. There are strong scientific and other reasons for the reduction of the use of animals in scientific research. There are also valid reasons for continuing to use laboratory animals in such research. Those involved should pay close attention to the more moderate aspects of the debate. It will be interesting to evaluate the role and impact of the animal-advocate member of animal care and use committees, once animal advocates have served on such committees for several years. Will the addition of one or more persons have any consequence? Will other committee members be reluctant to discuss or support experiments which may involve substantial pain to animals, even when these are determined to be of potentially great medical or scientific value?

Other seeming conflicts also need to be addressed and resolved. Traditionally, the animal welfare or advocacy viewpoint on these committees has been the responsibility of the veterinarian. The veterinarian's opinions have credibility because of his/her scientific and clinical background and training. The new lay appointees may not have any training in experimental science or medicine, and as a result lay appointees may not have much impact on committee deliberations. However, the main purpose of having public membership on committees is to bring an outside and different perspective to the review, with the hope of providing mutually beneficial and useful exchange and understanding.

In any event, lay appointees will be given the responsibility of reviewing protocols for reasonable and humane care and use of laboratory animals. There is clearly a need for the animal-advocate community to work closely with laboratory animal veterinarians to become better informed about the appropriate analgesics and anesthetics, the indications and risks for different species to be used in experiments, and other pertinent knowledge of laboratory animal husbandry and medicine. Presently, there is considerable dialogue between the public and scientific proponents of animal welfare and biomedical research administrators about committee membership issues. This type of dialogue should be expanded to include all representatives of the scientific effort (e.g., technicians, graduate students, fiscal and plant personnel, junior and senior scientists, and veterinarians).

Improving Animal Research

Since a dialogue implies an exchange of views and ideas, what can the public or lay appointee offer to an animal care committee? The very presence of this person serves as a reminder to the other committee members of their responsibility to animals. While some may consider this role superfluous, it can help to assure and maintain acceptable standards for animal care and use and to improve those areas that are deficient. If these objectives can be achieved, public support for biomedical investigation will be bolstered, and scientific pursuit of knowledge for the benefit of people and animals will be advanced in a more humane and responsible manner.

a critical thinking activity

Evaluating Sources of Information

A critical thinker must always question sources of information. Historians, for example, distinguish between *primary sources* (eyewitness accounts) and *secondary sources* (writings or statements based on primary or eyewitness accounts or on other secondary sources). The account of an animal rights activist at a sit-in protesting against a laboratory is an example of a primary source. A historian evaluating the incident by using the activist's account is an example of a secondary source.

To read and think critically, one must be able to recognize primary sources. This is not enough, however, because eyewitness accounts do not always provide accurate descriptions. Animal rights activists and biomedical researchers remembering the same incident in which a lab was illegally broken into may give differing accounts of the event. The historian must decide which account seems most accurate, keeping in mind the potential biases of the eyewitnesses.

Test your skill in evaluating sources of information by completing the following exercise. Imagine you are writing a report evaluating whether animal rights groups have helped animals. You decide to include an equal number of primary and secondary sources. Listed are a number of sources which may be useful for your research. *Place a P next to those descriptions you believe are primary sources.* Second, *rank the primary sources* assigning the number 1 to what appears to be the most accurate and fair primary source, the number 2 to the next most accurate, and so on until the ranking is finished. *Next, place an S next to those descriptions you believe are secondary sources and rank them also, using the same criteria.*

If you are doing this activity as a member of a class or group, discuss and compare your evaluations with other members of the group. Others may come to different conclusions than you. Listening to their reasons may give you valuable insights in evaluating sources of information.

P = *primary*
S = *secondary*

1. An article in a scholarly journal titled "A Review of Recent Studies on the Treatment of Laboratory Animals."

2. A journal written by an imprisoned member of the Animal Liberation Front.

3. The meeting notes of an animal liberation group that raids chicken farms.

4. A book called *Animal Rights or Animal Welfare?* written by an anthropologist.

5. An article in a monthly magazine summarizing animal welfare legislation in five countries.

6. A public television documentary on the animal rights movement in Australia.

7. A US government study evaluating how protests by animal rights activists have affected primate research centers.

8. A free-lance journalist's book titled *The Humane Society: Origins and Accomplishments.*

9. A book titled *How I Stopped the Slaughter of Seals.*

10. An article in *The Journal of European History* titled "Animal Welfare in Victorian England and the Anti-Vivisection Movement."

11. An article in *Farm Journal* discussing how improving the ventilation in sheds can speed the growth of farm animals.

12. A radio commentary on the harmfulness of violent acts by animal rights groups.

Periodical Bibliography

The following articles have been selected to supplement the diverse views presented in this chapter.

Jerry Adler — "Emptying the Cages," *Newsweek*, May 23, 1988.

The Animals' Agenda — "The ALF: Pros and Cons," May 1985.

Katherine Bishop — "From Shop to Lab to Farm, Animal Rights Battle Is Felt," *The New York Times*, January 14, 1989.

Stephen Budiansky — "Winning Through Intimidation?" *U.S. News & World Report*, August 31, 1987.

Matt Cartmill — "Animal Rights and Wrongs," *Natural History*, July 1986.

Madeline Chinnici — "A Frog's Day in Court," *Discover*, December 1987.

Maria A. Comninou — "Perspective," *The AV Magazine*, July 1988.

Dennis M. Feeney — "Human Rights and Animal Welfare," *American Psychologist*, June 1987.

Carol Horn — "Animal Rights Movement Gains Ground," *The Utne Reader*, November/December 1988.

Helen Hooper McCloskey — "Pity the Poor Animals," *The Wall Street Journal*, December 23, 1987.

Nick Ravo — "Company Admits Using Spies in Animal-Rights Groups," *The New York Times*, January 26, 1989.

Harriet Ritvo — "With Friends Like These," *The Nation*, December 12, 1988.

Howard Rosenberg — "Animal Rights Activists Get a TV Hearing," *Los Angeles Times*, February 1, 1989.

Mike Sager — "Inhuman Bondage," *Rolling Stone*, March 24, 1988.

Successful Farming — "All Animal Rights Activists Are Not the Same," January 1987.

Trans-Species Unlimited — "The Grass-Roots Struggle," *T S Update*, Spring 1988. Available from Trans-Species Unlimited, PO Box 1553, Williamsport, PA 17703.

Organizations To Contact

The editors have compiled the following list of organizations which are concerned with the issues debated in this book. All of them have information or publications available for interested readers. The descriptions are derived from materials provided by the organizations themselves. This list was compiled upon the date of publication. Names and phone numbers of organizations are subject to change.

The American Anti-Vivisection Society (AA-VS)
Suite 204 Noble Plaza
801 Old York Road
Jenkintown, PA 19046-1685
(215) 887-0816

The Society is devoted to the abolition of vivisection. AA-VS conducts programs in public outreach, research, and lobbying. It publishes many brochures, including *Why We Oppose Vivisection* and *Point/Counterpoint: Responses to Typical Pro-Vivisection Arguments*.

American Association for Laboratory Animal Science (AALAS)
70 Timber Creek Drive, Suite 5
Cordova, TN 38018
(901) 754-8620

AALAS is an organization of scientists, veterinarians, and others who work with laboratory animals. It believes animal experimentation is essential in the study of human diseases. AALAS publishes the journal, *Laboratory Animal Science*, six times a year. It also publishes a newsletter, the *AALAS Bulletin*.

American Association of Zoo Keepers, Inc. (AAZK)
National Headquarters
635 Gage Blvd.
Topeka, KS 66606

AAZK is an organization of zoo keepers and other interested persons from the US, Canada, and eighteen foreign countries. Its goal is to promote the best possible care for exotic animals in captivity. Its monthly journal, *Animal Keepers' Forum*, carries updates on current legislation affecting zoo animals.

American Farm Bureau Federation
225 Touhy Ave.
Park Ridge, IL 60068
(312) 484-2222

The Federation is one of the largest farm organizations in the US. It distributes educational materials on current agricultural methods. It publishes the weekly *Farm Bureau News*, the brochure *Farm Animals*, and distributes a videotape, *The Business of Laying Eggs*.

The American Vegan Society
501 Old Harding Highway
Malaga, NJ 08328
(609) 694-2887

The Society is dedicated to advocating a purely vegetarian diet. It publishes books on Buddhism, non-violence, and vegetarianism. Its booklets include *Why Veganism, Present Status and Aims of Veganism*, and *A Month of Menus*.

California Biomedical Research Association
48 Shattuck Square
Box 114
Berkeley, CA 94794
(415) 644-0829

The Association believes animal research is vital to the health of human beings. It publishes fact sheets on the importance of animal research for treating a variety of diseases, including alcoholism and diabetes. It also publishes many brochures, including *Health Research To Benefit People and Animals.*

The Committee To Abolish Sport Hunting (CASH)
PO Box 43
White Plains, NY 10605
(914) 428-7523

CASH seeks to abolish hunting in New York State. It is organizing a lawsuit attacking wildlife management boards which CASH feels are dominated by hunters. It publishes *Exploring the Abolition of Sport Hunting* and a series of pamphlets against hunting and trapping.

Council for Agricultural Science and Technology (CAST)
137 Lynn Ave.
Ames, IA 50010-7120
(515) 292-2125

CAST is made up of scientific societies, corporations, foundations, and individuals interested in the science and technology of food and agriculture. It supports the use of animals as a food source. It publishes *NewsCAST* and *Science of Food and Agriculture* quarterly.

Farm Animal Reform Movement (FARM)
PO Box 70123
Washington, DC 20088
(301) 530-1737

FARM aims to stop animal abuse and factory farming. FARM endorses a ban on veal. One successful campaign resulted in Burger King withdrawing their veal parmigiana sandwich. It publishes a newsletter, *The Farm Report,* and many booklets and fact sheets, such as *Diet and Health, The Myth of Farm Animals,* and *Can We Afford Our Diet?*

Food Animals Concerns Trust (FACT)
PO Box 14599
Chicago, IL 60614
(312) 525-4952

FACT believes factory-farming methods should be abolished and animals should be raised humanely. FACT sets standards for the care of veal calves, laying hens, and other farm animals. It funds the operations of farmers who are willing to meet these standards. Its trademarks are NEST EGGS and RAMBLING ROSE BRAND free-range veal. It publishes a quarterly newsletter, *FACT Acts,* as well as fact sheets such as *Veterinarians Concerned About Animal Husbandry.*

Foundation for Biomedical Research
818 Connecticut Ave. NW, Suite 303
Washington, DC 20006
(202) 457-0654

The Foundation works to educate the public on the importance of animal research in treating human illnesses. The Foundation considers itself "a formal opposition to animal rights activists who formerly went unchallenged." It publishes several booklets, including *Caring for Laboratory Animals* and *Health Benefits of Animal Research.*

The Humane Society of the United States (HSUS)
2100 L St. NW
Washington, DC 20037
(202) 452-1100

Founded in 1954, HSUS is the nation's largest animal protection organization. While the Humane Society is "not opposed to the legitimate and appropriate utilization of animals" for human needs, it believes humans have "neither the right nor the license to exploit or abuse any animals in the process." The Society has information on establishing humane shelters for pets and publishes the quarterly *HSUS News* and *Animal Activist Alert*. It also publishes numerous brochures, such as *Companion Animals, Fur Seals, Factory Farming,* and *The Living Science: A Humane Approach to the Study of Animals in Elementary and Secondary School Biology.*

Institute of Laboratory Animal Resources (ILAR)
2101 Constitution Ave. NW
Washington, DC 20478
(202) 334-2590

ILAR was established in 1952 to develop and distribute scientific and technical information on laboratory animals. The ILAR staff operates an Animal Models and Genetic Stocks Information Program through which individuals can obtain information about the humane care and appropriate use of laboratory animals. In addition, ILAR distributes information about the importance of animals to the nation's research efforts. It publishes the *ILAR News* quarterly.

International Primate Protection League (IPPL)
PO Drawer 766
Summerville, SC 29484
(803) 871-2280

IPPL works for the well-being of primates everywhere. It has field representatives in twenty countries who work to create national parks and sanctuaries for primates. It also maintains a sanctuary for gibbons who are discarded by laboratories. It publishes a newsletter.

International Society for Animal Rights (ISAR)
421 S. State St.
Clarks Summit, PA 18411
(717) 586-2200

ISAR seeks to abolish vivisection, hunting, laboratory experiments, and other forms of animal abuse. It publishes a monthly newsletter, the *International Society for Animal Rights Report,* as well as numerous brochures, such as the *Experimental Psychology* series and *Cosmetic Tests on Animals.*

International Wildlife Coalition
320 Gifford St.
Falmouth, MA 02540
(617) 540-8086

The Coalition seeks to "challenge the cruel abuse being inflicted on wildlife worldwide." They have launched postcard campaigns to protest the hunting of grizzly bears, whales, elephants, and other animals. They publish two newsletters,

Wildlife Watch and *Whale Watch.* They also publish brochures such as *Fashion Fur Cruelty* and *Why Jail Whales?*

National Cattlemen's Association
PO Box 3469
Englewood, CO 80155
(303) 694-0305

The Association is a lobbying group for beef growers. It distributes information on beef production and plans to publish brochures on animal rights issues.

National Hunters Association (NHA)
PO Box 16
Eagle Rock, NC 27523
(919) 365-9289

The Association lobbies to protect the individual's right to carry firearms and to hunt. It also provides "organized support, both ethical and political," to state conservation departments. It runs hunting camps for teenagers and outdoor survival programs for adults. It publishes the *NHA Newsletter.*

National Livestock and Meat Board
444 N. Michigan Ave.
Chicago, IL 60611
(312) 467-5520

The Board represents farmers, meat packers, and others in the livestock industry. It promotes meat and meat products, grants money for research, and distributes materials to schools in support of meat as a part of good nutrition. It publishes *Beef Promotion, Food and Nutrition News,* and several other newsletters.

National Rifle Association (NRA)
Hunter Services Division
1600 Rhode Island Ave. NW
Washington, DC 20036
(202) 828-6246

The NRA lobbies to protect the right of the individual to own and use firearms. It distributes literature that argues that hunting is a vital part of animal conservation. It publishes two monthly magazines, *The American Hunter* and *The American Rifleman.* It also publishes numerous brochures, including *Improving Access to Private Land.*

National Shooting Sports Foundation
1075 Post Road
Riverside, CT 06878
(203) 637-3618

The Foundation believes the individual has a right to hunt, and that hunting is a necessary part of wildlife management. It publishes a brochure called *What They Say About Hunting* as well as other brochures such as *The Hunter and Conservation* and *Un-Endangered Species.*

National Wildlife Federation
1400 16th St. NW
Washington, DC 20036-2266
(202) 637-3700

The Federation encourages the intelligent management of our natural resources and promotes the appreciation of such resources. It operates Ranger Rick's Wildlife

Camp, sponsors National Wildlife Week, and produces *Nature NewsBreak,* a daily radio program, and *Environment Today,* a weekly program. It also has a large library of conservation-related publications. Its publications include *Ranger Rick's Nature Magazine* and *National Wildlife Magazine.*

People for the Ethical Treatment of Animals (PETA)
PO Box 42516
Washington, DC 20015
(202) 726-0156

PETA works to stop animal research and to end the mistreatment of animals on factory farms. It advocates vegetarianism and the use of "cruelty-free" products that do not involve animal testing or contain animal products. It publishes *PETA News* bimonthly, as well as many fact sheets, including *Alternative Methods: Healing Without Hurt,* and *Factory Farming: Mechanized Madness.* It also publishes *The PETA Guide to Compassionate Living.*

Physicians Committee for Responsible Medicine (PCRM)
PO Box 6322
Washington, DC 20015
(202) 483-1312

The Committee promotes alternatives to using animals in medical research and education. It publishes a newsletter, *PCRM Update,* the brochure *Alternatives in Medical Education,* and *Animals: Ethics and Medical Research.*

Psychologists for the Ethical Treatment of Animals (PsyETA)
PO Box 87
New Gloucester, ME 12983
(207) 926-4817

PsyETA consists of psychologists who wish to lessen the suffering of animals in research laboratories, but who still recognize the importance of animal research. It has developed a bibliography of films that can replace animal dissection in the classroom. It publishes the quarterly *PsyETA Bulletin.*

Regional Primate Research Center
I-421 Health Sciences Building, SJ-50
University of Washington
Seattle, WA 98195
(206) 543-0440

The Center performs research on primates and publishes the results in professional journals. It operates a primate information center and will conduct searches for scientific publications related to primates. It distributes several publications, including *Current Primate References.*

Society for Animal Protective Legislation
PO Box 3719
Georgetown Station
Washington, DC 20007
(202) 337-2334

The Society lobbies for stronger laws to protect animals. It has worked for laws to improve the standards for the care of laboratory animals and to protect endangered species. It is currently working toward a bill to end the use of steel-jaw leghold traps. It publishes a brochure on federal animal protection laws from 1955 to 1986. Transcripts of the Society's testimony before Congress are available on request.

Student Action Corps for Animals (SACA)
PO Box 15588
Washington, DC 20003-0588
(202) 543-8983

SACA is an animal-rights group for high school students. It promotes vegetarianism and encourages the avoidance of animal products such as leather and fur. It supports students who refuse to dissect animals in the classroom. It publishes a newsletter, *SACA News*.

Trans-Species Unlimited
PO Box 1553
Williamsport, PA 17703
(717) 322-3252

Trans-Species Unlimited believes that the human is just one of many species inhabiting the earth and as such does not have dominion over other species. It supports animal rights by advocating vegetarianism, the avoidance of animal products, and an end to hunting, trapping, and fishing. It also suggests boycotts of products tested on animals, of pet stores and breeders, and of rodeos, circuses, and similar events. It publishes numerous brochures, including *What Can I Do for Animals?*

Vegetarian Resource Center
PO Box 1463
Baltimore, MD 21203
(301) 752-8348

The Center works to educate those interested in vegetarianism. It publishes the monthly *Vegetarian Journal* and the brochure *Vegetarianism in a Nutshell*.

Wisconsin Agri-Business Council, Inc.
1400 E. Washington Ave., Suite 185
Madison, WI 53703-3041
(608) 255-7976

The Council believes US farmers can efficiently feed the nation because of modern farming advances such as large-scale agriculture, the use of insecticides, and the addition of proteins and other additives to animal feed. It publishes brochures, such as *When It Concerns Groundwater, No One Cares More than the Farmer, That All May Eat,* and the forthcoming *Our Farmers Care.*

World Wildlife Fund (WWF)
1250 24th St. NW
Washington, DC 20037
(202) 293-4800

The Fund works to save species from extinction, to establish parks, and to conduct research related to wildlife. It publishes an endangered species list and the newsletters *WWF Letter* and *Primate Conservation.*

Yerkes Regional Primate Research Center
Emory University
Atlanta, GA 30322
(404) 727-7707

The Center is one of eleven federally-funded centers for laboratory research involving primates. It uses primates in research but supports treating them humanely. The Center also sponsors research related to conservation to prevent the extinction of endangered ape and monkey species. It publishes several pamphlets, including *The Importance and Benefits of Animals to Human Health.*

Bibliography of Books

Animal Liberation Front   *Against All Odds: Animal Liberation 1972-1986.* London: ARC Print, 1986.

Animal Welfare Institute   *Factory Farming: The Experiment That Failed.* Washington, DC: Animal Welfare Institute, 1987.

James A. Bailey   *Principles of Wildlife Management.* New York: John Wiley & Sons, 1984.

Ron Baker   *The American Hunting Myth.* New York: Vantage Press, 1985.

Seaton Baxter   *Intensive Pig Production.* Dobbs Ferry, NY: Sheridan House Inc., 1984.

John R. Campbell and John F. Lasley   *The Science of Animals That Serve Humanity.* New York: McGraw-Hill Book Company, 1985.

James G. Fox, Bennett J. Cohen, and Franklin M. Loew   *Laboratory Animal Medicine.* Orlando, FL: Academic Press, Inc., 1984.

Michael Allen Fox   *The Case for Animal Experimentation.* Berkeley, CA: University of California Press, 1986.

R.G. Frey   *Interests and Rights: The Case Against Animals.* New York: Oxford University Press, 1980.

Steven M. Geary   *Fur Trapping in North America.* San Diego: A.S. Barnes & Company, Inc., 1981.

Jane Goodall   *The Chimpanzees of Gombe.* Cambridge, MA: The Belknap Press, 1986.

R.J. Hoage, ed.   *Animal Extinctions: What Everyone Should Know.* Washington, DC: Smithsonian Institution Press, 1985.

William Humphrey   *Open Season: Sporting Adventures.* New York: Delacorte Press, 1986.

Junichi Kawamata and Edward C. Melby Jr.   *Animal Models: Assessing the Scope of Their Use in Biomedical Research.* New York: Alan R. Liss, Inc., 1987.

Coral Lansbury   *The Old Brown Dog: Women, Workers, and Vivisection in Edwardian England.* Madison, WI: The University of Wisconsin Press, 1985.

Frances Moore Lappé   *Diet for a Small Planet.* New York: Ballantine Books, 1982.

Aldo Leopold   *A Sand County Almanac.* New York: Oxford University Press, 1949.

Andrew Linzey   *Animal Rights: A Christian Assessment of Man's Treatment of Animals.* London: SCM Press, Ltd., 1976.

Jon R. Luoma   *A Crowded Ark: The Role of Zoos in Wildlife Conservation.* Boston: Houghton Mifflin Company, 1987.

Jim Mason and Peter Singer   *Animal Factories.* New York: Crown Publishers, 1980.

Farley Mowat — *Sea of Slaughter.* Boston: The Atlantic Monthly Press, 1984.

National Institutes of Health — *Guide for the Care and Use of Laboratory Animals.* Bethesda, MD: National Institutes of Health, 1985.

National Research Council — *Use of Laboratory Animals in Biomedical and Behavioral Research.* Washington, DC: National Academy Press, 1988.

Office of Technology Assessment — *Alternatives to Animal Use in Research, Testing, and Education.* Washington, DC: Government Printing Office, 1986.

John Robbins — *Diet for a New America.* Walpole, NH: Stillpoint Publishing, 1987.

S.F. Sapontzis — *Morals, Reason, and Animals.* Philadelphia: Temple University Press, 1987.

James Serpell — *In the Company of Animals.* New York: Basil Blackwell, Inc., 1986.

Robert Sharpe — *The Cruel Deception: The Use of Animals in Medical Research.* New York: Sterling Publishing, 1988.

Peter Singer, ed. — *In Defence of Animals.* New York: Basil Blackwell, Inc., 1985.

Susan Sperling — *Animal Liberators: Research and Morality.* Berkeley: University of California Press, 1988.

Marjorie Spiegel — *The Dreaded Comparison: Race and Animal Slavery.* Philadelphia: New Society Publishers, 1988.

William F. Tapley — *Those Hours Spent Outdoors: Reflections on Hunting and Fishing.* New York: Scribner & Sons, 1988.

John Vyuyan — *In Pity and in Anger: A Study of the Use of Animals in Science.* Marblehead, MA: Micah Publications, 1988.

Index

233